ADLAI STEVENSON

A STUDY IN VALUES

Books by Herbert J. Muller

ADLAI STEVENSON: A STUDY IN VALUES

FREEDOM IN THE MODERN WORLD

RELIGION AND FREEDOM IN THE
MODERN WORLD

FREEDOM IN THE WESTERN WORLD

FREEDOM IN THE ANCIENT WORLD

ISSUES OF FREEDOM

THE LOOM OF HISTORY

THE SPIRIT OF TRAGEDY

THE USES OF THE PAST

THOMAS WOLFE

SCIENCE AND CRITICISM

MODERN FICTION

Adlai E. Stevenson with Mrs. Roosevelt at the U.N.

ADLAI STEVENSON

A STUDY IN VALUES

HERBERT J. MULLER

Harper & Row, Publishers

New York, Evanston, and London

FIRST EDITION

LIBRARY OF CONGRESS CATALOG CARD NUMBER: 67-22503

H-R

TO CASS CANFIELD

CONTENTS

ACKNOWLEDGMENTS

I am deeply indebted to friends and political associates of Adlai Stevenson who kindly granted me interviews or answered questions by correspondence. Herewith I thank William Attwood, George Ball, Cass Canfield, Mrs. Dan P. Caulkins, J. Edward Day, Thomas K. Finletter, John Fischer, Clayton Fritchey, Senator William Fulbright, Lloyd K. Garrison, Mrs. Ernest L. Ives, Homer A. Jack, Walter Lippmann, Senator Eugene McCarthy, Judge Carl McGowan, Senator Mike Monroney, Reinhold Niebuhr, James Reston, James H. Rowe, Eric Sevareid, Robert Tucker, James Russell Wiggins, W. Willard Wirtz, and Charles Yost. In the text I neglect to cite their authority only because I assume full responsibility for all judgments.

I am also pleased to express my gratitude to Edwin W. Kenworthy for his genial services as a guide to the political scene in Washington, to Jeannette Hopkins for helpful suggestions, and to Cass Canfield, William DeWitt, John Fischer, and Arthur Jensen for critical readings of my manuscript.

PREFACE

First and last, my interest in this study has been Adlai Stevenson as a rare person. He was a thoroughly civilized man, sensitive, reasonable, gracious, humorous, urbane, and a man of true style, a distinction only made more manifest by the felicities of his literary style. He was an especially rare sort in politics as a civil idealist who was most earnest and high-minded, raising both the intellectual level and the moral tone of our political debate, yet who remained genial, humbler, and more magnanimous than most idealists, never pompous or self-righteous. For much the same reasons that William James was called an "adorable" philosopher, Adlai Stevenson was for many of us an adorable statesman. I wish to contribute a memorial to one who deserved the conventional tributes as a "great and good American," especially because he won them as an also-ran, and was great more for what he was and stood for than what he directly accomplished, or by popular historical standards was perhaps not clearly great.

Yet I am writing as a historian, not merely an admirer. My study is an effort to size up his political career in a historical perspective, place him against the background of our revolutionary era. Although I have naturally been concerned with his inner thoughts and feelings, his satisfactions, disappointments, and regrets, I have introduced only such biographical detail as seems necessary for a full understanding and appreciation of his public life. Still less have I attempted a psychological study or depth analysis. His friends often remark what a complicated character he was—how worldly and oblivious, convivial and lonely, merry and sad; but he does not strike me as a mysterious, elusive, or baffling character who cries out for plumbing of unsuspected depths, exposure of unconscious motives. I see only the normal complexities and conflicting impulses of an honest, thoughtful man not given to self-deception, and much freer than most in talking about his doubts and misgivings. One reason why he was beloved is that his "public image"—not created by ghost writers or Madison Avenue men—was essentially his real self, saving only the foibles and the reticences of any normal man.

The serious complexities lie rather in the issues he raised by his public life. These embrace almost all the basic issues—political, social, cultural—of American democracy today, and finally of modern civilization. The rare person may therefore appear to be chiefly an exhibit for a too common kind of reflection, or an excuse for me to roam all over the world again; but I have taken this risk. One can hope to do Stevenson full justice only by a survey of the many problems that concerned him, what he was up against, what troubled him, and what heartened him.

By the same token this book is by no means a "definitive" study. John Bartlow Martin and Walter Johnson, to whom Stevenson's private papers have been entrusted, will report much more about his inner thoughts and feelings. I am largely confining myself to what appears on the public record, on the assumption that his many public speeches and articles bring out all the matters of public concern in which he was seriously interested, and that in these matters he can be taken at his own word with less reservation than almost any other important statesman past or present, including his beloved Abraham Lincoln. Although I have checked up on my conjectures about the implications of the record by interviewing some of his close friends and political associates, their judgments naturally were not uniform. But in any case my study was never intended to be definitive, for the simple reason that it could not possibly be so even had I had access to his private papers and all other relevant documents. Apart from my nearness to Stevenson as a contemporary, in a world that is very much with us, I am constantly dealing with controversial issues, the kind that keep historians debating endlessly over statesmen of past centuries, and that can never be settled. Naturally I have tried to be as objective and dispassionate as possible, but for this reason I feel obliged to repeat what I have said in many a preface, that a historian never can be wholly objective, and that he may come closer to the ideal of impartiality by being aboveboard, stating openly the values he is committed to, the grounds of his partial judgments. My judgments reflect essentially the same liberal, democratic faith to which Stevenson was committed. Sometimes diffident, sometimes downright, they are tempered by a rather more skeptical spirit than his, but they are always as debatable as the faith on which they rest. Now and then I introduce the first person, quite deliberately, though I hope not obtrusively, to remind the reader that in the spirit of Adlai Stevenson I am not pronouncing the verdict of History or God.

1

The Importance of Stevenson

'Tis not in mortals to command success,
But we'll do more, Sempronius; we'll deserve it. . . .
—*Joseph Addison*

"A funny thing happened to me on the way to the White House," Adlai Stevenson told the Gridiron Club in Washington shortly after his first defeat by General Eisenhower; and he went on to say, "I think the chroniclers of our time have overlooked the meteoric beauty and brevity of my political career." Upon his death thirteen years later some thought his epitaph had been spoken by Hamlet: "The time is out of joint: O cursed spite, that ever I was born to set it right!" His political career might indeed be summed up with melancholy brevity. Having made his name as Governor of Illinois, he twice failed to win the Presidency, he then hoped to be Secretary of State under John Kennedy, and he ended instead as Ambassador to the United Nations, away from Washington. Throughout he played no key role in any major decision. In his one high national office he only defended policies made by others, some of which made him unhappy, supporting the common view of him as a lonely, tragic figure, doomed to frustration. One may doubt that he will figure prominently in the chronicles of the future.

Yet if there is a future for our world, I think it will owe something to Stevenson. He was by no means so ineffectual as might appear to us children of perpetual crisis. In defeat he did not curse his time or fate but continued to raise an eloquent voice, still heard in words that remain more memorable than their occasion. Retaining a large, devoted following, he became famous all over the world long before he served as official spokesman of America in the United Nations. At home he had far more influence on his party than President Eisenhower had on the Republican Party. By both specific policy and high example he lighted the way for President Kennedy, and Lyndon Johnson then carried out much of the program he had urged for a "New America." Certainly he was important to a great many of us as a spokesman of the best in American tradition, in a day that as certainly is no mean day as history goes. He knew that it might turn out to be the last day on our "little spaceship," the earth. If it does not, Adlai Stevenson might well enter the national pantheon as the legendary figure he already is, the brightest symbol in our time of the idealism typified by the Abraham Lincoln he revered. Just possibly he belongs in the company of Lincoln.

Meanwhile we need not worry over what posterity will make of him. Our sufficient concern remains the issues he forced by his effort to "serve our great tradition greatly," in particular to adapt it to an age more revolutionary than Lincoln could dream of. A time out of joint proved to be the right time for Stevenson. His qualities of greatness, which were hardly apparent in his early years and might never have been realized in a peaceful era, were called out by "the ordeal of the twentieth century," and by his awareness that the ordeal would go on indefinitely, there could be no simple or certain solution for either America or mankind. This awareness, which hardly suggests a high road to political success in America, nevertheless fortified his resolution to go on devoting himself to public affairs, as he did to the last day of his life. Thereby he implied a concern for the welfare of posterity, with no doubt some aspiration to be remembered by it. My immediate concern is the reasons why he is in any case important to us, his contemporaries—the main themes to be developed in the chapters that follow.

The story of the funny things that happened to Stevenson may begin with the new word that entered national politics with him—"egghead." By the standards of the intelligentsia he was not learned or bookish enough to be considered a full-fledged member of the class. He was liable to be misunderstood because he differed from most intellectuals in that he was less a man of theory, more at home in the world of practice, and never an innocent among the political wolves. Brought up in a family that for generations had been active in politics, he considered this a quite respectable vocation. Public life was his natural element—always a sufficient ordeal, but not because he felt it a menace to his dignity or integrity. In his last years he therefore disappointed many of his admirers when he appeared to betray his principles by defending in the United Nations Presidential policies that in private he confessed troubled him; and he was more troubled when some writers called on him to resign as Ambassador. But while his role at the end may provoke the most melancholy reflections about his career, it was ambiguous because Stevenson was still acting on principle, in good faith, believing that by resigning he would surrender his chances of influencing American foreign policy. The high call of duty in public life was not so simple or clear for him as it seemed to liberal intellectuals on the sidelines.

By American political standards, however, he remained unquestionably an egghead. It was enough that he was a highly literate man at home in the world of ideas, at ease in the company of intellectuals, and that he talked like one. In the public eye he became pre-eminently an egghead when he ran against General Eisenhower, whom nobody would ever accuse of such proclivities. He himself gaily accepted the challenge: "Eggheads of the world, unite! You have nothing to lose but your yolks." The new word, which was only a variant of the long familiar "highbrow," recalls the national tradition of anti-intellectualism. In Europe the intellectual in public life is still widely respected. In America he had been made familiar by Woodrow Wilson and the "Brain Trust" of Franklin Roosevelt, but he remained a suspect type, represented in cartoons as a loony with cap and gown. Most popular "Ike" shared the traditional mistrust of men devoted to ideas, or "mere theory," unless it was the kind of obsolete theory that passed for common sense. The contrast between these two brings up the most obvious issues of Stevenson's career.

"Let's talk sense to the American people," he said fervently in his great speech of acceptance when first nominated for the Presidency. "Let's tell them the truth." In sounding this keynote of his campaign Stevenson pointed to a basic necessity for a healthy democracy, above all in a time of crisis. The truth was hard, he at once added. Ahead lay "great decisions, not easy decisions," and a long, arduous, costly struggle with "the great enemies of mankind," poverty and tyranny. Although in campaigning he indulged in some of the usual simplicities of political oratory, essentially he ran true to form, rising to what he saw as "a great opportunity to educate and elevate" the people. To this task he would devote the rest of his life, and by his "call to greatness" found his own claims to greatness.

By contrast, General Eisenhower undoubtedly believed that he too was talking sense to the American people, but for him this involved little disagreeable truth or difficult challenge. The message in his speech of acceptance was simple and cheering: the good soldier would lead a "great crusade" to secure freedom both at home and abroad, while demanding no sacrifice to speak of in blood, sweat, or tears. At as little cost he promised to "build a sure foundation for sound prosperity for all here at home and for a just and sure peace throughout the world." There was no need to elevate the American people because he took for granted that they were naturally good, essentially always right; all that was necessary was to clean up "the mess in Washington." In victory he proceeded to make everything absolutely "sure" by staffing his administration with big businessmen, who to him represented the best brains in the country.

Now, it is too easy to gibe at the intellectual limitations of Eisenhower, made more glaring by his ineffably complacent memoirs. Nevertheless any study of Stevenson's career makes it necessary to dwell on them. Eisenhower was the popular spokesman of a humorless era of complacence—all the platitude, myth, and slogan that a truth-teller had to contend with, and that were more discouraging

because the good General was sincerely self-righteous, never a hypocrite. (As Stevenson said, he dedicated himself so often that he must
have felt like the cornerstone of a public building.) But since the
duty of exposing these limitations may give a possibly unwholesome
pleasure, I should say at once what Stevenson himself realized—that
the lesson of his defeat was neither simple nor simply depressing.

The American people had good reasons for electing Dwight
Eisenhower. He was no ordinary politician, either, but an uncom-
monly decent man of great good will and proved ability, a national
hero respected by Stevenson too. He made sense when he cried that it
was "time for a change," from an administration that had bred
enough corruption to look sluggish and tired. He represented a
change as well from the Republican Old Guard, having been nominated by the moderate wing of his party, and in his campaign he
promised to retain the basic reforms of the New Deal that the Republicans had stubbornly opposed. Stevenson ridiculed the "two-headed
elephant," the nominal alliance of the Old Guard with Eisenhower,
which reminded him of the Australian bushman who was given a
new boomerang and spent the rest of his life trying to throw his old
one away; but he did not question the sincerity of his "distinguished
opponent." Nor was the General an ordinary military hero; unquestionably he was a peace-loving man. And in 1952 he most likely
made a better President than Stevenson for a divided people, prone to
hysteria in their feeling of frustration over the stalemated war in
Korea. Granted that the Republicans had done more than their share
to deepen and exacerbate the divisions by their reckless charge that this
was "Truman's war," and their exploitation of the fears and hatreds
stirred up by Senator McCarthy, Eisenhower's transparent good will,
his popular reputation as a man above party, and his own illusion that
he was such a man enabled him to unite the country, end the war in
Korea without victory, and eventually help to dispose of McCarthy.
Stevenson would have had a much harder time quieting the many
solid partisans in Congress and the country at large.

More significant were his own limitations. A reluctant candidate
for the Presidency, Stevenson had freely expressed his doubts of his

capacities to lead the nation, and in his speech of acceptance said he had asked the Merciful Father "to let this cup pass from me." Most obviously he had the defects of his virtues as an ultracivilized, thoughtful, fair-minded man who could see at least two sides to every question, and so struck even many of his supporters as "indecisive." When in 1960 Arthur Schlesinger, Jr. announced that he was going to work for the nomination of John Kennedy, explaining that he still considered Stevenson the American best qualified for the Presidency but believed it impossible for him to win the nomination, James Reston guessed that he summed up the predominant feeling at the Democratic Convention: "I'm nostalgically for Stevenson, ideologically for Humphrey, and realistically for Kennedy." No doubt the reverence for Stevenson is still colored by nostalgia. Although to my mind he was the best American statesman of the day, the warmest of his admirers may wonder whether he was the best qualified for the Presidency when they consider the nature of the office, or "the politics of leadership." This calls for considerably more than statesmanship, beginning with effectiveness in dealing with Congress, bureaucracy, party, and public opinion. Even the moderation and reasonableness of Stevenson may raise some question when one recalls that all the great Presidents of the past, including Abraham Lincoln, were feared and hated more than he ever was. One cannot dismiss out of hand the judgment of his many thoughtful supporters, backed by his impressive record as Governor of Illinois, which is not widely known; but I think an admirer may do him fuller justice by granting that he might not have made a great President. Enough that he would never have been a mediocre one.

As it was, at any rate, the campaign immediately brought out the best in Stevenson. This appeared at the outset in a rare exhibition of political courage. Stevenson distinguished himself by not only attacking McCarthyism, then in its heyday, but choosing an American Legion convention for the occasion. He pointed out the serious menace in what Eisenhower treated as only an excess of patriotic or partisan zeal. "Patriotism," he told the unsympathetic Legionnaires, "is not the *fear* of something; it is the *love* of something." The rampant fears that were discrediting America's capacity for leadership abroad were more dangerous because they betrayed a lack of faith in democratic principles of liberty, the ideals that made America worthy of love. In adding that "it is often easier to fight for principles than to live up to them," he introduced a theme he sounded to the end of his life—the responsibilities of freedom, the discipline of democracy, the need of actual devotion to its announced moral ends. At a time when the fashion among political scientists was to concentrate on the "realities" of democratic processes or political behavior ("Who Gets What, When, How,") Stevenson dared to sound naïve by continuing to emphasize that the first and last issues of democracy were moral issues.

General Eisenhower himself remained sincere, but his campaign contrasted by featuring the most depressing characteristics of American politics, first of all its engrained tradition of irresponsibility. In his political naïveté he began his great moral crusade by picking out Richard Nixon for a running mate, an ambitious young man not eminent for his moral scruples. He made his peace with party leaders, including "Honest Bob" Taft, who had managed to couple their irresponsible attacks on "Truman's war" in Korea with charges that the President and the Secretary of State, Dean Acheson, were "soft on communism." He himself cheapened his promises by endorsing reckless talk about "liberating" the satellite peoples in East Europe. Granted his personal integrity, he could play the part of nonpartisan crusader more easily because he allowed his cohorts to keep on playing politics as usual. Nixon concentrated on the hatchet work, making personal attacks on Stevenson in which he perfected his tactics of innuendo, or the "middle-of-the-gutter" approach. Senator McCarthy helped out by fully exploiting all the uses of the gutter. Although Eisenhower obviously disliked the man, he put the interests of the party first, called for the Senator's re-election, and never disavowed his vicious attacks on Stevenson's patriotism in a national broadcast sponsored by the Republican National Committee.

At best the General hardly cooperated in Stevenson's effort to educate the American people. He never got around to actual debate of the issues. His conception of sincerity made him think it more dignified just to tell the people what he thought instead of wrangling with his opponent (not to mention Stevenson's unseemly proposal that if the Republicans "would stop telling lies about us, we would stop telling the truth about them"). The General was least prepared for serious debate over his main idea, "It's time for a change." To him the slogan meant only a change in administration, not at all any bold experiment or innovation. The only change he proposed was a restoration of "fiscal responsibility," which meant a reversion to Republican policy of the past, much ado about nothing but economizing, reducing taxes, balancing budgets, calling a halt to "creeping socialism." As for educating the people, he would learn to call the kind of creeping he preferred "dynamic" or "progressive" conservatism.

Hence Eisenhower raised a troublesome issue—the mentality of American voters. In promising to talk sense to them, Stevenson had emphasized his faith in democracy by adding, "The people are wise." After his defeat he reaffirmed this faith, saying that he was sure he had not talked over the heads of the people; the trouble was that they had cared little about the issues because they were weary of conflict, impatient for the repose promised by Eisenhower. Studies made of the voters, much closer than had been made of any previous election, confirmed their indifference to the issues he was concerned about, but gave further reason to doubt their wisdom. Most of the voters were unimpressed by Stevenson's efforts to talk good sense. They were much more impressed by Eisenhower's obvious kind of personality, displayed in his engaging grin and played up in the slogan "I like Ike." Richard Nixon added on his own a lurid demonstration of their insensitivity. In defending on television his acceptance of a "secret fund" contributed by businessmen when he served in Congress, he won the hearts of uncounted millions by baring his soul and his bankbook, parading his wife, daughters, and dog Checkers to prove how wholesome a life he led. The millions included Ike, who called this corny performance "magnificent," later writing that never before had he witnessed such an example of courage.[1]

More depressing was the popular response to one of Stevenson's most engaging traits. Like the General, many voters questioned his integrity because of his wittiness, or violation of what he called the "Republican law of gravity." In fact he was violating national tradition. However fond of the horse laugh or today the wisecrack, Americans have typically preferred to keep their politics solemn or stuffy. The vast majority of their politicians have obliged them, if with no pains to speak of. The tradition was epitomized by the advice a Senator Corwin gave General James Garfield: "Never make people laugh. If you would succeed in life you must be solemn—solemn as an ass. All the great monuments are built over solemn asses." Garfield learned his lesson well enough to become President.

After his second, more crushing defeat, Stevenson expressed some doubts about the wisdom of the American people, in particular about their moral and spiritual values, which President Eisenhower thought were tops. Yet he never despaired of the people, still less of democracy itself. The continued faith to which his public career testified was not simply stoical either. "Let us never forget," Murray Kempton wrote in 1960, "that if a light still rises above this dreary land, it is

[1] I should confess that despite conscientious efforts to be objective and fair-minded, I still find it impossible to respect and trust Richard Nixon. One may condone his ruthless ambition because he had to work his way up, without the advantages of either Stevenson or Kennedy, and for eight years had to endure the strain of his complete dependence on the uncertain intentions of President Eisenhower. He may even appear pathetic, as he did when he complained angrily of his treatment by newsmen after his defeat by Governor Brown in California; no wily politician would have felt or exposed such bitterness. Had he achieved his ambition, the responsibilities of the Presidency might well have brought out the best in him, as they did in Harry Truman. But from his book *Six Crises,* as from his whole political career, I have been able to get no clear idea of what the best in him may be, or what kind of person there is beneath the politician. Although he tells of his new resolve to appear at all times "sincere," he expresses only contempt for Stevenson, who could have taught him that so deliberate a concern with appearances was a poor way of becoming sincere. With newsmen and others on the Washington scene whom I consulted I had no more success; when pressed, none could find a good word to put in for him. Eventually I sought out a devil's advocate in a well-known conservative journalist, but he praised Nixon's executive abilities, not his statesmanship.

because for so long and so lonely a time this man held it up"; but however Stevenson may have suffered from feelings of loneliness, he was never in fact lonely as a public figure, any more than was his good friend and comrade Eleanor Roosevelt. For an egghead running against a national hero he had won remarkably warm popular support, and thereafter he retained an ardent following. A study of his career seems to me an excellent means to a toughened faith in American democracy, revealing most clearly the reasons for being dismayed and depressed by it, but also for not despairing of it.

Likewise Stevenson illumines its liberal tradition. Recently there has been a sophisticated tendency to play down this tradition in America, minimize the historic conflict between alleged progressives and conservatives, and emphasize instead the consensus on the values of free enterprise and the American Way, in a nation that never developed a strong radical tradition. Stevenson might appear to support this tendency since he was a moderate, never so militant as were the traditional liberals, crusaders for social and political reform. Hence he is criticized by some contemporary liberals, such as Irving Howe, who wrote that he was "certainly" not one of them, only another exhibit of the increasing conservatism of the fifties on which Eisenhower prospered. Today Stevenson seems still tamer to the "New Left" of the younger generation, with whom Howe also disagrees. Evidently no one can say authoritatively just what a "true" liberal is.

As I read American history, however, Stevenson spoke out of a tradition come down from Jefferson and Jackson that deserves this name by its proclaimed ideals, the reforms it supported on behalf of the common people, and the sharp opposition it always met from conservatives defending the status quo or business interests. To my mind he represented the maturity of this liberal tradition. He had a far more complex vision than most Populists, Progressives, and other crusaders for the common man, with never so simple a faith in progress or perfectibility, to be achieved by throwing out rascals and rooting out evils. He carried on in a temper more genuinely, philosophically liberal than the crusaders, never so doctrinaire. Like William Jennings Bryan, they were too often not only naïve but provincial, narrow-minded, self-righteous—illiberal.

Stevenson's own answer to the question whether he was headed left, right, or center was given in 1952: "I think it would be more relevant to ask: Is the man moving forward or backward, or is he grounded?" Stevenson was clearly a liberal in his welcome of change. He was much more aware than General Eisenhower of the deep changes that were going on willy-nilly all over the world, and saw as much more clearly the problems they created, at once the profound uncertainties, the terrible hazards, and the wondrous new possibilities. "I believe that man stands on the eve of his greatest day," he told the patriots at the American Legion convention. He would grow more uncertain about America's readiness for this eve, speak out with more sense of urgency; but such shifts in his views marked another major theme of his political career—a deepening understanding of his time, and with it a steady growth in his stature as a statesman.

In the 1952 campaign Stevenson offered hardly any new ideas, proposing chiefly a continuation of the policies of Roosevelt and Truman; often his program sounded much like that of General Eisenhower, even to promises of economy, a balanced budget, and resistance to the encroachments of the federal government. As a private citizen again he had more time to read and reflect. He started on the travels all over the world from which he learned much at firsthand, especially about the problems of non-Western peoples. At home he could ponder more deeply an affluent, postwar America rather different from that known to either Eisenhower or Harry Truman. He then moved forward enough to warrant the slogan of his 1956 campaign, a call for a "New America."

To be sure, his new ideas were hardly startling to thinking persons. No student of the modern world should look to Stevenson for new or profound insights into economic, social, or political problems. He had an active, alert mind, but not a particularly original or acute one; he was never far ahead of his time. Still, neither was Abraham Lincoln, nor were in our own day Franklin Roosevelt and Winston Churchill. Great leaders need not be great thinkers. For a statesman

Stevenson was far enough ahead of his time—just enough to be twice defeated, and then vindicated. In the 1956 campaign, for instance, he was much abused for his proposal of a ban on unlimited testing of hydrogen bombs—what Eisenhower branded as a "theatrical gesture" and Nixon "catastrophic nonsense." Always Stevenson could drive home the living truth of commonplaces by an eloquence that was not political rhetoric or literary embellishment, but a natural expression of his earnestness in endeavoring to educate and elevate the American people. And with the approach of 1960 he began coming into his own.

Although President Eisenhower at the outset of his administration had helped to quiet the worst in the American people, by the end he had done little to bring out the best in them, chiefly fortifying their tendencies to complacence. As it became plainer that his "progressive" conservatism had led to both economic and intellectual stagnation, it became as plain that Stevenson out of power had been a far more successful educator. His many ardent supporters sprang to political life again. Perhaps the most heartening of all tributes to Stevenson were the tremendous ovations he received in 1960 at the Democratic National Convention. As Senator Eugene McCarthy said in nominating him, he "made us all proud to be Democrats." The steam-rollered nomination of Kennedy accordingly seemed to his supporters another bitter disappointment: the old leader was being left a prophet without honor, discarded for a young man he did not at that time much admire. But at least one of the faithful pointed out the truth perhaps unrealized by either the victor or the loser: "It was 1952, not 1960, that marked the end of an era, the rising of a new order."

Kennedy's "New Frontier" called for substantially the same program the old leader had offered for a "New America." In his speech of acceptance he talked in the style of Stevenson, on as high a level. He too recalled Americans to their lost sense of historic purpose, stressing not only the opportunities but the perils of an uncertain future, and the need of sacrifices. Stevenson's supporters could therefore work for Kennedy's election, as he himself did. The new leader stirred a growing enthusiasm, especially among the young, as he developed a true style of his own and his public image became more like his real self. Once President, he made a truer prophet of the old leader who had sacrificed votes by farsighted proposals like the test-ban treaty.

As the heir of Stevenson, Kennedy affords a more interesting, suggestive contrast than the obvious one with Dwight Eisenhower. Most conspicuously he was a more ambitious, practical, effective politician. The notorious diffidence or "indecisiveness" that had made Stevenson reluctant to accept his first nomination was still apparent in 1960, when he wavered enough to encourage some supporters, discourage others, and kill what at the last moment seemed a good chance of being nominated. Kennedy never faltered after launching his drive for the Presidency, devoting all his energy and political skill to winning the power he had frankly set his heart on. He was as completely confident of his ability to measure up to this highest responsibility. Once in the White House he was at home both in the world of power and the world of ideas. Devoted to essentially the same national ends as Stevenson, he kept a closer, shrewder eye on the necessary political means. He had more clearly, I think, the potentialities for becoming a great President.

These potentialities were far from realized, however, in the few years left to him. It took the shock of his assassination to make Kennedy a national idol. Stevenson had displayed much more consistent political courage than the youthful author of *Profiles in Courage,* whose admiration of Daniel Webster and Robert Taft suggested some heedlessness of irresponsible means and dubious ends. As a Senator, Kennedy had long remained silent on the evils of McCarthyism. In his campaign against Nixon he did not dare to talk sense to the people about some dangerous issues, such as Castro's Cuba. In the White House he continued to dismay many of his supporters by his failure to press hard for the reforms needed to make good his promise of a New Frontier. Granted that he had good excuses for his timid dealings with Congress, since his very close victory had given him no clear mandate, the point remains that he was not a bold, gallant leader on the domestic front. And another excuse was that he had to live down the Bay of Pigs fiasco—an almost incredible venture that Stevenson would never have been guilty of.

We now know that Kennedy had misgivings all along about the invasion of Cuba, but in view of his halfhearted consent to it we may reconsider Stevenson's reputation as an indecisive, Hamlet type. This he earned by his irresolution in key decisions about his personal career, sometimes about specific policy, and always by his habit of talking freely about doubts that a shrewder politician would have kept to himself. Yet he was rarely if ever indecisive about matters of principle. Once he had made up his mind he was typically vigorous in action, often bolder and more resolute than Kennedy proved. What most plainly gives his whole political career its basic consistency was his moral courage. Even his hesitancies were linked with this. In the words of Archibald MacLeish, he had "the courage of his doubts," and was not only willing to consider all possible alternatives but unwilling not to consider them.

Historically more significant was the plainest difference between Stevenson and Kennedy—simply in age and origins. As he said after Kennedy's death, the young President was the "contemporary man." He himself had grown up in a simpler prewar America, specifically in a Midwestern family rooted in its agrarian tradition, and he could therefore sound like an antiquated idealist, clinging to such outworn Jeffersonian beliefs as that our democratic society "rests on an agricultural basis." In his last years he still described himself as a "country boy" at heart. Kennedy, a city boy without deep roots in the native soil, belonged to the generation born during World War I and had lived with crisis all his days. He was more skeptical, perhaps more tough-minded, certainly cooler and more reserved. Always keeping his head, he was a worthy heir of Stevenson's visions because his skepticism never blighted the hopes of a better world that he had fought for in World War II, but toughened an idealism comparable to Stevenson's. Once he had developed his own style he could speak more effectively to his generation, make good the promise of his speech of acceptance. It was time for another change, he there declared: "a new generation of leadership—new men to cope with new problems and new opportunities," young men "not bound by the traditions of the past." With his youth and charm, and the gracious aid of a cultivated wife, Kennedy became popular the world over, for both young and old a radiant symbol of the "New America" at its best.

Yet Stevenson—the spiritual father of this America—may appear to advantage in this perspective too.[2] As I see it, Stevenson provided something like an ideal transition between the old and the new America. He had a deeper sense of the past than either Kennedy or Eisenhower, and as deep a loyalty to the tradition symbolized by Lincoln; yet he was not "bound by the traditions of the past," much less "blinded by the old fears and hatreds" that Kennedy warned against; and he kept as abreast of the times, if anything further ahead of them in international affairs. For Stevenson too was very much a contemporary man. He was more fully aware of the revolutionary changes because he had lived, after all, through even more crises, including World War I and its aftermath. If he remained more optimistic, his experience in the Eisenhower years was not calculated to give him more illusions about America. If less cool, he kept as clear a head. To my mind he had a riper wisdom.

At the United Nations this appeared in the fundamental issue underlying the many difficult issues Ambassador Stevenson had to deal with—the uses of power. In the now highly publicized conflict between the "doves" and the "hawks," he was by no means pure dove. He had supported the policies of Truman and Acheson in the early years of the cold war, in particular the war in Korea. Always he valued the power of America—economic, political, and military—as a means of containing Communist aggression and aiding both our allies and the non-Western world. The main reason for his support of the war in Vietnam—the stand that many of his admirers most regretted—was his conviction of the necessity of halting the aggression of Red China. Yet military power was no answer to the problems

---

[2] Let me say that I write sympathetically as a slightly younger contemporary of his, who also has memories of prewar America. But I may write about it more objectively because I do not feel rooted in it, having grown up in the Bronx—stony ground to sink roots in.

that Stevenson had grown sensitive to before Kennedy. He was among the first statesmen to dwell on "the revolution of rising expectations" in the non-Western world, and the need of economic aid on a large scale quite apart from all jockeying with the Soviet for military and diplomatic advantages. In America he was among the first to argue that disarmament should be made "our top priority national interest." For he saw most clearly the terrible dangers of power: first and last the obvious horrors of a nuclear war, which nobody could win, but also the inflexibility of realists mistrustful of mere diplomacy, of anything but military supremacy, and in a pinch always prepared to risk a military showdown; and finally the insidious dangers of the mere possession of such immense, unprecedented wealth and power as postwar America had built up. This obscured the fundamental challenge to America, which he characteristically saw as a moral, spiritual challenge. It obscured as well the elementary reality of human interdependence that dwarfed the mighty powers of America and Russia, and the elementary contradictions between the awesome technological feats of man today and the appalling inanities of his conduct of human affairs. "Just as Europe could never again be the old, closed-in community after the voyages of Columbus," Stevenson said in his last speech at Geneva, a week before he dropped dead, "we can never again be a squabbling band of nations before the awful majesty of outer space."

To which anyone may answer, "Oh yeah?" In fact we are squabbling, and the wise money is betting that we will go on squabbling indefinitely. Meanwhile the professional realists continue to deride or deplore Stevenson's faith in efforts at reasonable persuasion, and with them in the power of ideals. (Dean Acheson's word for him was "softheaded.") It may well be that his faith was too optimistic. Nevertheless I assume that if there is any hope for us we must bank on the power of ideals too. Simple sanity demands a recognition that economic and military power alone can never save us.

And so, lastly, with Lyndon Johnson's call for the "Great Society," echoing Stevenson's early "call to greatness." On the obvious question, by what standards one determines greatness in a society or people, he would doubtless agree that the popular standard of wealth and power obviously won't do, since this would make us already far greater than any past society ever dreamed of being. He has implied a more pertinent standard by his concern with civil rights, Medicare, the war on poverty, and other social reforms urged by Stevenson on moral grounds: the clearest claim of America to greatness is the rights and opportunities it has extended to the common people. The President has also implied a cultural standard by his support of federal aid to education and a foundation to promote the humanities and fine arts, but his interest in culture seems superficial and perfunctory; he has displayed nothing like the concern that Stevenson often did over the blatant vulgarity of popular culture, or the failings that keep America far short of greatness by the standards implicit in the judgment of the human race to date. The societies and ages of the past that are commonly considered great are valued chiefly for their great creative works in art and thought, in the pursuit of truth, beauty, goodness, and sometimes holiness—not merely happiness. The most cherished values preserved by the human race are strictly civilized values.

The race may be wrong. But I would still say, flatly, that no society that simply mistrusted or ridiculed Adlai Stevenson as an "egghead" would deserve to be called great. A final reason for preserving the memory of a most civilized man who became a political leader is that he won the respect and affection of so many Americans, and that few men of our day represented more fully, expressed more eloquently, our hopes of becoming a Great Society. The final reason for studying his political career is the questions he forces by his fidelity to the best in our tradition. In a moving tribute to him President Johnson concluded: "He believed in us, perhaps more than we deserved. And so we came to believe in ourselves, more than we had." One might add "perhaps" to the last sentence too; for do Americans actually believe in their better selves? Are they in fact devoted to the great idea of America that Stevenson embodied? In Walter Lippmann's words, "Shall we see his like again? Or was he the last of his noble breed? On this question hangs the American future." It is an open question—or so we must hope. I would not venture a confident answer; but I would say that no question is more pertinent.

2

The Formative Years

Had our ears remained deaf to the cry of the stricken and
starving at our doors, we would not have been guiltless in
the high court of conscience, and before the dread judgment seat of history. The plea "Am I my brother's keeper?"
—whether interposed by individual or nation—cannot be
heard before the august tribunal of the Almighty.

—Adlai Ewing Stevenson I

By contemporary standards, Adlai Ewing Stevenson II lived an
abnormally normal life during his first thirty years, in which he
matured slowly and gave no sign of his future role as an egghead
running for the Presidency. Born in 1900, at the beginning of the
most tumultuous century in history, he enjoyed a serene boyhood in
the small city of Bloomington, Illinois, a typical Midwestern county
seat. As he grew up he developed a fondness for reading, especially
history and fiction, but this was still a quite normal pleasure for boys
in an era without comic books, radio, and television; he was no little
egghead and displayed no exceptional interests or abilities. Neither in
public high school nor later in Choate School did he distinguish
himself as a student, taking a livelier interest in extracurricular
activities; at Choate his principal distinctions were his elections as
captain of the tennis team and vice-president of the senior class. In
college he became a typical well-adjusted "Princeton man," con-

tinuing to distinguish himself more in extracurricular activities than in his studies. His classmates honored him by some recognition in voting for "biggest politician," "the man most likely to succeed," and "best all-around man outside athletics," but he ran far behind the winner on each of these exalted counts. He went on to study law at Harvard, at first with distaste and again without distinction. He showed no signs of brilliance either when he started his professional career as a clerk in a law firm in Chicago. His gifts were more apparent as a popular member of a wealthy young social set, in which he found his wife, Ellen Borden, a beautiful heiress. She would grow estranged from him when he finally settled down to public life, after prolonged formative years that on the surface had little prepared him for such a life.

The most notable exception to the generally even tenor of young Adlai's development was a tragic accident in his boyhood: he killed a girl while playing with a companion's supposedly unloaded gun. Given the ways of American journalism, this was inevitably brought to light when he became nationally prominent. In 1952 a reporter who inquired about it wrote that after a moment's hesitation Stevenson told the whole story "in a quiet, matter-of-fact way." The quietness could not have been easy, and the painful memory may have had something to do with his lifelong habit of deprecating his abilities and accomplishments, possibly with his tendency to agonize over crucial decisions. Otherwise I see no reason for dwelling on this tragedy in a study of his political career. His self-deprecation was typically humorous, not painful, and after agonizing he carried out vigorously enough his decisions, which kept him in public life to the end.

A Freudian might also make something of his devoted mother and her most earnest, high-minded concern for his character. In later years she said proudly that Adlai had been a "saintly" little boy. On his twenty-first birthday she wrote him a letter that summed up her pride in her tutelage:

> Your babyhood, boyhood, and young-manhood have been a natural sweet unfolding and gradual development! Round upon round. There

are no dark, muddy spots thus far in your career. Since you have become a reasoning being, you have always made an earnest, honest effort towards high living. This effort is character-building. The rewards are secondary in importance. . . . And so whatever in rewards come to you, you can rejoice over Right for the sake of Right! These, my dear, are the only principles that make for permanent success or happiness, and better never be rewarded or successful than to allow these to be forgotten for one moment. Character is better than all success and it brings success more certainly than friends, fortune or talents.

Again, however, I see no reason to believe that his mother warped Stevenson's political career by saddling him with feelings of guilt or anxiety, or with any perilous aspirations to saintliness. As a boy he got his nose broken more than once in fights, and as a grown man he was never priggish or stuffy. For her time and place her intentness on character-building was not preternatural, nor did he rebel against it as young intellectuals today might; he went his way as a good Princeton man with evident ease. Those who have never received such a letter (as I have not) might ponder the possible wholesomeness of such upbringing. The chief influence of Stevenson's mother on his political career might well be what appears on the surface—some contribution to the high seriousness that made him stress so much the moral basis of democracy, and that kept him devoted to "Right for the sake of Right," at some expense of immediate political success.

At any rate, the most significant influences on the young Adlai that I make out are the most obvious ones. They naturally begin in the home with the care of fond, proud parents and the company of an older sister, "Buffie" (Mrs. Ernest Ives), who was always as devoted to him as he was to her. To the end of his life he loved their old house, in which his experience confirmed his mother's old-fashioned belief that the home was "the foundation of civilization," the primary means of "the salvation of the race." The Stevenson home was a spacious one with a wide lawn, like many in Bloomington. Its backyard, an acre deep, sloped to a pasture with a small stream, where the children had more room to play and enjoy the simple pleasures of the countryside. A hitching post on the curb in front still recalls the leisurely life of rural America with its slow, natural rhythms, not yet distracted or disrupted by mechanization. In one respect young Adlai was perhaps more unsophisticated than most farm boys. Mrs. Ives reports in *My Brother Adlai* his brave or innocent reply to his mother's question about what he and his playmate had been doing in the fields: "We were watching the snakes do s-s-sex."

In most respects, however, Adlai was much more sophisticated than the ordinary farm boy. As the business center of the second richest agricultural county in America, Bloomington was a bustling town. Besides a Majestic Theatre and an Opera House, where the children enjoyed vaudeville and plays, it had some industry, railroad shops, and a college (Illinois Wesleyan). Stevenson's home town was accordingly not really typical of rural America. He was prone to an idealized conception of this America because he grew up knowing only by hearsay the poverty of many sturdy American farmers, the hard struggles to meet payments on their mortgages; his father managed some forty-five farms, with thousands of acres of rich soil, mostly belonging to a relative. Adlai had as little direct experience of the narrow, rigid conventions that warped or impoverished small-town life, made Main Street no citadel of either personal freedom or culture.[1] Wanting her children to find and be themselves, his earnest mother gave them an uncommon freedom. So far from constantly mothering them, she sent them off to summer camps and boarding schools.

Hence Stevenson was not actually the "country boy" at heart that he liked to think he was. He never spoke so authentically for small-town America as did William Allen White, the country editor famous in his day, and he was never so popular with it; farmers knew he was not one of them. True, he always loved Bloomington, the state of Illinois, and the farm he bought near Libertyville, outside Chicago, where to the end of his life he periodically returned for rest and refreshment. Shortly before he dropped dead he told Eric Sevareid,

[1] I am reminded of an inquiry I received from a small-town college when a young instructor. If interested in a position there, I was asked to answer twenty questions—did I dance, drink, smoke, gamble, etc. The only question I could have answered No honestly was the last one: "Do you believe in a personal Devil?"

"Oh, what I would really like to do is just to sit in the shade with a glass of wine in my hands and watch the dancers." Yet this kind of wistful longing is known to all harried men of affairs, and it scarcely harked back to specific memories of life in rural America. Had he actually yearned to retire to the simple life of the farm, he could easily have done so at any time after his defeat by General Eisenhower. The plainest reason why he never did was his greater love of public life, for which his upbringing had prepared him more than at first appeared. There he could better realize the benefits of his roots in rural America, having known its virtues and charms without suffering from its provinciality and bigotry. "I have Bloomington to thank for the most important lesson I have learned," Stevenson told the townspeople when he ran for Governor, "that in quiet places, reason abounds, that in quiet people there is vision and purpose, that many things are revealed to the humble that are hidden from the great. . . ."[2]

His chief debt was obviously to his devoted family. Although not rich, the Stevensons were always comfortably well-off and disposed to give their children every advantage within their means. They owned one of the first automobiles in Bloomington, which young Adlai could revel in without the least awareness of how profoundly it would transform American life. They were able to afford such luxuries as travel and private schools, or even such indulgences as the frugality Stevenson was extravagantly prone to in his freedom from serious financial worries. (He pinched pennies to the end of his life.) As a boy he was widely traveled, spending vacations in different regions of the country and making the first of his many trips abroad.

---

[2] For a well-documented contrast with the America Stevenson tended to idealize, see *The Talk in Vandalia* (1962) by Joseph P. Lyford. Originally the capital of his beloved Illinois, Vandalia is now a quiet place of 5,500. It belies the literary clichés about Main Street, being made up of all kinds of people, many of whom themselves complain about the town's conventionality, complacency, and lack of culture; yet their complaints are warranted. It is pretty much a cultural desert, as one said, and it is losing most of its bright young people, whom it has little to offer. Another typical comment indicated that reason does not abound: "People here are interested in what other people are up to, not in what they think." As the center of a farming region, Vandalia also illustrates the revolution in agriculture that has radically transformed the life of the farm that Stevenson knew only at secondhand.

Always eager to see new sights, he learned the elementary lesson of travel—to be pleased, not surprised or annoyed, by the discovery that foreign lands are inhabited by foreigners, with un-American ways. Hence he could feel at ease at Choate and Princeton, being no raw provincial from the Midwest, nothing of the "yokel" or "hayseed" then ridiculed by city people. At the same time he was free from snobbishness, for he had no reason to feel acutely class-conscious or in the least uneasy about his social status. As a Princeton man he was not troubled by the ambivalent attitudes of poor Scott Fitzgerald, a fellow Princetonian a few years before him—a precocious young writer who would make his fame by celebrating the Jazz Age as both beautiful and damned, and would always be dazzled by the wealthy smart set he saw through. Stevenson's easy familiarity with business-men, and as a young lawyer in Chicago with big business, contributed as well to his moderation as a liberal. The Great Depression would make him critical of the philosophy and ethic of capitalism, ripe for the New Deal, but he would remain less militant than most New Dealers and less hostile to big business.

Through his family young Adlai likewise acquired modest intellec-tual interests, above all the feeling that such interests were quite natural, as becoming to a normal American boy as his love of athletics. Although not intellectuals, his parents and relatives were cultivated people and the family living room was a library. His mother carried on the old custom of reading to her children, characteristically making a point of reading them nothing but "good" literature. Her favorites were the staples of the day, such as Greek mythology and the works of Hugo, Hawthorne, Dickens, Scott, and Cooper. Steven-son retained her old-fashioned tastes in literature. Similarly he learned from her to love poetry, again of a conventional kind.

Another, rather different favorite of his mother was William James, whom she quoted in letters to her son, and whom he came to resemble in his philosophical temper. Still another was the essays of Francis Bacon, from which Stevenson picked up one of his own favorite quotations: "If we begin with certainties, we shall end in doubts; but if we begin with doubts, and are patient in them, we shall end in certainties." This is not the key to his intellectual growth, since his basic faith does not appear to have been wrested from doubts, and toward the end he knew if anything more doubts; but the apothegm helps to define the kind of wisdom he shared with James, a rare balance of firm conviction and openness of mind. Young Adlai did not pick up, however, Bacon's enthusiasm for natural science. In college, where the social sciences had yet to become the vogue, his principal interest remained the humanities, especially literature and history. He knew just enough about science to lament in later years that he had not learned more. Altogether, the old-fashioned education he began getting in his home failed to prepare him adequately for an understanding of an age dominated by science and technology, but it did engrain a respect for the human values commonly slighted in this age, and its deficiencies were offset by a breadth of interest uncommon in up-to-date, highly trained specialists. I doubt that Stevenson's public life suffered much because he had little training in political "science."

Still another debt to his family was his liberal religious training. The Stevensons had a strong religious tradition, from which he got his Biblical name, owed to an ancestor in the eighteenth century. (The Book of Chronicles mentions "Shapat, the son of Adlai," who in the days of King David was placed "over the herds in the valley.") Though in the past they had been strict Presbyterians, his father was liberal and allowed his mother to bring up the children in the tolerant, humanistic Unitarian faith of her own ancestors, with reminders that these had included Quakers too. Adlai was taught to regard religion as neither a mere ritual nor an oppressive duty. In Sunday school he recited the credo that was as close as Unitarians came to dogma: "In the love of truth, and in the spirit of Jesus, we unite for the worship of God and the service of man." His mother wrote him that God stands for "universal Good" and "wants His children to be happy," not to mortify the flesh.

Accordingly Stevenson was spared the prejudice and intolerance that flourished on the common Fundamentalism of rural America. Although he was not a devout young man, and for a period was like most others an irregular churchgoer, he remained all his life a Unitarian by mature conviction. He therefore did not feel inconsistent when in later years he distressed some members of his fellowship by joining a Presbyterian church for a time. If this suggested that he might be placed somewhat right of center in the broad spectrum of Unitarianism, he thought he was only being as liberal as his Presbyterian father. Political considerations did not trouble him even though as a candidate he was handicapped somewhat by his Unitarianism in the South and the Bible Belt, where an advertisement or so protested against Americans who didn't believe in the divinity of Christ; he wrote that he was hurt very little because of the "dangerous popularity" of religion. For most Americans (as for President Eisenhower) it was enough that a man went to some church and seemed to believe in something or other. By contrast Stevenson was ever loyal to the tradition represented by Emerson and Channing, whom he often cited: believers unorthodox by ordinary Christian standards, yet not skeptical or casual, who took their religion quite seriously and whose thought had an unmistakable spiritual quality.

There remains the direct contribution of Stevenson's family to his political career—the family tradition of having some such career. As a boy he was much aware that his ancestors on both sides of the family had settled in America before the Revolution, and that their descendants had typically been active in public life. His wife would remark acidly that the Stevensons "must have Chinese blood in them, they all worship their ancestors so." Most of all the young Adlai worshiped his maternal great-grandfather, Jesse Weldon Fell, of whom his mother and her father loved to talk. This idol, whom he even called his "favorite historical character," incarnated the faith stated in one of his political speeches: "America was built by visionaries, and our visionaries have proved to be our most practical men."

Setting out from his native Pennsylvania on foot in 1828, Jesse Fell had "paused for two years" (a phrase Stevenson loved) to study law in Ohio before settling in Bloomington, a village of about a hundred people, to become its first lawyer. He made a fortune buying and selling land, including some in the region of the village of

Chicago, and after losing it in the Panic of 1837 set about making another. He exemplified the rampant speculation on the frontier—a possibly sordid aspect of the building of America that Stevenson might overlook—but he backed up his vision of the future of the Prairie State by building roads and founding a number of towns in the region. Everywhere he started making over the prairie by planting many thousands of trees. After failing twice in another pioneering venture, the founding of a newspaper in Bloomington, he succeeded with the *Pantagraph,* which a son-in-law built up into one of the most reputable, influential papers in central Illinois—a proud tradition it maintains today under family ownership. (Its editorial page runs a heading: "Founded January 14, 1837 by Jesse W. Fell.") A political leader too, he fought to bring the railroad to Bloomington. In the adjoining town of Normal, one of those he had founded, he helped to establish the State Normal School, donating the land for the first teachers' college west of the Alleghenies. In Bloomington he and his brother set up the Unitarian church. As an old man he actively supported the new cause of women's suffrage, entertaining Susan B. Anthony in his home.

Most important for young Adlai, Jesse Fell was a close friend of Abraham Lincoln. It was he who proposed the famous debates with Stephen Douglas, one of which Bloomington legend places in a grove of old oak trees still standing. He then pushed on Lincoln the idea of his becoming a candidate for the Presidency, a goal that his son-in-law helped to achieve by serving as floor manager in the Republican convention of 1860. For this purpose Jesse persuaded Lincoln to write a brief autobiography, the manuscript of which was in Stevenson's youth one of the family's choicest possessions. Brought up in the land of Abe, familiar with the scenes of his career in nearby Springfield, the boy developed through such intimacy much more than the conventional reverence for the favorite national hero.

Hence it should be noted how utterly different his youth was from that of his idol. Life on the frontier on which Lincoln grew up was not only poor and rude but not far removed from savagery. His shiftless father and his mother were alike illiterate. His one blessing was his stepmother, who though also illiterate brought a few books into the family. With the help of a bit of schooling, he learned to read and then grew to love reading, in part because of his laziness. Both his aversion to work and his uncommon ability to read led him into politics at an earlier age than Stevenson. He also acquired religious views somewhat like Stevenson's, but by revulsion against the primitive, often hysterical religion of the frontier. Otherwise they were alike only in that they were both lawyers and slow to develop. Stevenson's appreciation of Lincoln as a self-made man presumably contributed to his later modesty about his own achievements; though he may have heard the saying that self-made men often relieve God of an awful responsibility.

Meanwhile his reverence gave more point to another lesson he learned from the stories he was told about Jesse Fell. After the assassination of Lincoln a local pastor, an ardent Abolitionist, outraged his congregation by a sermon in which he traced the crime to the Founding Fathers, who had accepted slavery when writing the Constitution, and to the moral failure of Lincoln himself, who had supported this "slave constitution" until the Civil War forced him to issue the Emancipation Proclamation. "He had not the moral courage to step forth like a strong man in his might and do what his better nature told him was his highest duty." The congregation thereupon met to demand the pastor's resignation. Jesse Fell, who had led the public mourning for his dear friend, nevertheless staunchly defended the pastor. In this church, he told the meeting, every man must have the right to express his views freely, and he persuaded them to adopt a resolution censoring not the pastor but an angry "mob" that had almost drowned out the sermon. Stevenson remained more faithful to this ideal of free speech than did the Republican Party his great-grandfather helped to found.

He was no less indebted to his grandfather Adlai, whom he knew personally in his boyhood, and who he said had done most to kindle his interest in the nation's history. As a Democrat Adlai Ewing Stevenson I twice won election to Congress from a normally safe Republican district by championing the interests of farmers and

debtors, calling for reduced tariffs and bimetallism. He became
nationally known when he was appointed Assistant Postmaster General in Grover Cleveland's first administration. Here he distinguished
himself by replacing forty thousand Republican postmasters with
good Democrats, earning the name of "The Headsman" by a whole-
sale execution that was still fair enough, inasmuch as for years all
postmasters had been Republicans. His Populist views helped him to
win the nomination as Vice-President in Cleveland's second administration, but chiefly for less seemly reasons common in American
politics: he "balanced" the ticket because the President was strong for
the gold standard. His views also assured his defeat when he ran for
Vice-President again, more logically, with William Jennings Bryan.
At his home the boy who was destined to become more famous in
defeat was introduced to the Great Commoner.

The elder Adlai Stevenson left a book, *Something of Men I Have
Known* (1909), filled with the lavender fragrance of a bygone era
that he kept alive for his grandson. He penned many generous, uncritical tributes to "great statesmen" now considerably reduced in
stature when not forgotten. Of Grover Cleveland, "patriotic to the
core," he concluded typically: "Take him all in all, we may not look
upon his like again." He also devoted chapters to humorous anecdotes, including some from Lincoln, of the kind his grandson would
like to introduce into his speeches; they have a much more genial
humor and wit than the modern wisecrack. Most old-fashioned is a
chapter on "The Lost Art of Oratory," with samples of eloquence
ranging from Daniel Webster to Bryan. Contemporaries may find
some of this antique eloquence still moving, and then consider in
humility the possibility that our own tastes in style may go out of
fashion. At any rate, Grandfather Adlai Stevenson shamelessly indulged in the lost art of oratory, for which he had no particular flair
beyond genuine feeling. His book ends with a long oration delivered
at a homecoming in Bloomington, in which he edified his fellow
citizens by a proud review, studded with superlatives, of the growth
of their town, county, and state, appealing to the youth of this
"magnificent county" to study the history of Illinois and our "grand

republic," ending with a paean to its democracy—and a reminder to the youth of the "tremendous responsibility" of their privilege.

There is "no dead past," wrote Adlai Stevenson I; but already his America seems far away and long ago. Dying shortly before World War I broke out, he rapidly faded into obscurity. He was in this respect more fortunate than William Jennings Bryan, who lived on to bow out of history grotesquely at the Scopes trial over the teaching of evolution, making a sorry exhibit of his provincial Fundamentalism. Young Adlai, then working on the Bloomington *Pantagraph,* wrote editorials deploring the last stand of the Great Commoner. He retained a green memory of his grandfather, however, as a great person in his own right. If "The Headsman" helped to prepare him for the realities of American politics, the simple, sincere democrat contributed more to his political philosophy. In the United Nations he was still upholding the credo of his grandfather, stated in 1898, that is prefixed to this chapter.

Adlai's father, Lewis Stevenson, carried on the family tradition in a more modest but still active role. Employed for some years by the mother of William Randolph Hearst as manager of her estates in California (where Adlai was born), he settled down in Bloomington as a farm manager, devoted to scientific agriculture, but he became engaged in politics through his father, for whom he had worked as private secretary in Washington. When an Illinois Secretary of State died in office, he was prominent enough to be appointed to serve out his term, and in 1912 he ran for the office. Although defeated—the normal fate of Illinois Democrats outside of Chicago—he had the consolation of running well ahead of both Woodrow Wilson and the rest of the state ticket. When America entered the World War, he went to Washington to serve under his friend Josephus Daniels, Secretary of the Navy. The Stevensons were accustomed to associating with prominent people, and among those they ran into now was a younger Assistant Secretary of the Navy, Franklin D. Roosevelt.

Previously Lewis Stevenson had given his son a memorable experience by taking him along to meet Woodrow Wilson, then running for the Presidency, who would become another of the great Democrats in Adlai Stevenson's book. In 1916 he had furthered the political education of his youngsters by bringing them to Chicago to observe the Republican National Convention. Harold Ickes, later to become a New Dealer, took them as well to the Bull Moose convention that was meeting simultaneously, trying to get Teddy Roosevelt to accept its nomination on a Progressive ticket. Ickes bitterly spelt out the lesson when Roosevelt sent it a message not only declining but urging the Progressives to become good Republicans again. Adlai was learning about both the Old Guard and the facts of political life under the American two-party system. William Allen White, another ardent Progressive he would later meet, was slower to learn: he dutifully supported the regular Republican ticket.

Stevenson's political education continued at school, in ways indirect but still pertinent for his as yet undreamed-of career. At exclusive Choate he was lonely as but one of three students who were Democrats, and the only one who was much concerned about the 1916 elections. (In Bloomington he had sat on the platform when Josephus Daniels made a campaign speech.) Most of his classmates were in effect born Republicans, simply because of their social class; some looked askance at him as a dangerous radical like Wilson himself, shocking in his disrespect for the hallowed rights of private property. At Princeton, which the original Adlai had also attended (class of 1768), he was thrown among many more such class-conscious young Republicans. He was never a pariah here, to be sure, if only because Princeton men included a large number of Southern Democrats, and he was enjoying college life too thoroughly anyway to be much disturbed by social and political prejudice; in his letters home he wrote chiefly about all the "fine fellows" he was meeting. Still, he caught some inkling of why most of the fine fellows would not support him in his campaigns for the Presidency, or why the majority of college graduates unfailingly vote Republican.

When he entered Princeton in 1918 he enrolled in the Naval Reserve; the World War was still a serious distraction. With the end of the war a couple of months later, however, Princeton quickly returned to college life as usual, Stevenson as happily as others.

When president of the university, Woodrow Wilson had failed in his effort to make it over in his own image, tone down the aristocratic social life and the emphasis on extracurricular activities that distracted students from his dream of inculcating a passion for both scholarship and public service. Stevenson was among the majority who had no such passion; he wrote home much about his extracurricular activities, little about his studies. But his father helped to keep alive his interest in politics, always a main subject of conversation at home. They talked over the issues of Versailles, Wilson's crusade for the League of Nations, and the prospects of the election in 1920. During the campaign Stevenson helped to organize a Cox-Roosevelt Club and to bring Governor Cox to Princeton for a rally. The great issue of the campaign, he believed, was obviously the League of Nations, the chief hope of world peace. He got another sobering lesson in American politics when a huge majority of the voters responded to Warren Harding's ringing call for "not heroism but healing, not nostrums but normalcy, not revolution but restoration—not sub-mergence in internationality but sustainment in triumphant nation-ality."

As a law student Stevenson gradually overcame his initial un-happiness at Harvard, which he found very different from Princeton —"a city club rather than a country club." He learned to love New England too. Nevertheless he was not stimulated as some students would be by Felix Frankfurter; the more rabid Republican news-papers that later attacked him as another Harvard pinko were wrong on both counts. His political education in this period was still due primarily to his father.

At the Democratic National Convention of 1924 Lewis Stevenson secured him an appointment as assistant sergeant at arms. Hence he had an inside view of the long, bitter, futile struggle between the forces of William McAdoo and Alfred E. Smith. They split irrev-ocably at the outset in a platform battle over the Ku Klux Klan, which was then at the peak of its power, dominating a number of states even outside the South. Like the Republicans, who in nominat-ing "Silent Cal" Coolidge had carefully ignored the issue, the

McAdoo men favored a harmless plank that merely deplored racial and religious intolerance. The Smith men fought for a plank condemning the Klan by name. Having lost by a very close vote, on what they regarded as a moral issue, they refused to break the deadlock of a hundred ballots by withdrawing their candidate. It seems, however, that Stevenson was not greatly inspired by Al Smith, even though he heard Franklin D. Roosevelt, on crutches, deliver the speech nominating him; he thought more highly of a speech his father gave nominating a dark horse, David Houston. He also learned more about practical politics by sitting in on strategy conferences headed by his father.

At about this time Stevenson's education was further varied by his interest in journalism, which grew naturally out of his family's ownership of the Bloomington *Daily Pantagraph*. At Choate he had become editor of the school paper, at Princeton managing editor of the *Princetonian*—the principal honor he won in college. He was more interested in journalism than law as a profession, indeed, even dreaming of becoming a creative writer; he entered law school only because of the insistence of his father, who reminded him that both his grandfather and Jesse Fell had started out as lawyers. But in 1924 he took a year off to practice journalism before completing his studies at Northwestern University. Since another branch of the family was contesting the ownership of the *Pantagraph,* he maintained the Stevenson interests by serving as an editor pending a decision by the courts. Feature stories he wrote indicate a real but scarcely brilliant promise; he had yet to develop his distinctive style. What he learned about American life included some acquaintance with its seamy side. In reporting the devastation of a tornado that struck southern Illinois, killing about seven hundred people, he noted a doctor who "thought it more important to patch up his house than to help with the injured and dying. . . . Slacking, next to looting, is the greatest sin throughout the stricken area." In later years he would grow more troubled by tendencies to slackness.

In the summer of 1926 Stevenson took "one last fling" before settling down to the practice of law. Struck by the wild fancy of going to the Soviet Union and scooping the news world by getting an interview with Chicherin, the Foreign Minister, he managed to get the credentials as a foreign correspondent necessary for admission to a promised land not open to foreigners who were not Communists. Although he knew no Russian and had no connections, he also managed by perseverance and resourcefulness to get into the country by way of Turkey and the Caucasus, and then to find his way to Moscow. There he spent a month sitting in an outer office, waiting vainly for his interview, but profiting by meeting daily some first-rate correspondents, such as Walter Duranty of the *New York Times*. At length he returned home with sober impressions of the latest in new worlds. Upon arriving in Moscow he had been at once struck by the signs of abject poverty, perhaps without making sufficient allowance for the devastating civil wars and terrible famines that had followed the Bolshevik Revolution. He had better reason for feeling depressed by the atmosphere of fear created by Stalin, then on his ruthless way to complete autocratic control of the country; he knew that Russians were afraid to be seen talking with him. Because of his natural moderation Stevenson would most likely not have been deluded by Stalin's pretense of rugged idealism, as many liberals were, but while he could appreciate the humanitarian motives that during the Great Depression led some to become Communists or fellow travelers, his firsthand experience of the tyranny precluded illusions on this score. The man whom Dwight Eisenhower's party would charge with being soft on communism knew much more about it than the General did.

Once started as a law clerk in Chicago, no longer dreaming of becoming a writer, Stevenson worked conscientiously and cheerfully, making a good impression, but still giving little sign of a brilliant career. What he learned about law seems to have been less stimulating than the friendships he made in both business and social life. Most of his associates were relatively level-headed people, considering that for the young this was the Jazz Age, for businessmen the giddy boom days. One friend, a Republican, even urged him to run for the Illinois legislature—an idea he found attractive enough to mull over for some weeks, but gave up as impractical. He was facing a bright enough future in private life. Toward the end of 1928 he married Ellen Borden in a fashionable ceremony suited to their prospects. Early in 1929 his father, felled by a heart attack, whispered to Stevenson on his deathbed something about the hazards of politics; but this survivor of the era of Woodrow Wilson apparently had no more premonitions than his son of the great crash that was soon to end the fantastic boom.

In 1954, when Stevenson returned to Princeton as he often had for his class reunion, this time to receive an honorary degree, he warned the seniors at their class banquet that the hunting season was now on, they were "fair game for all of us uplifters, viewers with alarm, Chautauqua-style orators, even for occasional unemployed politicians." Nevertheless he went on to say that in 1922 he had graduated into a world "happier and more hopeful" than the one they were entering. "Optimism was boundless and people proclaimed that we were on the threshold of the new era of universal and perpetual peace and prosperity." He himself had basked in this glow, having enjoyed the advantage of always comfortable circumstances and the acquaintance of many "fine fellows." His sobering experiences had not dispelled the glow. On a summer tour of Europe in 1920 he brooded only in passing over famous battlegrounds of the World War, scenes of devastation and mass slaughter. In Berlin he wrote home complaining of the high prices charged Americans but remarking chiefly how beautiful the city was, how happy the people seemed, how likeable most of them were. En route to the Soviet Union in 1926 he stopped over in Mussolini's Italy, which inspired him to comment on the dictator's suppression of civil liberties in articles written for the *Pantagraph,* but his articles expressed little fear or horror of fascism. In the Soviet Union he had no dread premonitions either of its becoming a great world power. At home, where Woodrow Wilson had been humiliated and the League of Nations repudiated, he suffered little if any from dark misgivings about the future. If Stevenson was not taken in by Harding's "normalcy," he seemed otherwise a quite normal young American, no egghead. His real initiation into a revolutionary world began only now, with the Great Depression.

Still, his experience had on the whole prepared him well for this initiation, and for the career in public life that followed upon it. It gave him a solid bedrock in his sense of the American past and its ideal tradition: a sense that was uncommon even in the simpler world he grew up in, inasmuch as the schools typically offered shallow, perfunctory courses in American history. With the help of his upbringing at home, his formal education had cultivated both his head and his heart and made him a better-rounded man than most bookish students, less self-conscious about his culture or sophistication, more sensitive to the simplicities of goodness as well as beauty and truth. He had kept on learning steadily, maybe more than he realized, because of his active, eager interests in the world about him—another reason why he was not given to brooding. His growth to maturity was perhaps healthier for being slow; at least he had no extravagances or obsessions to outgrow. The style he had yet to develop would be the style of a genuinely mature man, not at all flashy or superficial, like that of too many bright young men. And once started on the new career he had not consciously prepared for, he was never the novice in politics that General Eisenhower was.

3

Initiation into a Revolutionary World

From now on, history is a race between education and catastrophe.

— *H. G. Wells,* after World War I

Although his wife's income fell off and her father lost millions, Stevenson himself remained among the fortunate who were not hard hit by the Great Depression. Later he remarked that he was not a very thoughtful person at that time. One excuse was that it was about the happiest period of his private life. He and his attractive wife, to all appearances still ideally coupled, continued to enjoy the company of their many friends at many a party. In 1930 their first son was born to them, Adlai Ewing Stevenson III. Stevenson was also distracted by hard work at his law firm, which had more business than usual because of the many corporations in trouble. And since he was on easy terms with many wealthy people, he was never inclined to be so indignant as the ardent New Dealers over the "money-changers" and the "economic royalists"—an epithet he later declared unfortunate and unfair. Stevenson kept his head, perhaps too easily.

Yet he could not help doing some sober thinking. Daily he saw everywhere the ragged victims of the depression, begging on street corners; unemployment in Chicago ran up to 40 percent. He began taking a more active interest in civic affairs, working with such organizations as Hull-House and the Lower North Side Community Council. As a good Wilsonian Democrat he was naturally critical of President Hoover's way of thinking—the characteristic insistence on government aid only to businessmen, not to the millions of unemployed, on the theory that someone described as "feeding the sparrows by feeding the horse." Much less devoted than his many Republican friends to their common class interests, he struck some of them as radical. No doubt he would have voted for Franklin D. Roosevelt in any case, but the call for a New Deal sharpened his awareness of the changes that had come over America. It crystallized his belief in both the tradition of Jefferson and Jackson and the necessity of adapting the tradition to the economic needs of an industrial, urban society radically different from the society they had known. No devotee of big federal government, and still inclined to the old belief that the less government the better, he nevertheless recognized the plain need of more government to deal with the national emergency, even to protect business itself from its shortcomings and abuses.

Having gone to Washington with his wife on invitation to attend the inauguration of Roosevelt, Stevenson felt the excitement in the air over the idea that now at last the government would make a bold effort to combat the depression, and there was "nothing to fear but fear itself." Eleanor Roosevelt thought more somberly that the inauguration was a "little terrifying" too. "One has a feeling of going it blindly," she noted, "because we're in a tremendous stream, and none of us knows where we're going to land." Certainly the President didn't know, any more than Stevenson did. He had immediately to deal with the banking crisis, since just before the inauguration all the banks of the country had closed their doors, and when he and his advisers discovered that the bankers had no plan, they hastily improvised one acceptable to conservatives; some New Dealers lamented that he had missed a golden opportunity to nationalize the banks. Another of the hodgepodge of *ad hoc* measures rushed through in the early days was an Economy Act, designed to make good his campaign promise to reduce the cost of government and balance the budget; his budget director, Lewis Douglas, talked precisely as Eisenhower would of the supreme importance of balancing the budget, even though Roosevelt had also promised to do much more for the unemployed. But it seemed enough that the government was taking vigorous action on all fronts, restoring the confidence of a panic-stricken country. Countless bright, eager young men were flocking to Washington as never before to enter government service. And like Roosevelt, Stevenson accepted from the beginning what was to be the "permanent revolution" of the New Deal: the recognition by the federal government of its responsibility for maintaining a sound economy, immediately for providing the security and relief that private enterprise and local government were unable to.

A few months after the inauguration Stevenson left home to join the horde of young New Dealers in Washington, feeling more deeply excited as he embarked on his first venture in government service. Another crisis Roosevelt had to deal with promptly was the literally desperate state of the farmers, who in the Middle West were not far from revolution; they had fared poorly even under "Coolidge prosperity," and since the crash farm prices had dropped more than 50 percent. The New Deal response was to set up the Agricultural Adjustment Administration, designed to raise farm prices and put agriculture on something like a par with industry. It was put in charge of George Peek, a veteran of the battle for farmers who had been a close friend of Lewis Stevenson. Adlai was called to Washington to serve as assistant to Jerome Frank, general counsel of the AAA, who also called in such keen young men as Thurman Arnold and Abe Fortas. He saw something of the ardent confusion and conflict that heightened the excitement of the New Deal. In the "tremendous stream" many captains and lieutenants had quite definite ideas about where to land, only different ideas.

Old George Peek was bent only on helping the farmers, without regard to the rest of the economy. Suspicious of all the young New Dealers, whom he described as "chain talkers," he sought to raise farm prices by drawing up marketing agreements with food processors, protecting farmers by high tariffs, and if need be dumping surpluses abroad. He was opposed to the production controls favored by his superior, Henry Wallace, Secretary of Agriculture, a "visionary" who took a longer view of the farm problem, worried over the huge surpluses already on hand, and had no faith in tariffs or dumping. Peek gave in grudgingly on controls of cotton, wheat, corn, and hogs, but he continued to clash with Jerome Frank, an ardent liberal who wanted to reduce the excessive profit margins of the processors and distributors, and to introduce permanent reforms on behalf of farmers, including sharecroppers and farm laborers. All had to contend with the hostility of businessmen to any kind of government "planning," except for their own benefit. Henry Wallace was no happier than George Peek in spite of the success of his production controls. He anticipated the uproar in 1933 when ten million acres of cotton were plowed under and six million little pigs were slaughtered. No "sane society" would do such a thing, he agreed, especially when hundreds of millions of people in the world went ill-clothed and underfed, but these emergency measures had been made necessary "by the almost insane lack of world statesmanship" from 1920 to 1932; critics should blame the profit system, not the AAA. As for the particular uproar over the baby pigs, he could not understand the apparent assumption that it was more humane to slaughter big hogs, and that every little pig had "the right to attain before slaughter the full pigginess of his pigness."

The bureaucratic infighting over farm policy was aggravated because Peek had sought and got "direct access" to Roosevelt, reporting to him instead of to and through Secretary Wallace. This was in keeping with the notorious looseness of the New Deal, the proliferation of new agencies with uncertain and overlapping authority, which gave Roosevelt the reputation of being a poor administrator. The professionals in these matters always wanted logical organization with clearly defined functions, proper channels, and an orderly "decision-making process," as political scientists now love to call it. Later Roosevelt's disorderly methods would be hailed as a proof of his administrative genius. Wanting above all to keep the New Deal flexible, imaginative, and inventive, he rightly distrusted the old-line bureaucracies, and in setting up new agencies he made a point of keeping authority incomplete and overlapping in order to assure a steady flow of diverse information and advice, in particular to keep power securely in his own hands. In *Presidential Power* Richard E. Neustadt pays Roosevelt the highest tribute as a master in the White House.

In Stevenson's time, however, these methods seemed due more to haste than to genius or deliberate design. Thus George Peek had to contend with not only Henry Wallace above but Jerome Frank within the AAA; at the end of 1933 he was eased out of his job by the President; Wallace then appointed his successor, who also clashed with Frank; and in another year the Secretary reluctantly asked Frank to resign, to the President's sorrow too. Stevenson, at any rate, seems not to have been much impressed by Roosevelt's genius in this regard. He would never be such a virtuoso in the exercise of power, have anything like his love of making decisions and cheerful readiness to risk making wrong ones. His respect for Roosevelt was based on more obvious qualities—the genuine concern for the common people, the zeal for educating them, the sensitivity to the needs of the future, the willingness to adventure, and always the basically simple idealism underlying the devious, even deceitful ways of a leader who often baffled his intimates.

For the rest Stevenson was happily engrossed in drafting marketing agreements for the AAA, touring the country both to advise and to listen to farmers on their problems. The work was complicated, he wrote a friend, even "too complicated," but "interesting and vastly important." As he saw it, he was helping in the creation of "gigantic trusts in all the food industries, to raise prices and eliminate unfair competition, thereby increasing returns to the farmers ultimately." He did not then remark that these price-fixing "trusts" were a radical violation of the canons of the American Way, which might raise some questions about the interests of consumers as well as the sovereign virtues of free private enterprise. The AAA was well on its way to the immediate success that within a few years brought about a recovery in agriculture more substantial than the rest of the economy enjoyed. By the end of 1933 it was running smoothly enough to permit Stevenson's transfer to the Federal Alcohol Control Administration, the latest of the fifteen new agencies already set up by the New Deal, where he served another eight months as assistant general counsel. He left Washington just as the extraordinarily virulent hatred of Roosevelt, concentrated in his own wealthy class, was beginning to come to a head.

An incidental by-product of Stevenson's experience with the AAA was due to cause him trouble in later years. Among the keen young men whom Jerome Frank hired for his staff was Alger Hiss, a protégé of Felix Frankfurter who had served as secretary to Justice Oliver Wendell Holmes. Hiss persuaded Frank to bring in Lee Pressman from Harvard Law School, and following him came John Abt and Nathan Witt—all three alleged Communists or fellow travelers who held secret meetings in what amounted to a little cell. Stevenson had only a slight acquaintance with Hiss, later to be charged with belonging to the cell, and he had no reason to suspect him or any of the group of being Communists. They kept to themselves their revolutionary purposes, if any, having no chance of insinuating them into the operations of AAA; relieving the plight of the farmers was a poor way to promote communism, which they knew Frank was opposed to. Since Stevenson did not meet Hiss again until more than ten years later during the early days of the United Nations, where again the alleged conspirator betrayed no Communist sympathies, he could give only one answer when asked to testify about his reputation: it was good. His experience in Washington suggested an important consideration that was generally forgotten in the national uproar over the Communists who had wormed their way into government—that there was no evidence of their having swayed any major policy decision, determined or altered in any significant respect the course of the New Deal.[1]

[1] During World War II, I might add, my own experience working in both an old-line department and a new war agency led me to doubt that the government was honeycombed with Communists. Several times I was interviewed by Civil Service or FBI agents about friends who were applying for jobs in the government, and I was always asked whether they had any pinko inclinations—this at a time when the Russians were our allies. I was never asked whether they had ever displayed any Fascist sympathies.

Upon returning to his law firm in Chicago, Stevenson was presently honored by being made a partner, but he grew more active in public life in spite of a heavy load of work in his office. He began acquiring a considerably wider and more varied experience than most professional politicians, or than businessmen who would dismiss him as an egghead. Thus he was appointed government member of the code authorities for the flour-milling and wine industries, and a little later was asked by the Governor of Illinois to draft a law liberalizing the sale of wine and beer. He served as vice-president of the Illinois Children's Home and Aid Society. Joining the Legislative Voters' League to promote good government, he was made president and in conducting its affairs vigorously learned much about corruption in state politics; in the years ahead he would have to work with some of the politicians attacked by the League. In the Presidential campaign of 1936 he held a high position in the Democratic National Committee and made his first important political speech, sweating over it even more than he would over his own campaign speeches. As a director of the Immigrant's Protective League of Chicago he caught the eye of Frances Perkins, Secretary of Labor, who offered him the post of Commissioner General of Naturalization and Immigration— an offer he thought flattering but turned down. Another characteristic interest led him to serve as chairman of the Civil Rights Committee of the Chicago Bar Association.

But most important for Stevenson's future was his work with the Chicago Council on Foreign Relations, on which he had served as president before he went to Washington. He again became its president in 1935, when Congress began passing a series of Neutrality Acts, and with the growing menace of Hitler he became engrossed in the Council's educational program. It was in presiding over its meetings, and on its behalf addressing other professional societies, that Stevenson developed the style for which he became famous. His reputation for wit, grace, and eloquence spread through the upper circles of Chicago. He had increasing need of these qualities, and of courage too, "grace under pressure." While he had distinguished associates on the Council, it was stirring a powerful opposition that wanted nothing to do with foreign affairs except to keep out of them. In 1937 the opposition created an uproar when President Roosevelt chose to give in Chicago his "quarantine" speech, in which for the first time he publicly warned the country that it could not hope to escape the dangers of the "reign of terror and lawlessness" instituted by Hitler and Japan. Roosevelt then ate some of his words, not yet daring to combat boldly the illusions cherished by most Americans.

The Middle West was still the stronghold of the national tradition of isolationism that had defeated Woodrow Wilson, and that was now flourishing on the disillusionment with his crusade in World War I. This was in part a matter of geography; Midwesterners were more provincial than Easterners and Far Westerners because more remote from Europe and Asia. As provincials they likewise retained more of the old native feeling of moral superiority over the corrupt, decadent Europeans. The American conquest of a continent, at the expense of Indians and Mexicans, was in their eyes utterly different from European imperialism—it was simply the march of democracy, with the blessing of God. Hence few of the leading isolationists were pacifists on principle, as William Jennings Bryan had been. Most suffered from less honorable delusions, fortified by smugness. In Chicago Americanism was translated into pure xenophobia by Colonel "Bertie" McCormick. His Chicago *Tribune,* self-styled "the world's greatest newspaper," daily trumpeted the cause of innocence by the methods that made newsmen consider it one of the world's worst—a blatant distortion of the news in headlines and lead stories, to assure the brainwashing of readers who failed to reach his rabid editorial page.

When the war broke out, the Colonel consolidated the repute of Chicago as the citadel of isolationism by working still harder on his million customers. Stevenson responded by accepting the chairman-ship of the Chicago chapter of William Allen White's Committee to Defend America by Aiding the Allies. Thereby he laid himself open to violent attack in the news columns of the *Tribune,* whose milder names for him included "cookie pusher," "professional bleeding heart," and "warmonger." He also drew the fire of the America First Committee, headed by General Robert E. Wood of Chicago and handsomely supported by other wealthy contributors; some of the patriots put pressure on Stevenson's law firm, withdrawing their business. However sincere their patriotism, the American Firsters were pretty careless of their associations. Although disavowing the support of the German-American Bund, they distributed the propaganda put out by George Sylvester Viereck, a Nazi agent. They flourished on some of the ugliest traditional prejudices, failing to repudiate the support of the Ku Klux Klan and such Fascist organizations as Pelley's Silver Shirts. Charles A. Lindbergh, the national hero who was their most popular spokesman, announced that "the three most important groups which have been pressing this country toward war are the British, the Jewish, and the Roosevelt Administration." The America First Committee neglected as well to disavow the Christian Front of the popular radio priest Father Coughlin, who was more frankly anti-Semitic. So the isolationists waged sorry battle until the day of Pearl Harbor. As this neared, the Firsters proclaimed: "We have nothing to fear from a Nazi European victory." The Chicago *Tribune* proved the Colonel's authority as a military expert by pointing out that we had nothing to fear from Japan either: "She cannot attack us. That is a military impossibility. Even our base at Hawaii is beyond the effective striking power of her fleet." After Pearl Harbor William Allen White summed up the lesson of this ignominious period by observing that the general and the admiral in charge there were not the real culprits—the blame for the disaster rested on the American people and Congress.

Nevertheless White himself had complicated the issues, for reasons that illuminate the career of Stevenson. A liberal, democratic spokesman of small-town America, he still differed from Stevenson as its true son and folk hero. Like most of his fellow Kansans he was a Republican by baptism, who voted Republican in every election, even supporting the egregious Harding. Although he welcomed most of the New Deal, as he had the reforms of the Progressives long before, he continued to support the Republican Party, which had grown more bitterly opposed to Roosevelt and all his works. Stevenson was as habitual a Democrat, but for more philosophical reasons: by class and association he would normally have been a Republican too. Such political differences now disrupted the White Committee. Many of its leaders, including Stevenson, wanted to battle isolationist Congressmen. White balked because this would have meant attacking the overwhelming majority of the Republican delegation in Congress, including every single Kansan. In the 1940 elections he went so far as to write on behalf of Hamilton Fish, the most notorious of these isolationists, announcing his "support of the Republican ticket from top to bottom in every district and every state." Soon after the elections he distressed Stevenson as much by resigning from the Committee. He then continued to applaud the statesmanship of Roosevelt and to deplore the voting record of the Republicans in Congress, which down to Pearl Harbor he remarked gave nothing but comfort to Hitler and encouragement to Japan; but until his death, in 1944, he remained a staunch Republican.

Another difference between them was at first less pronounced. Apart from his weariness as an old man, William Allen White was troubled by the charges that he was a warmonger. Throughout his career as a Progressive he had never been far ahead of public opinion, and he was always liable to the confusions of small-town America, its uncertain awareness of the profound changes that had come over an industrial nation and the world from which it could never be isolated. Now he still clung to the traditional belief that America could and should go its own way. He stirred up more trouble in the Committee by a public announcement, on his own, that "the only reason in God's world" he was heading the organization was to keep the country out of war. "If I was making a motto for the Committee to defend America by Aiding the Allies, it would be 'The Yanks Are Not Coming.' " Like most Americans, he was all for the defeat of Hitler, but he could not face up to the grim probability that sooner or later this would require the coming of the Yanks. Stevenson too was at first confused, and so more troubled when the issue was forced by an intelligent spokesman of the America First Committee with whom he held public debate. "Is this our war?" asked his opponent. If the answer was Yes, then we ought to get into it at once, knowing that it would mean a much harder job than the First World War. Stevenson began to realize that from the beginning he had felt that this was indeed our war, and that it now demanded our intervention; to support the popular opinion that we could and should keep out of it would be intellectually dishonest. He might have pondered the devious tactics of Roosevelt that would enable Clare Boothe Luce to charge, with her customary grace, that "he lied us into war because he could not lead us into it." He was looking for a way of quietly resigning from the Committee when his problem was solved by another invitation from Washington.

To strengthen bipartisan support of his efforts to aid Great Britain, President Roosevelt had appointed Frank Knox Secretary of the Navy. Knox was an Old Guard Republican, the running mate of Alf Landon in 1936 and a bitter opponent of the New Deal, but on foreign affairs he had been educated by the distinguished foreign correspondents of his newspaper, the Chicago *Daily News*. After a painful bout with his Republican conscience he had accepted the appointment out of simple patriotism, knowing that he would be charged with treason by other Old Guard leaders and the cohorts of Bertie McCormick. Stevenson he had come to know and admire through his work on the Council on Foreign Relations, and when Roosevelt proclaimed "an unlimited national emergency," the Secretary asked him to serve as his special personal assistant. Stevenson returned to Washington in July 1941—shortly after Hitler attacked Russia—with a three months' leave from his law firm; but he was to stay on for three years. Working intimately with Frank Knox as his troubleshooter, he gained a deepening admiration and affection for a man who was nothing of an egghead but intelligent as well as honest, kind, and brave, and who worked himself to death doing what at first had been a painful duty. Stevenson's inclinations to tolerance and moderation were strengthened by this intimacy with a conservative Republican unlike the fanatical breed in Chicago.

His first important assignment involved him in the problems of labor relations. A big private shipyard, working on a half-billion-dollar contract, was threatened with a work stoppage by a CIO union that demanded a maintenance-of-membership clause in return for a pledge not to strike during the national emergency. As a first test of the President's emergency powers, Knox and the other top officials decided that in case of a shutdown the government must seize and operate the shipyard; Stevenson was asked to prepare the necessary plans and take care of all the legal problems. Denied its guarantee, the union struck, and when the company rejected a compromise recommended by a mediation board, the government used the machinery set up by Stevenson to take over the shipyard, as it would many another plant during the war. He passed on to the admirals in Washington something of this liberal education in labor problems, which could arise from the stubbornness of management too because of some tendency to put the interests of private enterprise above the national interest.

The seizure of the shipyard, which Stevenson's superiors regarded as a most urgent affair, gave him a more dramatic, potentially more instructive experience. He was assigned the task of getting at once the President's signature to the necessary executive orders, and at the last moment was also asked to deliver in person an alarming secret—Admiral Nimitz had just heard from a reliable source that Stalin had started negotiating again with Hitler. The task was difficult because Roosevelt was somewhere at sea with Winston Churchill, drafting the Atlantic Charter of the Four Freedoms. After a series of nerve-racking mishaps, out of which Stevenson later made an amusing story at his own expense, he finally managed to catch up with Roosevelt on a train in Maine. Roosevelt greeted him genially and remained quite unperturbed by the news of the emergency; there was no need of signing the executive order right away—he would call a meeting at the White House in the morning after reading all the papers about the case. He also waved away the dreadful news from Admiral Nimitz, saying simply that he didn't believe it and saw no reason to worry. Stevenson might have been much impressed by the President's buoyancy in this crisis. To judge by the record, however, he never acquired a deep admiration of Roosevelt. In his public addresses he paid him only brief, conventional tributes, lacking the reverential spirit of his tributes to Lincoln, Jefferson, and Wilson. Like most of the war workers in Washington, he was engrossed in his own job, and might have thought more about his ludicrous adventure than the historic Four Freedoms.[2]

Stevenson seemed to be little bothered either by the "reliable" sources that had misinformed Admiral Nimitz, reflecting the engrained suspicions of the military about the Reds, soon to be our allies. Their distrust could be amply justified by Stalin's record, but could also justify his own dark suspicions of the democracies—a mutual ill-feeling that would complicate Stevenson's task as a peacemaker at the United Nations. Another matter that on the record he never brooded over as much as one might expect was the "military-industrial complex," due to achieve increasing power in the cold war. But at the time there was good reason for such possible oversights. The big job in Washington was precisely to build up this "complex." As an intimate and admirer of Frank Knox, Stevenson was more disposed to a favorable view of the Navy because he became acquainted at firsthand with its vast operations, the spectacular recovery from the disaster at Pearl Harbor. Following inspection tours of both coasts and the Caribbean zone, he accompanied Knox and Admiral Nimitz on a long tour of the whole Pacific theater (where John F. Kennedy was to distinguish himself for bravery). At home he did yeoman service as a ghost writer, if in a style rather unsuited to the bluff Knox, and gave as well speeches of his own for the Navy. He got along well enough with the admirals to help liberalize the Navy's

[2] Stevenson's private papers may disclose more interest in Roosevelt than appears in the public record, but talks with a number of his associates have confirmed my impression that he had some reservations about FDR and no great interest in him.

In this chapter I am also drawing on my own experience in wartime Washington, in particular as an editor of a confidential weekly put out by the War Production Board, which gave me some impressions rather different from Stevenson's. Among other things I learned why the Navy was not loved by the war agencies and the other branches of the military in Washington. An incidental reason was the battle of the spittoons, fought with the War Production Board when the admirals insisted that their spittoons be made of the traditional brass even though the supplies of brass were too short for more urgent war purposes.

policies in informing the public about its activities, and particularly in providing more opportunities for Negroes. On the side he secured a commission for a young Texan Congressman, Lyndon Johnson. His reward for the efficient discharge of these and other duties was the Navy's Distinguished Civilian Service Award. It was among the remarkably diverse accomplishments that remained generally unknown when Stevenson won his national notoriety as an egghead.

Another tribute to his abilities was a special assignment in late 1943 that acquainted him with the postwar problems looming up, giving him insights that would prove more useful. At Roosevelt's request Stevenson was loaned by the Navy to the new Foreign Economic Administration, to head a mission to Sicily and Italy to size up the needs of relief and rehabilitation in the regions freed from German and Fascist control. He at first had some difficulty because the Army had neglected to arrange for the transportation and lodging of his party, not being disposed to welcome civilians. (As I learned in Washington at the time, the Pentagon was unhappy over its responsibilities in liberated areas, but unhappier at the thought of turning them over to civilians or sharing its authority.) With the Navy's help, however, he was able to tour Sicily and south Italy for six weeks, during which he incidentally had a chat with General Eisenhower in Naples. He prepared an impressive secret report of over a hundred pages covering the political and economic problems of Italy. While it no doubt stressed the extreme poverty of the people, he may or may not have stressed a question that he jotted down in his notes when a passing peasant cheerfully contrasted his miserable state with that of the American liberators: "How is the American taxpayer to be persuaded that to help Italy at his expense is to help himself?" Fear of the Soviet Union would partially answer that one in the cold war, but not another troublesome question that occurred to Stevenson in Italy. Here he read about a public opinion poll reporting that seven out of ten American parents didn't want their sons to go into politics or public service. In the Mediterranean as in the Pacific he was impressed by the tremendous war effort and the unpretentious heroism of the soldiers and sailors—the sons at the front. Later he summarized the lesson: "Fight, suffer, squander our substance, yes; but work in peacetime for the things we die for in war, no!" In Italy he resolved that if he ever had a chance he would go into politics.

Stevenson's mission to make "politics" a respectable word might have been diverted by the death of Frank Knox in the spring of 1944. Not wishing to embarrass the new Secretary, James V. Forrestal (who would later crack up under the strain), he resigned and returned to Chicago. When a group of men on the *Daily News* asked him to head a syndicate to purchase Knox's controlling stock, and then to be publisher of the paper, Stevenson welcomed the idea enthusiastically, having visions of honoring the memory of his good friend by building the *Daily News* into one of the truly great newspapers of the world. Given its celebrated foreign news service, he might have fulfilled this dream, and America have gotten a good publisher instead of a great statesman, had not his syndicate been outbid by a more respectable Republican. As it was, the paper later dropped this service when it discovered that fewer than one out of a hundred of its Chicago readers read its foreign correspondents.

In the fall Stevenson returned to war service to assist his friend George Ball, a director of the Strategic Bombing Survey appointed to assess the damage done to Germany and perhaps to evolve basic theories of air power. His mission was to study the effectiveness of tactical bombing. On it he spent two months in England, France, and Germany, rounding out his comprehensive experience of the war by a tour of the Western front. On the side he presumably got some inkling that the mass air raids on Germany had crippled its war production much less than the Air Force maintained, apart from the habitually exaggerated claims of the communiqués. (Elsewhere I have noted that I stopped reading its communiqués about its mass raids on Berlin when I added up and learned that the city had been 140 percent destroyed.) But again the public record does not indicate that Stevenson brooded over this revelation or its possible implications when the Air Force became the most popular and influential of the services in the cold war. Though in the United Nations he was in no position to dwell on the evident inadequacies of the old basic theories in the bombing of North Vietnam, which failed completely to achieve its declared objectives of discouraging infiltration and demoralizing the populace, the lessons of Germany would not apply anyway to a primitive agricultural country with no industry to speak of.

Briefly, Stevenson's experiences in the war hardly made him either an authority on military affairs or an acute analyst. They did give him vivid impressions of the mighty war effort, its immediate success, and also its human costs, the problems of rehabilitation after the terrible devastation. Upon reflection, once he was no longer in the exciting thick of things, he could realize as vividly both the value and the dangers of the unprecedented power that America had built up in so few years. Shortly after his return from Europe he accepted another government appointment that encouraged such reflection, in effect enlisted him in the peace effort. In February 1945, when the war with Germany was nearing the end, he became a special assistant to Secretary of State Edward R. Stettinius, Jr. He was to work directly with Archibald MacLeish, Assistant Secretary, on problems of postwar international organization, immediately on a program to educate the public about the activities of the hitherto too stately Department, and to prepare the public for the forthcoming conference on the establishment of the United Nations.

In this congenial mission of education—one that Stevenson had started on in the Chicago Council on Foreign Relations, and would be engaged in for the rest of his life—he had as congenial company in Archibald MacLeish. As an eminent poet, and therefore an egghead in government, MacLeish incidentally prepared Stevenson for the reception in store for him. He incurred even more hostility from newspaper editors and Congressmen than did professors in government, who had likewise never met a payroll; it made no difference that he had been a flier in World War I. But immediately he and the still unlabeled Stevenson had more serious problems on their hands in educating the public about the proposed United Nations Organization. Many of the old isolationists sprang to arms again, and though now a dwindling minority, they were as vociferous as ever. When word came out that Roosevelt at Yalta had agreed to Stalin's demand for a veto provision in the Security Council, they charged that he had sold out to Stalin—even though the United States would surely have demanded the right of veto, and they themselves first of all. Other concessions to the Soviet, at first unknown to MacLeish and Stevenson, embarrassed them because they had been broadcasting that voting in the U.N. would be based on the principle of "absolute equality." On April 12, 1945, came the worst shock—the sudden death of Roosevelt. MacLeish was charged with the official proclamation of his death (in the writing of which Stevenson did not collaborate). They knew that no one could at once take his place in diplomacy because for all important purposes he had been his own Secretary of State.

When two weeks later the delegates of fifty nations assembled at San Francisco to write the U.N. Charter, the American delegation was nominally headed by Secretary of State Stettinius, an inexperienced diplomat who was unable to resolve the disagreements among its strong-minded members. Newspaper correspondents were soon angered by the scanty, garbled information handed or leaked out about its decisions on policy. (Among them was a novice, John F. Kennedy.) Stevenson was then called in to handle its press relations. In his words, his job was to serve as "official leak," but by newsmen it was called Operation Titanic. Though harried by the conflicts within the delegation, he soon managed admirably not only to keep the reporters sufficiently informed but to educate them on the complex affairs of the conference, which he had first to master himself. When the conference finished its work two months later, he expressed his basic satisfaction with its Charter in an article in the Bloomington *Pantagraph*. Unlike many idealists, he did not believe that a strong world government was feasible yet; it was enough that the Charter was a "long stride" toward world peace. If everything depended on the "good faith" of the Big Five, particularly the United States, Britain, and the Soviet Union, their collaboration rested on "the most solid of all foundations—national self-interest." Stevenson therefore agreed to return to the State Department to help it in getting the Charter ratified by the Senate. He stayed on in

Washington until the Senate did so, by a huge majority that suggested that Americans—always excluding the Chicago *Tribune*—had at last outgrown their isolationism.

Upon his return to Chicago in midsummer, Stevenson settled down with his family to enjoy his first vacation in five years. He did not enjoy it long. In August the atom bomb was dropped on Hiroshima, suggesting to the thoughtful that hereafter the maintenance of world peace would be no longer a fond ideal but an imperious necessity of human survival. A little later he was called up by James F. Byrnes, the new Secretary of State, who urgently requested him to serve as deputy of Stettinius on a Preparatory Commission that was meeting in London to complete the structure of the U.N. before the scheduled meeting of its General Assembly at the beginning of 1946. Stevenson gave in to the pressure, and in London he soon found himself in a bigger job than he had anticipated. He was put in charge of the American delegation when Stettinius had to return home because of illness; or as the Chicago *Tribune* put it, American interests were handed over to "the boy orator of Bloomington." Colonel McCormick's temper was not improved by the debate over where to locate the permanent headquarters of the U.N. Although Chicago was among the twenty-odd American cities that were lobbying for the honor of becoming the world capital, Stevenson diplomatically announced that these lobbies did not represent the official policy of the United States, which would welcome the honor but was not seeking it. Thereupon the *Tribune* headlined its editorial "Mr. Stevenson Votes for Europe," and went on to explain why: "He and his kind profess an interest in foreign affairs only because they wish to get away from America and associate with foreigners, to whom they pay fawning obeisance." The insidious foreigners nevertheless voted two to one to make the United States the home of the U.N.[3]

Stevenson's chief difficulties, naturally, were with the Russian

[3] One may regret the selection of New York, which offered only a few acres for the site. Although San Francisco offered its Presidio, with 700 acres, the State Department plumped for New York. On the small plot it offered, at the commercial heart of the city, the big slab of the U.N. building looks still less like a radiant symbol of the hopes of world peace. I do not know how Stevenson felt about these matters.

delegates. The Soviet Union was now emerging as one of the greatest powers in the world, and communism as the menace it had never been during the Red hysteria after World War I. Unwilling to trust the "good faith" of their allies, the Russians kept insisting that the Soviet Union and its satellites be given a third of the membership on all U.N. bodies. While Stevenson could always count on a large majority to vote them down, he preferred efforts at reasonable negotiation to showdowns that would only stiffen their backs; he had written earlier that the great task was to prevent the United Nations from being split into two camps, as the United States had been before the Civil War. Without giving in on fundamentals, he managed to keep relations decently smooth by inexhaustible patience, reasonableness, good humor, and wit, winning the esteem even of the dour Gromyko. Responsible American foreign correspondents praised his skill in handling the various delegations with their conflicting interests, especially in handling the Russians. He contributed as much to the success of the historic first meeting of the General Assembly in Westminster, which got off to a surprisingly amicable start.

Altogether, Stevenson's experience at London was perhaps the most satisfying of his political career. Although he knew that the United Nations fell well short of an ideal federation, by American or any other standards, it appeared to be working well enough to justify hopes that in time governments would be less fearful of ceding to it any of their sovereign powers. He could rejoice that the American delegation included such stalwarts as Republican Senator Vandenberg, a thoroughly converted ex-isolationist, and above all Eleanor Roosevelt—an ideal exemplar of American devotion to the cause of peace and good will. Although she at first impressed him as too didactic, they were soon on the way to becoming the fast friends they remained to the end of her life.

We can now see that like most Americans at the time Stevenson was too optimistic about the United Nations. Winston Churchill proved to be more realistic in his mistrust from the beginning in Stalin's good faith, which a few months later got him denounced as an imperialist and a warmonger when he expressed it publicly in his speech at Fulton, Missouri. Stevenson doubtless relied too much on his personal charm in dealings with the Russians, just as Roosevelt had been much too confident of his ability to charm Stalin out of his distrust of the democracies. He did not realize what now seems clear from Stalin's whole record, that "national self-interest" as the dictator saw it precluded any genuine collaboration with the "capitalist-imperialist" democracies. Yet as clearly a serious effort had to be made to get along with the Russians if there was to be any hope of world peace. Stevenson's experience in dealing with them at least gave him no illusions that this effort would ever be easy. To my mind he was approaching an ideal mean between the traditional utopianism of American foreign policy and the hard-boiled realism it had lacked.

While sharing Woodrow Wilson's vision of an international order to maintain world peace, Stevenson was much more aware of the difficulties, and worked with as much more patience, tact, and willingness to compromise. He soon proved his flexibility and his sufficient sense of America's own national interest; when the cold war broke out, he gave speeches supporting Truman's policy of aiding Greece and Turkey to resist Communist aggression, and praising the "bold" Marshall Plan. At the same time, he welcomed this plan for moral reasons, not merely as a measure of expediency. As American optimism over the United Nations gave way to anger over the cold war, realists got more attention in their stress on the necessities of power politics, but they were still likely to be as shortsighted as the old isolationists. Stevenson always knew that for the long run mere expediency would never do, vision was essential for American leadership of the Atlantic Community, and a measure of idealism was as essential for any realistic hopes of world order and peace. America was especially vulnerable if it surrendered its traditional idealism, for it would be left with the conspicuous materialism for which it was also known the world over.

At any rate, Stevenson's experience was an excellent education for his later role as Ambassador at the United Nations, whose survival vindicated his early faith in it. He became well acquainted with the leaders of many nations and confident of his ability to deal with them. His work in London, in the intimate company of James Byrnes, Charles Bohlen, John Foster Dulles, Ralph Bunche, Eleanor Roosevelt, and other diverse types, capped his richly variegated experience in wartime Washington, where he had also come to know many prominent people. It made life in Chicago seem relatively tame when he returned there early in 1946 to practice law again.

At this he worked conscientiously, as usual, but without evident enthusiasm over the resumption of his normal career. His uncertainties about his life's work were aggravated by domestic troubles, a growing estrangement from his wife. She had been unhappy in Washington and grew unhappier as his various missions took him away from home; his public life, in which she took little interest and less pride, was among the reasons for their eventual divorce. In the next eighteen months he turned down a number of offers of high posts, including one from George Marshall to be Assistant Secretary of State, but he accepted when President Truman twice appointed him as an alternate on the American delegation at meetings of the United Nations. He continued giving public speeches, chiefly about foreign affairs. These suggested the interest he had shown in entering public life, like his ancestors, even before he read in Italy what most Americans thought about politics. Now the World War helped to crystallize his decision, in unpremeditated and ultimately ironic ways.

One of his speeches excited Louis A. Kohn, a Chicago lawyer who had served three years in the Pacific, brooded in the heat over the causes of the war, and returned with a determination to eliminate one of them—Senator Wayland (Curly) Brooks, an isolationist and right-winger who was among the most egregious darlings of Colonel McCormick. What excited Kohn was the idea that Stevenson would make an excellent replacement of Brooks. Getting in touch with his white hope and finding him willing to entertain the idea, he at once went to work on it with all the enthusiasm of an amateur. Before Pearl Harbor there had been a tentative movement to run Stevenson against Brooks, and periodically some talk of his possibilities for high office, but Kohn started the first real boom for him. He drummed up enthusiasm for the cause among other amateurs, including some

Republicans who could offer little but enthusiasm because they knew few Democrats. Their main problem derived precisely from the superb qualifications of their man for the Senate—by their nature these were known to few voters, especially downstate. Immediately they also needed the support of Colonel Jacob Arvey, head of the Cook County Democratic machine, about the most powerful of the old city machines. But here they had some good fortune. Sobered by the war, Arvey had been converted to the "modern" belief that providing good government was good politics. Another aid was a chance meeting he had had in Washington with Secretary of State James Byrnes when looking for a respectable man to appoint as U.S. attorney for northern Illinois. "You have a gold nugget in your own backyard," Byrnes told him, naming Stevenson. Arvey was more inclined to risk supporting so distinguished an unknown because he had been impressed by another nugget in his backyard—Paul H. Douglas, a professor of economics who had proved himself a vote-getter by winning election as city alderman. After careful inquiries, he at length decided to back both of them to head the state ticket as candidates for Governor and Senator.

The obvious difficulties that lay ahead were summed up by a precinct leader. "Where the hell did you dig up this guy Add-lay?" he asked. "Let alone not knowing him, the voters can't even pronounce his name. He'll get his ears beat back." Colonel Arvey has denied the common belief at the time that since it looked like a Republican year he picked Stevenson only because he expected to lose the state (which in almost a century had elected but three Democratic governors), and so could dignify the ticket at no cost to the Cook County machine. He has admitted, however, that he found it easier to sell "Add-lay" to his organization because many members believed that he had little or no chance of winning. But first the boss had given an ironical twist to his future career. Stevenson was interested only in the Senate, inasmuch as he had had no executive experience to qualify him for the governorship, and he thought Paul Douglas was more interested in this. Arvey decided to switch their roles for typically trivial but cogent reasons of practical politics. Curly Brooks had exploited his record as a bemedaled Marine in World War I, and Douglas could make a stronger race against him because he too had won a medal as a Marine in World War II; in campaign oratory he could match the Republican war hero "wound for wound and deed for deed." Stevenson at first balked when informed that he was slated for the governorship, and he spent some days in anguished indecision before he agreed at the last minute to accept the only nomination the party had open for him.

So he and his amateur backers settled down to a campaign that they had not bargained for, that almost all experienced observers agreed he had no chance of winning, and that he proceeded to win by 527,000 votes, the largest plurality in the history of Illinois. In making his crucial decision, Stevenson was hardly swayed by the thought that the rules of American politics gave governors a better chance than Senators to be nominated for the Presidency.

4

Apprenticeship in Politics: Governor of Illinois

I think that government is more than the sum of all the interests; it is the paramount interest, the public interest. It must be the efficient, effective agent of a responsible citizenry, not the shelter of the incompetent and the corrupt. It must be the positive business of all of us, and beneath the dignity of none of us. It must be the honorable calling the founders of a government by the governed meant it to be.
—*Adlai Stevenson*, Bloomington, 1948

"The New Look in Illinois Politics" proclaimed the volunteers for Stevenson when he campaigned for Governor. He was not indeed a wholly novel type in American politics, which had some tradition of new deals. The slogan, itself a commonplace of campaigns, was safer because he did not disturb voters by offering a radically new program. Still, it was true enough, especially for Illinois at the time. Stevenson's opponent, Governor Dwight Green, was a crony of Colonel McCormick, who still stood for isolationism, hatred of the New Deal, and all the prewar slogans of the Old Guard. While he made much ado about states' rights, his administration had guarded faithfully a particular right, the graft traditional in both state and municipal government. Shortly before the formal nomination of Stevenson, Colonel Arvey too had learned that his "blue-ribbon" candidate was more novel than he had known. When on a train to Springfield Stevenson submitted for his approval a tentative draft of a speech he had scribbled, Arvey recognized a "new style" in political oratory, at once urging him never to let anyone change a word of his speeches. Ward politicians likewise began learning that they could go with Stevenson—he had "class." And the new look in American politics was to prove newer than any of the campaigners realized.

The campaign itself was a novel experience for both Stevenson and the amateurs who managed it. From the outset they were underdogs, financially and politically. Having been put on their own by Arvey and the state chairman, they lived from hand to mouth on contributions that never came up to expectations, since many of Stevenson's wealthy associates let him down, and that totaled only a fraction of the money available to his Republican opponent, since he refused to accept money with strings attached, make any promises of political favors. Early in the campaign the betting odds quoted against him were ten to one, and all along no public opinion poll indicated even a close race. The unpracticed, unpaid volunteers who worked for Stevenson were presumably more dedicated because they knew he was an underdog, but in any case they had to contend with the American tradition summed up in baseball by Leo Durocher: "Nice guys finish last." As amateurs they were often disheartened because they appeared to be getting no help from the "organization" (the good word for what the opposition party calls "the machine"). They did not know that the pros never worked hard until October, when getting out the vote really mattered.

Immediately Stevenson proved himself the courageous fighter he would always be. From the outset he gave his all to his campaign—body, heart, and mind—working tirelessly for nine long months. No observer at this time would have guessed his future reputation as an indecisive Hamlet type. For a potential egghead he was more unusual in that he got along well with the organization leaders and their lieutenants, belying the future reports that he was always unhappy in the company of politicians. Colonel Arvey writes that he respected their experience, sought their advice, and learned quickly. Stevenson's intimates say he had an amused respect for them as hard-boiled professionals, dedicated without pretense to their wholly practical job; one could always know where they stood and what they stood for. His scorn he reserved for the mealy-mouthed, hypocritical leaders who avowed high principles and made promises to the people they did not expect to keep.

On the record there is no question that Stevenson was an effective campaigner too. He had a plain advantage in a vulnerable opponent whom he could attack vigorously in good conscience. Governor Green distinguished himself as a keynoter at the Republican National Convention by a blatantly reactionary speech that defied the moderate wing of his party, which nevertheless went on to nominate Thomas Dewey to run against President Truman. In mid-campaign the murder of a gambler in Peoria led to the exposure of the flagrant corruption of his administration: a newspaper reporter came up with evidence that law enforcement officers were in league with the gamblers. When Green's henchmen made the mistake of trying to discredit the reporter, more newspapermen began digging and soon piled up still more scandalous evidence. Among other things they revealed that dozens of editors were on the state payroll, paid handsome sums to keep them well behaved. Otherwise the exposure was a credit to American journalism, particularly to the St. Louis *Post-Dispatch* and the Chicago *Daily News.* In this campaign Stevenson was supported by most of the press; the Chicago *Tribune* was the only important newspaper to oppose him. (On election night it would give a celebrated example of the Colonel's manner of reporting the news, its early edition coming out with a headline about how Dewey had won by a landslide.)

Stevenson learned much more about America as he stumped Illinois, day in and day out. Campaigning was a literally "amazing experience," he wrote, making him wonder how anyone could presume to talk about America without having had the experience. He wondered as well about the secret or the curse of political success, "the illusive business of finding your way to the heart of the average man—when there is no such thing," often only something "encased in a pocketbook." In his speeches he appealed to both the heart and the pocketbook as he promised honest, efficient, economical government. But since Green made much the same standard promises, it must be presumed that Stevenson made some effective appeal to the head too in his initial effort to talk sense to the people. He gave them lessons in democracy, telling them that "no form of government demands such vigilance, such civic virtue, such public spirit and such intelligence." Although voters did not have to be very bright or vigilant to be aware of the corruption in Green's administration, which no doubt was the chief reason for Stevenson's overwhelming victory, many of them must have been impressed by the "new look," or specifically his new style, since his victory caught the professionals by surprise. Anyone at all sensitive to the uses of language could recognize the *tone* that distinguished Stevenson's speeches, gave real meaning to the commonplaces, revealed a rare person behind the familiar campaign orator. American political history suggests that most voters are insensitive to such nuances, politicians can count on their applause of blah-blah and go on substituting slogans for ideas, making patently insincere promises. It also suggests that they cannot count on fooling most of the people all the time. Stevenson's triumph in Illinois made plainest what his later defeats might obscure, that many voters are capable of recognizing a man of true style.

He campaigned with particular fervor because of another conviction that was novel enough—a real devotion to an old-fashioned cause. Good state government was now more important than ever before. Believing that "government should be as small in scope and local in character as possible," Stevenson had always been troubled by the increasing centralization of power in Washington, and by the aggressive New Dealers who wanted the government to take charge of still more business. He knew that the "tidal drift" toward big federal government would go on because of the organizational revolution that was making everything bigger, but also because of the services that the American people naturally wanted. It was therefore essential that the states take good care of their own proper business, provide efficiently all the services they could and should. As it was, he said, "Too many of the problems of states' rights have been created by states' wrongs." It was especially disgraceful that Republicans who professed such fear of Washington and horror of the New Deal had given Illinois such poor government. Stevenson felt more deeply about this because when he indulged in the hackneyed sentiments about "our great state" he really meant them too. Through his ancestors he had got an exalted idea of the history of Illinois, and of his own indebtedness to it. Once elected, he settled down to make good his campaign promises, summed up in his inaugural address as a government of "plain talk, hard work, and prairie horse sense"— another hackneyed pledge that was novel because he literally meant it. As Governor he laid the groundwork for the belief that he would have made a great President.

Immediately he had to clean up a mess considerably worse than the mess in Washington that Republicans would later exploit. Among his incidental legacies from the Green administration were almost two thousand automobiles owned by the state, many of them difficult to locate because officials used them for their private purposes and parked them at home. With them came thousands of superfluous men on the state payroll. Yet at worst Illinois was only an extreme example of the backwardness, inefficiency, and corruption that have been endemic in American state government. What makes Stevenson's governorship significant is that he faced all the problems obscured by the popular myths that state government is closer to the people than is the national government, that it takes care of their needs more cheaply and efficiently, and that the services it provides are somehow no such threat to their freedom as are services provided by Washington. He knew that in fact most people paid little attention to state affairs.

To begin with, Illinois was operating on an inflexible, archaic constitution, eighty years old. As in most states, it assured a grossly undemocratic legislature by giving rural districts a heavy preponderance, in effect disfranchising many city people, while it also made impossible both effective home rule in the cities and an equitable tax system. Among Stevenson's first major proposals to the legislature was a resolution calling for a popular referendum on a convention to draw up a new constitution. In spelling out the need for this, he quoted from a speech his Grandfather Adlai gave in 1903: "It will be strange indeed if changing conditions, augmented population, the growth of cities—especially of our great city—and commercial development along all lines, shall not render some alteration in the organic law of the state a necessity." But it was not strange that Stevenson here met his first major defeat. The natural opposition from vested interests was strengthened by fears that a new constitution would lead to a state income tax; he observed that too many businessmen who prided themselves on their efficiency preferred obsolete methods in "the biggest business of all—the public business." He had to settle for a weak compromise, a "gateway" proposal for the adoption of amendments that required the approval of two-thirds of the voters, though most states required only a simple majority.

The Republican-controlled Senate that put through this compromise was another difficulty he always had to contend with. Partisan politics usually made little sense in state government, since there were seldom serious differences between the parties on local issues, but tradition demanded that they aggravate when not invent differences. When Stevenson tried to moderate partisanship by efforts at cooperation with the Republicans, he could be sure only of complaints from regular Democrats. These in turn were aggravated by the patronage system on which party politics flourishes everywhere, always at some expense of efficiency in conducting the public business. Illinois was especially rich in hirelings appointed on a purely political basis; not only game wardens but the state police were Republicans to a man when Stevenson took over. Colonel Arvey confesses that he was stunned when the Governor informed him of his resolve to put the state police on a strict merit system and give the Republicans an equal share in the initial appointments. It seemed like a plain injustice, considering that Republican governors succeeding a Democrat had dutifully fired all the Democrats on the police force, and that such practices reflected a peculiar kind of honesty in politics. While campaign pledges made to the people could be forgotten, pledges made to party workers and contributors were sacred.

This fidelity was about the only kind that could be counted on in state legislators. "Now an' then an innocent man is sent to the legislature," said Abe Martin, a Hoosier small-town philosopher whom Stevenson liked to quote, but the rule was petty graft and bribery.[1] The Democratic delegation from Chicago included "the West Side bloc" from the river wards, headed by a lawmaker with a record of eighteen arrests and no convictions; it sealed the defeat of Stevenson on the new constitution issue by joining the Republican opposition because he was supporting bills to tighten up law enforcement in Chicago—bills that were also voted down. Downstate representatives from the favored rural districts, made more powerful by the normal "senility system" of promotion, were typically mediocre men who raised neither the moral nor the intellectual tone of the legislature. They were likely to be most hostile to calls for the new and expanded services required of the states in the twentieth century, for these cost money. Conservatives were always demanding economy, except when it interfered with patronage and logrolling. For Stevenson the problem was acute because Illinois ranked near the bottom in the nation in its provisions for welfare and education.

As in other states, one reason for the low caliber of legislators was their low salaries. In Illinois this applied as well to top officials; Stevenson's cabinet members were paid only $8,000 a year, in keeping with his own low salary of $12,000. It was accordingly difficult both to attract able men to public office and to keep them honest. Stevenson was embarrassed by several scandals in his own administration, even though he promptly investigated all charges of

[1] I may cite a typical example from Abe Martin's state some years ago when the liquor stores were trying to get the right to sell beer, which by law was reserved for grocers. My dealer was all confidence as he set out for the state capitol to join the lobby: this year they would surely win—they had greased all the necessary palms. When they lost, he reported ruefully but without bitterness that the chain stores had been more lavish in bribing the solons. He remained cheerful about the prospects of the liquor dealers because in the next session they could count on winning simply by raising their ante. So they did.

corruption and fired guilty officials. (One scandal involved the sale of horse meat for hamburgers, or what the *Tribune* called "Adlai-burgers.") Later he would be embarrassed by an expedient he adopted to keep good men in high office, supplementing the pay of some with money left over from campaign funds. Since he made no public announcement of this, but no secret of it either, a Republican who heard him talk about it at a dinner table later reported the "Stevenson fund" to offset the bad publicity Richard Nixon got when news of his personal secret fund made headlines.

In view of all these difficulties, Stevenson made a notable record as Governor. He began by presenting the 1949 legislature with the most ambitious legislative program in the history of Illinois. Although Colonel Arvey considered it too ambitious, publicly saying that no experienced governor would try to get so much done, the lawmakers enacted about two-thirds of the program. With experience Stevenson did not lower his sights. Two years later, when the Republicans had won control of both houses of the legislature, he managed just as well, or even better. On some important matters he failed, naturally, but by general consent he was a most effective governor. He proved that state government still could do well what it had to do if the people really wanted Washington to keep hands off.

Some of the reasons for his success may be called accidental or extrinsic. He had the advantage of an earlier demonstration by Governor Dewey of New York, whose efficient administration he admired and studied. He started out with a surplus of $150 million in the state treasury, built up during the world war when states were able to spend little on their own; though the Green administration claimed credit for it and critics could howl "spendthrift" when he began drawing on it, it made easier the large appropriations needed for improved services. Colonel Arvey gave him much help, lining up the Democrats in the legislature in support of his bold program, even persuading them to vote for the removal of politics from the state police system. And Stevenson was helped in a way by a personal tragedy.

Within a year after his election he made a public announcement: "I am deeply distressed that, due to the incompatibility of our lives, Mrs. Stevenson feels a separation is necessary. Though I do not believe in divorce, I will not contest it. We have separated with the highest mutual regard." His wife manifested no such regard. She had for some time been hurting him by a habit of belittling him and his achievements, and after the divorce she long hurt him deeply by ever more bitter remarks that were widely circulated as he grew more famous. Stevenson suffered in silence. Although his sister Mrs. Ives served as his hostess at the state mansion, and he always had many devoted friends, henceforth he appeared to be a lonely man in spite of his geniality. But another consequence was an utter dedication to his public duties. He had failed as a husband, he said, so he must succeed as a governor. The basic reason for his success was his absorption in his job, which he mastered thoroughly. In giving himself to it completely he came to love it.

Hence he displayed the qualities that might have made him a great President, and that in any case constitute his claims to greatness. Most unexpected and unappreciated, once more, was Stevenson's ability to get along with politicians. If he found few "innocent men" in the legislature, he found many with decent qualities he could appeal to. From the beginning he called for a bipartisan effort to give Illinois the good government that both parties could agree their great state deserved. He was always partisan enough, of course, periodically denouncing the Republicans, but he was never a narrow, dogmatic, arrogant, or vindictive partisan. Eschewing Harry Truman's method of "giving 'em hell," he depended instead on methods of conciliation suited to his natural moderation, reasonableness, and tact. He was rewarded by the admiration and personal liking of many of the Republican legislators he invited to the Governor's mansion. He was no wild-eyed radical, after all, but he won them over more easily because of his modesty. Whereas in previous administrations pictures of the Governor were always plastered on the walls of all state offices, Stevenson at once let it be known that he would prefer not to see his picture wherever he went.

He made out well enough too with Democrats who tended to

dismay over this "new look" in politics. Noel Busch reports the comment of a typical visitor to the state capitol: "This Stevenson, he seems to be surrounded by a lot of well-scrubbed college boys and I've seen all of them. Now, who the hell do you go to around here when you want to talk politics?" Actually Stevenson himself knew the language of politics, just as he knew the pros in Cook County. He acceded to the ordinary kinds of patronage, on the sensible assumption that Democrats were as good as Republicans at keeping books, driving cars, or scrubbing floors. In the legislature he won the loyal support of a notorious Cook County boss whom he had attacked when he headed the Legislative Voters' League. He played ball with "the machine" often enough, indeed, to upset some of his idealistic supporters. As he saw it, his program otherwise would fail to go through, decent men would be further discouraged from entering public life, and the grafters would have a still easier time.

The issue here is of some consequence because of the many amateurs who since World War II have clubbed together to combat the bosses and work for reforms, and have had considerable influence in such important states as California and New York. Stevenson was naturally a hero of this movement, inspiring the formation of more clubs when he ran vainly for the Presidency. While generally calling themselves Democrats, the amateur politicians have as naturally tended to be hostile to the professionals, whose main concern is simply winning elections, and sometimes they have concentrated on battling a particular boss, as they did DeSapio in New York. In any case they look attractive as high-minded men defending principles against vulgar politicians. Liberals may therefore forget that it was amateur politicians who managed the campaign of Barry Goldwater, refusing to compromise with moderate Republicans. A few years before this Republican disaster Stevenson had raised pertinent questions in reviewing a book about the movement: "What are the implications of all our election campaigning by highly vocal groups who assume little responsibility for legislative follow-up of either their nominees or their programs? What is necessary to prevent hit-and-run politics—even by one's high-

est minded political friends?" He gave no answer, but implicitly
he had given it when Governor. His policy was to work with, not
simply against, the organization—just as Eleanor Roosevelt did. He
knew that Abraham Lincoln had also been a practical politician, with
no scruples about using the power of patronage. He considered
himself loyal to his credo that government was properly the business
of all of us, beneath the dignity of none of us.[2]

Yet he was as loyal to another of his mottoes: "Those who treat
politics and morality apart will never understand the one or the
other." He did not compromise on fundamentals, make serious
concessions in appointments to high office, or ever tolerate outright
graft. He won the grudging respect of the professionals because they
knew he was incorruptible, and honest with them too. By contrast
Stevenson's associates report that his predecessor Dwight Green had
started out with good intentions, but given in often enough to the
customary graft so that he had no firm principle to stand on, could
draw no clear lines; the shady dealers felt he was not actually scrupulous; and in his last years he seemed demoralized, virtually giving up
and doing nothing. Stevenson was consistently tough on matters of
principle. The professionals could respect as well as deplore his courage too, his willingness to assume the full responsibility for unpopular acts. He cut the funds of the Illinois Veterans Commission, a pet
of the American Legion that he considered no longer necessary. He
was as unpolitic in addressing the Illinois Federation of Labor, attacking its opposition to a constitutional convention. In short, he established his habit of telling special interest groups in so many words
that the public interest came first.

As for the Governor's specific achievements, a few of the distinctive ones will suffice to substantiate his generally impressive record,
which prepared for his future career in ways sometimes ironic. Most
conspicuous and unambiguous was the high caliber of the men he
appointed to top positions, some of them Republicans. Those closest to
him were mostly young men, foreshadowing the many more he

[2] For a critical study of this movement, see *The Amateur Democrat* by James
Q. Wilson, 1966 edition. Wilson had once rung doorbells for Stevenson.

would inspire to enter public life. His chief assistants were Carl McGowan, formerly a law professor and destined to become Judge of the U.S. Court of Appeals, and William McCormick Blair, Jr. (a relative of Colonel McCormick), later Ambassador to Denmark and the Philippines. For the rest he sought out experienced professional men to fill his cabinet and other high state offices. He was content with an informal kind of administration, dealing with his lieutenants personally instead of setting up a staff system or any organization charts. His methods might not have availed for the much vaster government in Washington, but they worked well in Springfield by dint of both his own hard work and the stimulating atmosphere he created—something like the excitement of the early New Deal.

The new deal he gave Illinois may be typified by his appointment of Fred Hoehler to head the Welfare Department. The biggest of the state's departments, this was one of the worst in the country, staffed with politicians and their wards, and shot through with graft in the purchasing of supplies; the state had been paying top prices for the poorest grade of meat and spoiled fruit fed to the unfortunate inmates of its institutions. Hoehler, who had directed a large welfare agency, accepted the post on condition that a list of jobs be filled by professional people without regard to patronage. Stevenson then backed him to the hilt, as he did his other officials, against the constant pressure of politicians and seekers of favors. "He had to fight the battle over and over," Hoehler commented, "—those political fellows never give up." The director succeeded in building up the Welfare Department into one of the nation's best, praised by Dr. Karl Menninger. Among his innovations encouraged by Stevenson was the setting up of local clinics, in which the home town could contribute to the care of patients; the Governor believed that local communities, like the state, should take care of their own as much as possible and Americans practice more of the self-reliance they preached. Similarly he required contributions from relatives able to pay for the care of patients. Government aid should go to those who really needed it, such as the unemployed, the aged, and the blind, whose benefits and pensions he got increased.

Regarding other services, Stevenson was especially proud of what he did for education. Appropriations for the schools were almost doubled during his administration, with provisions that local communities also raise and spend more. Underpaid teachers in overcrowded schools got some relief in salary raises. Stevenson was quite aware, however, that he had only made a start. As he lamented in 1952, Americans were given to paying the lowest salaries "to those who handle, not our goods, or even our garbage, but our children's education."

He had an easier time improving the highways of Illinois, which had broken up during the war and were going to pieces under the pounding of trucks, but here too he ran into the sordid problems of financing a much needed service. When he proposed that truckers pay something like their share of the costs of maintaining the highways, the newspapers reported that their lobbyists promptly wooed the legislators with bundles of cash; he had to work hard to get their license fees raised. He was more hesitant about an increase in the state gasoline tax, since ordinary automobilists were no more willing to pay directly for the good roads they wanted more than good schools. The most conservative were quite willing to let Washington come in on this deal. The Eisenhower administration, all for economy and dead set against "creeping socialism," would be applauded when it proposed a $100 billion highway program while Congress kept voting down federal aid to education.

Stevenson's honeymoon with the voters and the press of Illinois ended when he presented to the legislature his first budget. Increases in salaries, pensions, relief payments, aid to the schools, and other services made it a record budget. It was balanced, but the balance was precarious, dependent on the prosperity of business; so when Stevenson recommended that a permanent revenue commission explore new sources of revenue, critics pointed out that this meant more taxation, maybe an income tax—what some said was the real reason for the newfangled constitution he wanted. Such complaints were to be expected in a state unaccustomed to spending freely, except on graft, but they grew ludicrous when coupled with the familiar charges of extravagance and demands for economy. Illinois had never had so economical a governor as Stevenson.

Notoriously close-fisted in his personal expenditures, he got no more pleasure out of spending the public's money. The increased expenditures for basic services were dictated by "prairie horse sense"; it was never economical to neglect education, health, and public welfare. Otherwise Stevenson had a passion for economy. If it too could look ludicrous when he went around the Governor's mansion at night turning out lights, he was proud of his record of vetoing more appropriation bills than any governor in the history of Illinois. He reduced the cost of government by eliminating much routine graft, lopping off the payrolls more than a thousand politicians who were doing nothing. Among his first projects was to rid the state departments of most of their press agents, who could always justify any expenditure. He blew up when some of his department heads came in with fatty budgets that included requests for new automobiles. In his last session he blew up again when the Republican-controlled legislature wrecked his carefully balanced budget by cutting out a few hundred thousand dollars and adding fifty million more. No Republican had more ardor for the "fiscal responsibility" on which President Eisenhower would pride himself than Governor Stevenson had.

By the same token he was least bold in tackling problems of taxation. Stevenson could boast that he had put through his new deal without any increase in general-purpose taxes, such as most states had adopted, but on this matter he was somewhat equivocal. Although at first he announced that he did not favor an increase in the sales tax, he later approved an extension of it to cover more items. He hesitated longer over a reasonable increase in the gasoline tax, recommended by a bipartisan commission; when he finally endorsed it, Republicans could charge that he had been trying to make them take the rap for it. In particular his thriftiness aggravated the most troublesome problem of his budget director—aid to the cities. Stevenson realized their difficulty in meeting the increasing costs of the services he wanted them to provide, inasmuch as they were restricted by law to inadequate, inequitable personal property and real estate taxes; he proposed legislation granting the cities more home rule and providing for a special study of their revenue problems. He was reluctant, however, to share with them the revenues from the sales tax on a per capita basis. For the great, most sorely pressed city of Chicago he offered at best some stopgap measures. In general, he was too absorbed in state affairs, too concerned with balancing his budget, and perhaps too attached to rural Illinois to worry enough over the problems of Chicago, or to anticipate the much worse headaches in store for the American city.

Stevenson seemed more disturbed by one of his legislative setbacks —a Fair Employment Practices Bill to ban discrimination on the basis of race, creed, or color. Passed by the Democratic House, this was defeated by the Republican Senate even though the Republican national platform in 1948 had advocated fair employment laws. "The day must come, and come soon," the Governor protested, "when we will practice the equality of opportunity we so loudly and proudly proclaim." What came first was one of the ugliest incidents of his administration, a race riot touched off when a Negro family tried to move into the all-white Chicago suburb of Cicero. The violence shook his cherished ideal of local responsibility. The local police failed to restrain the white mob, he had to send in the National Guard to restore order, and before long the federal government would step in to enforce laws defied by states. Stevenson had a rather painful education coming.

Most suggestive, meanwhile, were his many vetoes. His administration set records for both the number of bills passed and the number vetoed. The messages he carefully prepared for the latter, with the help of Carl McGowan, his legal counsel, were admirable examples of his style, proofs of his honesty and courage, and expositions of his philosophy of government. The best known of them was the most controversial and the most portentous for his future career—his veto of the so-called Broyles Bill. Passed by the legislature in 1951, when Senator Joe McCarthy was riding high, this set up elaborate procedures for detecting "subversives" and required loyalty oaths of teachers and state officials.

Stevenson ran into the hysteria early in the first year of his governorship when legislators began declaiming that the University of Chicago and Roosevelt College were infested with Communists, and appropriated money for an investigation. He allowed this bill to become law without his signature, but publicly declared that it was unnecessary and probably illegal, or in effect subversive itself. "Suppression and intimidation are not among the weapons we ought to use in the current warfare of ideas," he said. "Academic freedom, freedom to think and freedom to speak are the best antidotes to Communism and tyranny." He then got himself into more trouble by testifying, against the advice of some of his associates, that the reputation of Alger Hiss was good. In 1950, after the conviction of Hiss for perjury, he was repeatedly attacked, by Everett Dirksen among others, for whitewashing the traitor or being soft on communism. (Dirksen, who would become known as "the wizard of ooze," had not yet donned the mantle of elder statesman.) Stevenson could only protest that he had done his plain duty: "It will be a very sad day for Anglo-Saxon justice when any man, and especially a lawyer, will refuse to give honest evidence in a criminal trial for fear the defendant may eventually be found guilty. What would happen to our whole system of law if such timidity prevailed?" Later he would add, " 'Thou shalt not bear false witness' is one of the Ten Commandments, in case Senator Nixon has not read them lately." But at the time most Americans were little concerned about Anglo-Saxon justice. When the Broyles Bill came to his desk, Stevenson had no illusions about the popular state of mind. "I know full well that this veto will be distorted and misunderstood, even as telling the truth of what I knew about the reputation of Alger Hiss was distorted and misunderstood," he wrote. "But I must, in good conscience, protest against any unnecessary suppression of our ancient rights as free men."

In a characteristic effort to be scrupulously fair, he had first gone to the trouble of making an unpublicized trip to Washington to talk over the matter with the FBI.[3] He was informed that they were

[3] Carl McGowan told about this in 1966 in a talk to the Law and Legal Clubs of Chicago.

embarrassed by these activities of the states, since like as not the local
patriots turned up one of their undercover agents. In his veto message
Stevenson accordingly pointed out what should have been obvious to
all the Americans who were so proud of their own secret police, that
these inquisitions by the states were quite unnecessary. He also
remarked the obvious nonsense of loyalty oaths, that no really
dangerous subversive or saboteur would hesitate to sign one. He did
not mention what he was told in Washington, however, but assumed
the sole responsibility for his veto. While attacking the especially
obnoxious enforcement provisions of the Broyles Bill, which required
the State's Attorney of every county to look into charges of subversive
activities and pass along all rumor and hearsay, he went to the heart
of the problem, the basic principles at stake, and presented a clear
statement of the faith in freedom that too many Americans always
forget in times of anxiety:

> The stated purpose of this bill is to combat the menace of world
> Communism. That the Communist Party—and all it stands for—is a
> danger to our Republic, as real as it is sinister, is clear to all who have
> the slightest understanding of our democracy. . . .
>
> Agreed upon ends, our concern is with means. It is in the choice of
> methods to deal with recognized problems that we Americans, in and
> out of public life, so often develop differences of opinion. Our freedom
> to do so is a great source of strength and, if not impaired by mistakes
> of our own, will contribute greatly to the ultimate confusion of the
> enemies of freedom. . . . Public service requires independent and
> courageous action on matters which affect countless private interests.
> We cannot afford to make public employees vulnerable to malicious
> charges of disloyalty. So far as the employers are concerned—heads of
> departments and of schools and so on—the only safe policy would be
> timid employment practices which could only result in lowering the
> level of ability, independence and courage of our public agencies,
> schools and colleges. . . .
>
> The whole notion of loyalty inquisitions is a natural characteristic of
> the police state, not of democracy. . . . The vast majority of our
> people are intensely loyal, as they have amply demonstrated. To ques-
> tion, even by implication, the loyalty and devotion of a large group of

citizens is to create an atmosphere of suspicion and distrust which is neither justified, healthy nor consistent with our traditions. . . .

Basically, the effect of this legislation, then, will be less the detection of subversives and more the intimidation of honest citizens. But we cannot suppress thought and expression and preserve the freedoms guaranteed by the Bill of Rights.

All this Stevenson would have to say over and over in the years ahead, when an active concern for the Bill of Rights was identified as an un-American activity. Of his other veto messages, mostly dealing with relatively trivial legislation, a few may illustrate his habit of getting down to basic principles. A bill providing for state regulation of trailer camps, some of which were creating a health problem, he rejected because it conflicted with a cherished principle: "If local government refuses to accept and discharge its responsibilities, the people will have only themselves to blame for the expansion of central, and the shrinkage and impotence of local, governments." A routine logrolling bill that gave some legislator a new bridge in his district he denounced as incompatible with a businesslike administration of the highway system, a principle supposedy dear to Republicans. Of a bill that made it a criminal offense for any person to sell a motor vehicle on Sunday he asked, why not newspapers and ice cream cones? Why should any business group with political pull be allowed to dictate the hours of business of its competitors? "Surely such restrictive legislation as this is not compatible with our earnest convictions and constant proclamations about the merits of free enterprise." Stevenson found outrageous a bill obviously designed to win votes by granting a blanket raise in old-age pensions, without providing the necessary funds: "Perhaps such cynicism is good politics, but it seems to me cruel as well as fiscally irresponsible—and, may I add, futile, to the extent that its objective was political intimidation of the Governor."

Another of his best-known veto messages illustrates the novel humor for which Stevenson was not yet politically suspect. Over the years legislators had regularly introduced solemn bills restricting the movement of cats. In disapproving the latest of these he wrote:

I cannot agree that it should be the declared public policy of Illinois
that a cat visiting a neighbor's yard or crossing the highway is a public
nuisance. It is in the nature of cats to do a certain amount of unescorted
roaming. Many live with their owners in apartments or other restricted
premises, and I doubt if we want to make their very brief foray an opportunity for a small game hunt by zealous citizens. . . . Moreover,
cats perform useful service, particularly in the rural areas, in combating
rodents—work they necessarily perform alone and without regard for
party lines. . . .

We are all interested in protecting certain varieties of birds. That
cats can destroy some birds, I well know, but I believe this legislation
would further but little the worthy cause to which its proponents give
such unselfish effort. The problem of cat versus bird is as old as time.
If we attempt to resolve it by legislation, who knows but what we may
be called upon to take sides as well in the age-old problem of dog
versus cat, bird versus bird, even bird versus worm. In my opinion,
the State of Illinois and the local governing bodies already have enough
to do without trying to control feline delinquency.

Newspapers rejoiced in this message (though I have neglected to
look up a possible editorial in the Chicago *Tribune*).

For the rest Stevenson kept busy on the side in his mission of
educating the people—pocketbook, heart, and head. He supplemented
occasional fireside chats on the radio with a column on state government that was accepted by over 250 weeklies. He gave many talks
all over the state, prefaced by jokes and homely anecdotes he
was "reminded of," in the manner of after-dinner speakers, but
settling down to a patient explanation of state problems. He got
along well with the small local groups that provided most of his
audiences, and from all reports made a good impression on them;
though newspapers commented on his unusual vocabulary, it appears
that few voters except those who took their gospel from the *Tribune*
dismissed him as a cookie-pusher or an egghead. To young people, as
at commencement exercises, he often expounded a theme that to him
was never hackneyed:

You have a responsibility to acquaint yourselves with the political
life of your community, to interest yourselves in the selection of candi-

dates and the operation of the elective machinery. To be a responsible citizen you can't just criticize. You must participate in political activity. It's your government and you must help if you want to keep it that way.

And all along, despite his absorption in state affairs, Stevenson maintained his deep interest in foreign affairs.

At the outset, he had stated what was always in the back of his mind:

> Ours is a sad, disillusioned world. Too many people on this blood-soaked, battered globe live in constant fear and dread; fear of hunger and want, dread of oppression and slavery. Poverty, starvation, disease and repression stalk the world, and over us all hangs the menace of war like a gloomy shroud. But everywhere people cling to their hope and their faith in freedom and justice and peace—though fear, anguish, even death are their daily lot.

Periodically Stevenson warned the people that for a long time they were going to be "incessantly engaged in an aggravating, exhausting cold war." In his first years as Governor he took time off, for example, to write an article for the *New York Times Magazine* warning against the dangers of the "new isolationism," which was chafing at the stiff price of world order and peace. In his last year he contributed to *Foreign Affairs* a lead article on the Korean War, defending it against Republican criticisms. Defending as well the United Nations against critics impatient because it was not working perfectly, he returned to the theme of the new isolationism:

> The audible yearning to escape from it all, the murmurs and cries of disdain for the "meddlers," "the globalists" and the "foreigners" now sometimes heard in our midst, are strangely familiar.
>
> I think the eagle, not the ostrich, will continue to be the American emblem.

By this time Stevenson was a nationally known figure. At the end of 1951 he announced for the governorship again, but the newspapers were soon full of the talk about him as a Presidential possibility that had been started immediately after his amazing victory. In January 1952 he made the American peerage, the cover of *Time* magazine, which honored him by a laudatory biographical sketch. It appeared by accident in the nick of time, for President Truman had just called him in to invite him to be his heir, assuring him of the nomination. Truman was flabbergasted when Stevenson turned down the invitation, saying he had committed himself for Governor again and owed it to the people of Illinois to finish the job he had started—a position he maintained stubbornly down to the meeting of the National Convention that nominated him. So began the legend of his "indecisiveness." But before looking into this we must wind up the story of his governorship. Of the conflicting motives from which he suffered, the leading one was unquestionably a sincere desire to run for Governor again, backed by a sincere feeling of obligation to the people of Illinois. It raises the strictly un-answerable but nevertheless pertinent questions both of what "might have been" and what came out of his achievements in Illinois—how deep and lasting were the consequences of the new deal he gave it.

The Eisenhower landslide, which gave the General Illinois too, carried in a Republic governor, William G. Stratton. Stevenson's associates there differ on what might have happened had he run for the governorship instead. Some believe that his unquestioned popu-larity would have enabled him to survive the landslide and then to complete his program, make good his resolve to be tougher in a second term. Others think that even had he been re-elected, which was unlikely, he would have got nowhere to speak of with a Repub-lican legislature now flushed by the national victory. Given the atmosphere of the Eisenhower era, my guess is that he would have distinguished himself chiefly by more veto messages, and at best could never have made such a name for himself as he did in defeat on the national stage. As it was, he at least had the satisfaction of knowing that the basic legislation he had put through was not repealed.

Otherwise the aftermath was mixed. Although Governor Stratton was for some time regarded as one of the promising young Republi-cans, he scarcely had Stevenson's ardor for good government; he was finished when his second administration ended in scandals. Meanwhile many of the men who worked for or with Stevenson remained active in politics. After his defeat in 1956 many joined the Democratic Federation of Illinois, another amateur group, formed in part because it was thought the organization had let him down in this campaign. Like him, however, they sought to liberalize the party by working with, not against, the organization. They had some disagreements with Mayor Richard J. Daley, who succeeded Colonel Arvey as head of the Cook County machine, but they could support him in good conscience because he too believed that good government was smart politics. When Otto Kerner, his hand-picked candidate for Governor, won the election in 1960, he carried on in the Stevenson tradition, bringing many of the DFI men into his administration. Others went off to Washington to work in the Kennedy administration. On the whole, the best in Governor Stevenson lived after him.

There remains the truth that in 1952 he wanted most of all to run for Governor, return to the job that he said had given him the most rewarding years of his life. Various friends in whom he confided have told me of his anguish when Truman asked him to run for the Presidency. For months he suffered under the increasing pressures as he continued to insist he was not a candidate. He resented bitterly the charge that he was being indecisive, not to mention the cynical belief that he was merely being coy or playing smart politics; as he later told Lillian Ross, "My very decisiveness was attributed to what they called indecision." For he had other good reasons for not wanting to run, as difficult for ordinary politicians and voters to appreciate. To some extent he shared his ex-wife's hatred of the publicity their sons would inevitably get in the goldfish bowl of national politics. At times he thought that it might be better for the Republicans to take over for a change, learn to assume responsibilities, especially because he had a high respect for General Eisenhower. Above all, he knew that the Presidency was a fearful responsibility, and in his humility doubted his ability to measure up to it. He went so far as to tell the Illinois delegation a few days before the convention met that he was "mentally, temperamentally, and physically unfit" to be President. His good record as Governor was in fact no proof that he could manage as well the much bigger, harder job in the White House.

Yet there was some plain substance in the legend of his indecisiveness. Stevenson would not have suffered such anguish had he been positively resolved not to run for the Presidency. Early in the year when George Ball, his wartime friend, asked permission to set up a little information center on his behalf, he "reluctantly agreed" so long as Ball made it clear that he was acting wholly on his own initiative. In his repeated insistence that he was not a candidate, Stevenson never declared that he would refuse the nomination. He was not simply harried by all the attention he was getting in the newspapers, remarking, "The awful thing is, I can't say that I mind it much either." Flattery, he would often say, is all right as long as you don't inhale it. The attention strengthened his quite honorable reasons for leaving the door open. He could never believe wholeheartedly that it would be better for the Republicans to take charge while their Old Guard remained so powerful, and Senator Taft their possible nominee. Doubts about his capacities were offset by doubts about other candidates, none of whom were clearly better qualified than he. In humility he could recognize that he had a particular qualification that most governors and Senators lacked, and that he felt was most important at this time—an intimate acquaintance with international affairs. Always there remained a consideration that meant more to him than to ordinary politicians. Just as he felt an obligation to the people of Illinois, so he felt others to not only his party but the American people. As he wrote later, "Could anyone in good health and already in public life refuse the greatest honor and greatest responsibility in our political system?"

The appearance of indecision and the openly expressed doubts about his fitness could and did hurt Stevenson as he entered the national stage, for good. Americans were least accustomed to this kind of "new look" in politics. But once the decision was made he campaigned with all the energy, determination, and courage he exhibited in his campaign for Governor, again in the role of underdog. Or as he told the Gridiron Club in Washington after his defeat,

"Mindful of the Chinese maiden's philosophical acceptance of unwanted and aggressive attentions, I concluded to accept my fate gallantly and joyfully, with consequences that were reported by most of you publishers—also joyfully."

5

The Presidential Campaign of 1952

> Politics is the most hazardous of all professions. There is
> not another in which a man can hope to do so much good
> to his fellow creatures; neither is there any in which by a
> mere loss of nerve he may do such widespread harm; nor
> is there another in which he may so easily lose his own soul;
> nor is there another in which a positive and strict veracity is
> so difficult. But danger is the inseparable companion of
> honor. With all the temptations and degradations that beset
> it, politics is still the noblest career any man can choose.
> —*Andrew Oliver*, as quoted by Stevenson

To me, as to many of Adlai Stevenson's admirers, his campaign of
1952 was his finest hour. In it he gave some of his most eloquent
speeches, and on the whole the most memorable exhibition of his rare
style, his integrity and courage, his noble conception of politics, and
all the qualities that gave him not only dignity but eventually victory
in defeat. All are written plainly in the public record, where he who
runs may read. But since we have to run so hard to keep abreast of
yesterday, it is easy to overlook the deeper significance of a campaign
that may already seem like ancient history. To appreciate it, we have
first to consider the unique rituals of American politics.

The most distinctive of these is the national convention, at which every four years each party selects a candidate to assume the most solemn responsibility of the Presidency of the United States. It is an orgy of oratory, beginning with a keynote address. The keynote, repeated with variations by following speakers, is a declamation of the virtues and the achievements of "our great party," its undying devotion to lofty principles menaced by the other party. After a couple of days of this logorrhea the convention gets down to the serious business of nominating, which involves a great deal more oratory because each candidate is presented to the assembly with a speech, a rehearsal of all the exceptional qualifications of "a man who." Each nomination is followed by a wild demonstration, carefully contrived, in which for a quarter of an hour delegates mill about the convention floor carrying posters and banners, wearing the novelty hats or other insignia of the candidate; most of the demonstrators are hirelings who then retire to the wings to put on the trappings of the next candidate. All this might seem insufferably tedious were it not for the carnival atmosphere provided by bands, costumes, and pretty girls, and for the self-importance of the delegates, exalted by their participation in such high proceedings. Some of the delegates have been voted in at primaries, but most have been hand-picked by party leaders as a reward for the effort or the money they have contributed to the party. They are not a representative body under any direct control by the voters, and since with alternates they number a couple of thousand they can scarcely be a deliberative body either.

The champion who emerges from the quadrennial hullabaloo then has the summer to prepare for the next ritual, the campaign, which is distinctive as the most grueling ordeal that any nation imposes on its prospective leaders. The candidate could give a full enough statement of his views in a dozen speeches or debates, but tradition demands that he spend the full two months making himself known, heard, and seen all over the country, satisfying the American people that he is at once, in the words of Stevenson's sister, "a saint, superman and buffoon." For Stevenson, resolved to give his all again, this meant traveling thirty thousand miles and giving some 250 speeches. After the election he described the daily routine in the introduction to a collection of his campaign speeches:

You must emerge, bright and bubbling with wisdom and well-being, every morning at 8 o'clock, just in time for a charming and profound breakfast talk, shake hands with hundreds, often literally thousands, of people, make several inspiring, "newsworthy" speeches during the day, confer with political leaders along the way and with your staff all the time, write at every chance, think if possible, read mail and newspapers, talk on the telephone, talk to everybody, dictate, receive delegations, eat, with decorum—and discretion!—and ride through city after city on the back of an open car, smiling until your mouth is dehydrated by the wind, waving until the blood runs out of your arm, and then bounce gaily, confidently, masterfully, into great howling halls, shaved and all made up for television with the right color shirt and tie. . . .

After the imperishable speech, in the blinding spotlights, there is still no rest:

The real work has just commenced—two or three, sometimes four hours of frenzied writing and editing of the next day's immortal mouthings so you can get something to the stenographers, so they can get something to the mimeograph machines, so they can get something to the reporters, so they can get something to their papers by deadline time.

These fantastic rituals have an ominous aspect in the steadily increasing costs of the publicity they entail. Although exact, complete reports of the money spent are never available, the most careful estimates of expenditures for nominating and electing all public officials in 1952 ran well over $100 million and by 1964 reached $200 million. No man of ordinary means can hope for high office unless he can get powerful financial backing, which is always easiest for conservatives. The rituals may also stir some disagreeable reflections about the two-party system that Americans are so proud of. The business of a national convention is not to nominate the ablest man available, the one best qualified for the Presidency, or even necessarily the one most popular with the party workers—Senator Robert Taft was always the favorite of the Republican professionals. In 1952 General Eisenhower was nominated because he measured up better by the primary consideration, the question "Can he win the election?" The campaigns have grown more bizarre and expensive because the two big parties are more frantically dedicated than any others in all the democracies to their main function, to win elections; or as Frank Sorauf put it, they are "great and overt conspiracies for the capture of public office."

Hence European observers are always bewildered by the American two-party system. To them the major parties look almost indistinguishable as they go about their common obsession. Neither has a clear ideology, of course, in lieu of one offering chiefly pseudo-ideological slogans or resounding generalities. Both are at once embarrassed and aided by the vagueness of their alleged principles. Both embrace liberal and conservative wings that may battle each other more bitterly than they battle the enemy, as the Republicans did over Eisenhower and Taft; but then they blur or confuse the major issues by patching up their internal differences in order to give the appearance of consensus, to capture the public consensus, and to bolster the myth that they are dedicated to the interests of all the people all the time. They take their stand on a platform made up of miscellaneous planks in which the definite promises may be as empty as the meaningless ones because the winning party is not obliged to carry them out, and for that matter is often unable to. Although Stevenson made much of the ideals for which the Democratic Party stood, his party was not actually united, and had he been elected he could hardly have made good on promises repugnant to the coalition of Republicans and Southern Democrats that had long controlled Congress.

Yet all this myth and ritual accentuated his "new look," which in turn finally redounded to the credit of a political system in which he achieved such eminence. No national convention had ever been opened by anything like the welcoming address Stevenson gave in Chicago as Governor of the host state. While he made the expected attacks on the Republicans, who had convened in Chicago a week earlier, he indulged his distinctive humor:

For almost a week pompous phrases marched over this landscape in search of an idea, and the only idea they found was that the two great decades of progress in peace, victory in war, and bold leadership in this anxious hour were the misbegotten spawn of socialism, bungling, corruption, mismanagement, waste and worse. They captured, tied and dragged that ragged idea in here and furiously beat it to death. . . .

But we Democrats were not the only victims here. First they slaughtered each other, and they then went after us. And the same vocabulary was good for both exercises, which was a great convenience. Perhaps the proximity of the stockyards accounts for the carnage.

Stevenson proceeded with the expected praise of the Democratic Party, but then sounded a more uncommon note:

Where we have erred, let there be no denial; where we have wronged the public trust, let there be no excuses. Self-criticism is the secret weapon of democracy, and candor and confession are good for the political soul.

In this spirit of humility he introduced his solemn message to the delegates:

A great record of past achievement is not enough. There can be no complacency, perhaps for years to come. We dare not just look back to great yesterdays. We must look forward to great tomorrows.

What counts now is not just what we are *against*, but what we are *for. Who* leads us is less important than *what* leads us—what convictions, what courage, what faith—win or lose. . . .

And let us remember that we are not meeting here alone. All the world is watching and listening to what we say, what we do and how we behave. So let us give them a demonstration of democracy in action at its best—our manners good, our proceedings orderly and dignified. And—above all—let us make our decisions openly, fairly, not by the processes of synthetic excitement or mass hysteria, but, as these solemn times demand, by earnest thought and prayerful deliberation.

Thus can the people's party reassure the people and vindicate and strengthen the forces of democracy throughout the world.

The delegates applauded, as they had to, but the aftermath testified that they had really been impressed by Stevenson's unorthodox opening address. He was still not a candidate, and those who had nevertheless resolved to vote for him were still a minority; on the first

ballot he was only one of the many who ran behind Senator
Kefauver, the leading contender. On the third ballot Stevenson
forged so far ahead of Kefauver and the field that he was immediately nominated by acclamation. According to the Republicans, his
victory was contrived by Harry Truman and the "bosses," who
thereby made him their "captive." Actually the "bosses" had long
since lost the power that had enabled a few Republican politicians to
dictate the nomination of Warren Harding in a smoke-filled room; if
conventions are not purely democratic institutions, the closer attention
and much larger audience they now get from radio and television as
well as the press make it almost impossible for them to be so crudely
controlled. As for Truman, he unquestionably had the great influence
that retiring Presidents normally do, and in his own opinion it was
the decisive influence, exerted by asking Averell Harriman to with-
draw in favor of Stevenson. But Truman had first given up on
Stevenson, Harriman had urged his supporters to shift before he was
asked to do so, and the tide was by then so strong that Stevenson had
no need of the President's help. His nomination was essentially a
draft, at first due to the organization of enthusiasts who persisted in
spite of his refusal to declare himself, then to contagion that made it
spontaneous. As a genuine draft, it was very rare if not unique in
American political history. Inasmuch as he had made no political
deals, promises, or commitments, no candidate was ever less a
"captive."

No less rare was Stevenson's moving speech of acceptance. Although it too had conventional passages, it was again the unconven-
tional style and substance that made many listeners all over the
country—both simple people and sophisticates—feel that it was the
greatest political speech they had ever heard. At the outset he
confessed that he had been troubled, unable to seek the high office in
good conscience:

> I have asked the Merciful Father—the Father of us all—to let this
> cup pass from me. But from such dread responsibility one does not
> shrink in fear, in self-interest, or in false humility. So, "If this cup
> may not pass from me, except I drink it, Thy will be done."

After some good words for the platform and the conduct of the convention, and some ridicule of the schizophrenic Republican Party, he departed from the ritual text of a victory speech as he came to his peroration:

> I hope and pray that we Democrats, win or lose, can campaign not as a crusade to exterminate the opposing party, as our opponents seem to prefer, but as a great opportunity to educate and elevate a people whose destiny is leadership, not alone of a rich and prosperous, contented country as in the past, but of a world in ferment.
>
> And, my friends, more important than winning the election is governing the nation. That is the test of a political party—the acid, final test. When the tumult and the shouting die, when the bands are gone and the lights are dimmed, there is the stark reality of responsibility in an hour of history haunted with those gaunt, grim specters of strife, dissension and materialism at home, and ruthless, inscrutable and hostile power abroad.
>
> The ordeal of the twentieth century—the bloodiest, most turbulent era of the Christian age—is far from over. Sacrifice, patience, understanding and implacable purpose may be our lot for years to come. Let's face it. Let's talk sense to the American people. Let's tell them the truth, that there are no gains without pains, that we are now on the eve of great decisions, not easy decisions, like resistance when you're attacked, but a long, patient, costly struggle which alone can assure triumph over the great enemies of man—war, poverty and tyranny— and the assaults upon human dignity which are the most grievous consequences of each.

Thus, Stevenson concluded, "we will serve our great tradition greatly." He ended his brief address in the spirit he began it: "And finally, my friends, in the staggering task you have assigned me, I shall always try 'to do justly and to love mercy and to walk humbly with my God.' " God appears regularly on high political occasions in America, to bless them; but since Abraham Lincoln he has seldom been invoked in this spirit. Back in Springfield two days later, Stevenson invoked the spiritual aid of Lincoln too. In the middle of the night he quietly visited Lincoln's home and for an hour sat alone in his rocking chair, drawing strength for the staggering task.

These addresses force some qualification of the common charges against the two major parties. Their notorious lack of a clear-cut ideology is not simply deplorable, for it reflects the basic solidarity of America. Few but revolutionaries would like to see this solidarity broken up by a deep class or ideological hostility, a militant Left and Right. The plaintiffs might contemplate the fate of a European intellectual in politics who resembled Adlai Stevenson—León Blum.

Although he differed as a full-fledged intellectual and a socialist, Blum had much the same attractive qualities of political honesty, courage, fidelity, dignity, and generosity. He too gained in stature after his defeat as Premier, shortly before World War II, maintaining his principles under the Vichy regime; he was most admired in his last years before his death in 1950. In France, the holy land of ideology, he too passed as a moderate because of his fidelity to constitutional government. And for this reason he failed as Premier, faring much worse than Stevenson would in defeat. Lacking a clear majority behind his socialistic program, he could not put it through so long as he remained true to democratic principles; he was violently attacked by both the Left and the Right, the latter spreading the word "Better Hitler than Blum"; and both his party and the Republic he was trying to save went down, as the Left too opposed the war with Hitler when it came. With all its faults, the American two-party system may seem, as it did to Stevenson, better suited to a democracy.

Yet Stevenson also believed that there were real and important differences between the parties, and certainly he was sincere in habitually speaking of the Democrats as "the people's party." Polls indicated that most voters agreed with him, believing that the Democrats favored the little man, the Republicans favored business. The Republican National Convention itself provided evidence: of its delegates (incidentally 87 percent Protestant) fewer than 3 percent were trade unionists. And Stevenson plainly had history on his side. Behind him were the administrations of Wilson, Roosevelt, and Truman, which contrasted sharply enough with those of Harding, Coolidge, and Hoover to justify the description of the New Deal as a "permanent revolution." There was literally a world of difference between him and the Republican Old Guard—all the radical change that made the postwar world so different from their nineteenth-century America, and that made them the hopelessly impractical dreamers or "visionaries" they accused him of being. Most of the Republicans in Congress were men who had fought the New Deal.

Still, private polls indicated that when the campaign started Stevenson had only 35 percent of the people behind him. His most obvious handicap was the popularity of General Eisenhower as a war hero, which offset the chief liability of the Republican Party, its association with the Great Depression. Ostensibly a nonpolitical man, the General played the old party game better than he knew. He attracted many voters by his stand as a moderate, somewhere between the parties, and many more by the stereotyped generalities that placed him everywhere or nowhere, concealing his failure to offer a positive program. But he had a further advantage in the social changes brought about by wartime prosperity, which made voters more indifferent to such programs or any fundamental issues. Roosevelt had drawn his popular support especially from young people, low-income groups, and city-dwellers. Now the young no longer had memories of the depression, the low-income groups were largely a rising middle class, and many people were leaving the cities for the suburbs, the citadels of middle-class mentality. Voters were worrying about inflation instead of depression and were blaming it on government spending, complaining about high taxes. Able as never before to afford the luxury of such complaints, they took out all their grievances on the Truman administration. Truman had become so unpopular that they responded to the slogan "It's time for a change" even though—or more likely because—General Eisenhower proposed no basic change.

In another respect the slogan was still odder. President Truman had presided over a period of continuous, radical change—the dropping of the atomic bomb, the beginning of the cold war, the Truman Doctrine, the Marshall Plan, the Korean War. His bold, resolute leadership in foreign affairs belied the common view of him as an earnest little man doing his best in a job too big for him. In a poll of historians and political scientists years later he was ranked among the "near great" Presidents, well above Eisenhower. Moreover, most Americans had backed his crucial decisions. In polls an overwhelming majority approved the use of the atom bomb (a distressing 23 percent even subscribing to the statement that we should have quickly used many more bombs before Japan had a chance to surrender). As great a majority agreed that Truman did the right thing in sending American troops to Korea. And in 1948 the voters had risen to his gallant campaign, when with the odds heavily against him he went to the people. In his *Memoirs* he wrote that he decided to run again because the Republican-controlled Eightieth Congress proved that the Old Guard was as reactionary as ever, convincing him "of the urgent need for more liberalism in government rather than less." His surprise victory pleased liberals the more because he took a positive stand on all issues, even when he knew it might be an unpopular stand, whereas Governor Dewey was as careful to skirt most of the issues as he was to keep clear of the Republican Congress.

In the last years of his administration, however, Truman's popularity steadily declined, reaching a low of 26 percent in the polls. The most apparent reason was the stalemated war in Korea. Coming only five years after complete victory in the world war, it was especially frustrating to a people accustomed to victory. Republican leaders bent on exploiting the frustration over "Truman's war" saw their chance when General Douglas MacArthur, his vanity wounded because he had led the longest retreat in American history, defied the orders of his Commander in Chief, and Truman had the courage to relieve him of his command in Korea. One may still shudder over the popular hysteria that greeted this war hero on his return home, and the ovation he got in Congress when he said he would now "just fade away" like an old soldier; whereupon he began fading by stumping the country to attack limited warfare as just "appeasement of Communism." When General Omar Bradley told a Senate hearing that MacArthur's aggressive policy "would involve us in the wrong war, at the wrong place, at the wrong time, and with the wrong enemy," the Republican members of the committee issued a statement supporting this policy and denouncing the dismissal of the hero. But Truman's own shortcomings made it easier for Republicans to make him the scapegoat for all the grievances and anxieties accumulated over the years of Democratic rule. Although they exaggerated "the mess in Washington," there had been enough easygoing corruption to justify disquiet or even disgust. As a politician Truman was still a little man, inclined to be lax because of his party loyalties and his questionable taste in cronies.

Stevenson was clearly somewhat embarrassed by his role of heir. While he endorsed without flinching both the foreign and the domestic policies of Truman, he knew from his experience in Illinois that the corruption issue could hurt; so he took more pains to run his own campaign, or as Truman saw it, "to disassociate himself from the administration in Washington." He moved his campaign headquarters to Springfield, replaced the chairman of the Democratic National Committee with an Illinois associate, and again turned his campaign over to amateurs, headed by Wilson Wyatt. Truman wrote in his *Memoirs* that these were serious mistakes: "How Stevenson hoped he could persuade the American voters to maintain the Democratic party in power while seeming to disown powerful elements of it, I don't know." It is doubtful that this independence hurt Stevenson much, since General Eisenhower campaigned against Truman rather than him anyway; but the differences between the two men added something to the "new look."

As an ex-haberdasher, Harry Truman may be regarded as a vindication of Abraham Lincoln's faith in the dignity and wisdom of the common man. Quite aware that he was no Roosevelt or Churchill, he never brooded over feelings of inferiority but simply went about doing his duty to the best of his ability, never complaining either of his dread responsibilities. He was just what he seemed—a plain man with nothing complicated about him.[1] By his cheerful courage and integrity, exemplified by his desk motto "The buck stops here,"

[1] In 1948 one shrewd observer anticipated Truman's astonishing victory when he noticed that the crowds around his train not only were larger than those around Dewey's but always included some people who looked like Truman, and nobody who looked like Thomas Dewey. Stevenson lacked this advantage too.

he won the admiration of not only Stevenson but such aristocrats as Churchill and Dean Acheson (a man never disposed to be patient with fools, whom he saw all over Washington). On the other hand, Truman was thoroughly commonplace in his style. Lacking any power of eloquence, he could never rouse the people to serve a great tradition greatly. He could take on his appalling responsibilities more easily because he was not very sensitive or imaginative; the decision to drop the atom bomb on Japan cost him nothing like the anguish that Stevenson would have suffered. As a politician he was simply unable to understand the Governor's motives in rejecting his offer of the nomination. Richard Rovere reports that during the speech of acceptance he looked absent-minded when not uneasy—this was no fighting speech; and when Stevenson paid him a tribute he un-thinkingly joined the applause for himself. A loyal party man, he seemed wholehearted as he threw himself into the campaign, but he was a doubtful help in giving 'em hell again. He offended many voters by attacking General Eisenhower with the same hatchet he used on the worst of the Old Guard.

Making due allowance for the necessities of political campaigns, Stevenson remained true to the pledge in his speech of acceptance: "Better we lose the election than mislead the people." He paid folksy or fulsome tributes to whatever region he was in, hailing alike the "political genius" of the Old South and the bright promise of Los Angeles, "the city of the future" (God help us); he talked loosely about what "the Democratic Party" and "the American people" believed, how both were forever in search of new frontiers; he glided easily from what we "must" do to what we "will" do; and so forth. But always he settled down to an honest effort to talk sense to the people, taking up the issues one by one and appealing more to reason than to emotion. Later he apologized for his shortcomings by quoting Froude: "The excitement of perpetual speechmaking is fatal to the exercise of the highest powers."

The 250 speeches he gave call for a bow from an unsung, possibly unseemly newcomer in the ritual of American campaigns—the ghost writer. Before his nomination Stevenson had told George Ball that if he ran, "Every word I speak or write during the campaign must be mine"; he was more repelled by the idea of ghost writers because he remembered what most Americans have now forgotten, that once upon a time statesmen used to write their speeches themselves. No man, however, could possibly compose all the speeches required in a modern American campaign, and Stevenson ended up with the largest battalion of ghost writers to date. It was also by far the most distinguished. Beginning with William Blair and Carl McGowan, who knew intimately his ways of thinking and expressing himself, it included Arthur Schlesinger, Jr., Kenneth Galbraith, Willard Wirtz, David Bell, John Fischer, Eric Hodgins, and John Bartlow Martin, with occasional assists from Herbert Agar, Bernard De Voto, and other prominent writers. He gave his writers more trouble because he hated to repeat himself, and though he inevitably did, he refused to use the same talk at every whistle stop; so they were forever under pressure. (Mary McGrory has reported how many people tried vainly to tell him that it was not necessary to make the Gettysburg Address at every street corner, "particularly when the corner is not wired for sound.") But those of his writers who have gone on record give much the same report, intimating that Stevenson himself was the best of the lot; he set the basic style and by revision made the speeches essentially his own. With his major television speeches he distressed his whole staff by polishing and making additions up to the last minute, more than once running beyond his allotted time on the air and being cut off before he had reached his elegant conclusion. For the same reason he gave reporters constant trouble—they could never count on getting his copy in time to meet their deadlines. By contrast they could always count on getting Nixon's copy well ahead of time, since on tours he gave the same talk over and over, and he grew resentful when they gave it little publicity after the first time.

The contrast emphasizes an essential quality of Stevenson's new look. He despised the business of "public relations," the manufacture of "public images," the cult of superficial or artificial "personality." During the campaign James Reston commented on the difference between his diffident wave from his open automobile and Ike's arms flung up in a V for victory, and he added, "The difference can beat him." His managers did their best to make him alter his image somewhat at least on television, which in this campaign was playing an important role for the first time. They called in professionals to coach him in the arts of timing, gesturing, "projecting" for the cameras—the tricks of the TV trade that General Eisenhower was dutifully learning from Hollywood and Madison Avenue men; but they could get no more out of him than an occasional awkward gesture or nervous grin. Stevenson stubbornly insisted on being himself. The best-known photograph of him snapped during the campaign showed a hole in the sole of his shoe. After the campaign he remarked gaily that he always forgot to wear the right color shirt and tie when performing on TV.

He was as incorrigible about his speeches, which were criticized for opposite reasons. Some of his advisers thought he was talking over the heads of the voters, being too much the egghead; others thought he was indulging too freely his satirical humor, giving the impression of levity, with which the Republicans were charging him. Unquestionably his "image" suffered somewhat on both counts, which could reinforce one another. Whether humorous or in deadly earnest, he struck many voters as less serious than General Eisenhower, who got more thunderous applause for both his humorless stereotypes and his denunciations of the "Truman gang." Eisenhower had little respect for him because he could appreciate neither his seriousness nor his wit. At any rate, Stevenson went on talking to suit himself, in what for him had become his natural style. As another Happy Warrior he continued to defy "the Republican law of gravity." Soberly he said, "I believe you should talk up to people, not down." Whatever the political effects of his campaign speeches, their distinction lies in just this blend of humor and high seriousness. Today a reader of them will find much repetition, arid stretches of campaign rhetoric, ideas too familiar or outdated, in general plenty of dead wood; but he will also find many witty observations, much matter still worth thinking about, and periodically memorable passages, soaring to eloquence. The speeches are still a pleasure to read and to quote. I think an inadequate but suggestive measure of their distinction is a simple question: How many thoughtful Republicans today would be willing to read the campaign speeches of General Eisenhower or Richard Nixon?[2]

Stevenson's speeches were not all of a piece, however, apart from some natural unevenness. They reflect a significant change in his attitude toward General Eisenhower, for whom he lost much of his initial respect. His more and more direct attacks on the General were legitimate because of his growing awareness of the serious limitations of the man who was to become President at a time calling for great decisions. As political tactics they were nevertheless somewhat dubious. And finally they exposed more clearly his own shortcomings.

After his courageous attack on McCarthyism at the American Legion Convention, Stevenson periodically returned to this issue. He was shocked when Eisenhower called for the re-election of McCarthy, consented to cut out from a speech in Wisconsin a passage praising General Marshall (whom the Senator had charged with heading a conspiracy to deliver China to the Communists), and then gave his support to Senator Jenner of Indiana, who had called Marshall a "living lie" and "a front man for traitors." When Stevenson spoke in Wisconsin he denounced McCarthy again, and included Eisenhower: "My opponent has been worrying about my funny bone. I'm worrying about his backbone."[3] Though he still concentrated on the main issue, the menace to civil liberties, he was having to put up with the smear campaign of Nixon, who was constantly attacking him because of his deposition on behalf of Alger Hiss. Finally he felt obliged to devote a whole speech to the Hiss case. Once more he pointed out that he had simply told the truth, adding that if Nixon, a fellow lawyer, "would not tell and tell honestly what he knew of a defendant's

---

[2] I should confess that I myself was not up to this task, which conscientious historians of the future may feel obliged to tackle. It seemed to me enough to read the passages featured in the press, which did ample justice to their main ideas or the appearances thereof.

[3] To be fair to Eisenhower, he was unhappy about this affair himself. In his memoirs he wrote that when he learned that his managers had arranged a speaking tour in Wisconsin, it "occasioned the sharpest flareup I can recall between my staff and I [*sic*] during the entire campaign."

reputation, he would be a coward and unfit for any office." Stevenson then introduced some relevant evidence. At the time of his deposition Hiss was president of the Carnegie Endowment, of whose board of trustees John Foster Dulles was chairman and General Eisenhower a member. When rumors were reported to Dulles, he said, "I have confidence that there is no reason to doubt Mr. Hiss' complete loyalty to our American institutions." Eisenhower voiced no public disapproval when the board voted to reject the resignation of Hiss after he had been indicted. For the General's benefit Stevenson threw in the remark of another general, the Duke of Wellington, after inspecting his troops: "They may not frighten the enemy, but gad sir, they frighten me." He concluded, "I never would have believed that a Presidential contest with General Eisenhower would have made this speech necessary." Later Stevenson regretted having dragged his opponent into the Hiss affair, but I suppose few would blame him.

More questionable was the case he made against the General's Republicanism. From the beginning of his campaign he had good clean fun ridiculing "the two-headed elephant," the glaring discrepancy between the expressed intentions of Eisenhower and the record of the Old Guard. Often he pointed out that Eisenhower seemed to be running on the Democratic platform, adding that he welcomed "such a distinguished hitchhiker," only "it is just those one-eyed guys with knives in their teeth who are scrambling aboard with him that make me a little uncomfortable." He complained reasonably of his opponent's refusal to debate the issues with him, which made his long campaign road lonely—"I never meet anybody coming the other way." When Eisenhower came to terms with Senator Taft, however, announcing that they saw eye to eye on domestic issues, Stevenson saw a surrender to the Old Guard. He began giving up his mock pity for "my distinguished opponent," making more scathing remarks about the "General." He was justified by both the real power of the Old Guard and the apparent confusion of its new leader. Nevertheless his tactics may have hurt him politically, since they focused attention on the personality of the war hero—the Republicans' main selling point. They did some injustice to the General, who would prove his sincere intention to retain most of the New Deal reforms. Finally they cheapened Stevenson's campaign. At the outset he had said that he would not "run against Herbert Hoover," but toward the end he was often doing pretty much this. Again and again he recited the accomplishments of the New Deal and the Republican record of opposition to it, with the implication that if Eisenhower won, reaction and depression would come again.

In retrospect it is clearer that on domestic problems Stevenson offered little by way of the new ideas or the "fresh look" he urged. Now and then he spoke of a "new America," healthier, better educated, better housed, more secure, more prosperous, and he pointed to the deeper challenges of the cold war, which "has forced us to redefine our own values . . . restate the ideal of freedom for the complex industrial society of the twentieth century." But essentially he offered only a continuation of the New Deal and the Fair Deal, more of the same. He differed from Roosevelt and Truman chiefly by making more effort to placate businessmen. His program was therefore not very different from what Eisenhower vaguely promised, and it sounded less so because of their common insistence on the prime necessity of economy. The forward-looking Democratic program of action, said Stevenson, could only be carried out "consistent with our national solvency and with a sound national fiscal policy," which he still thought required balanced budgets except in times of war or depression. Otherwise he was much more specific than Eisenhower about means and ends, but for this reason he could seem vague at critical points, apart from his refusal to make easy or empty promises.

One example that has some biographical interest was his early speech on farm policy, a matter close to his heart because, as he said, "we Democrats" have always believed that "our society rests on an agricultural basis." Stevenson stoutly defended the plank in the Democratic platform that called for price supports at not less than 90 percent of parity—another of the planks that Eisenhower borrowed without due acknowledgment. (The Republican platform merely "aimed" at parity levels.) Saying that he knew farmers wanted nothing more than what was in the public interest, he did not dwell on one complication, that many who demanded the protection of price supports sturdily opposed accompanying controls as restrictions of their freedom, and that the chief beneficiaries were the big farmers, represented by the politically powerful American Farm Bureau at some possible expense of the interests of city people. He did mention that perishable products were not supported, though they accounted for about three-fourths of farm income, but on this difficult problem he could "only hope" that close study and consultation would provide a solution. Likewise he touched on the subject of family-sized farms —for him the ideal type—whose tillers were having a hard time making a decent living, a million of them having net incomes of less than $1,000 a year; about them he said only that "there must be ways to help the industrious small farmer who wants to help himself." In a later speech he mentioned more briefly the nasty problem of the million migrant farm laborers, observing that it "certainly invites our compassionate attention." Though I cannot speak with the least authority on any of these matters, I think it fair to comment that Stevenson did not come to grips with the problems of most American farmers in a mechanized society that favors bigness.

Yet much more important was the generally high level of his campaign discourse. On the eve of the election Stevenson said in his last broadcast that it was not easy to talk sensibly, honestly, candidly about all of our many problems, and that he was not wholly satisfied with his efforts; but his verdict on them was fair:

> Looking back, I am content. Win or lose, I have told you the truth as I see it. I have said what I meant and meant what I said. I have not done as well as I should like to have done, but I have done my best, frankly and forthrightly; no man can do more, and you are entitled to no less.

However vulnerable on specific domestic issues, Stevenson at least talked basic good sense. He got down to the elementary truth that most Congressmen, editors, and businessmen still seemed unwilling or unable to recognize, that our vaunted free enterprise system had long been in fact a mixed economy, a combination of government and private enterprise. With the New Deal the government had considerably enlarged its sphere, assuming more responsibility for both the health of the economy and public welfare, and there would always be room for disagreement about specific policies; but it was foolish to cry "regimentation" or "creeping socialism" whenever the government moved in to take care of basic needs, such as social security, that private enterprise was unable to. It was as foolish to assume that security and freedom are incompatible: "We know now that freedom and security are indivisible and that any society which chooses one loses both." Stevenson noted the irony in the position of the Old Guard:

> The strange alchemy of time has somehow converted the Democrats into the truly conservative party of this country—the party dedicated to conserving all that is best, and building solidly and safely on these foundations. The Republicans, by contrast, are behaving like the radical party—the party of the reckless and the embittered, bent on dismantling institutions which have been built solidly into our social fabric.

At the same time, he would not stoop to the tried-and-true refrain of 1948, "You never had it so good." There remained far too much poverty, insecurity, and social injustice for Americans ever to be complacent.

Much more uncommon was the courage of Stevenson. So far from tempering his views to please a special audience, he often went out of his way to express views likely to displease it. As he chose the American Legion Convention for his attack on McCarthyism, so on Labor Day he told an audience of Detroit workers that he was not really their "captive," but intended always to do what he thought best for all the people, including businessmen; and among other things he deplored the too common union practice of denying equality to Negroes. In the South he talked of the necessity of civil rights for Negroes, if anything more emphatically than he had in Harlem. In Texas and Louisiana he brought up the tidelands issue, declaring that he was inclined to agree with the Supreme Court decision that the

tidelands oil belonged to the country, not the states. To a delegation
of party leaders who came to Springfield to plead some regional cause
he thought contrary to the national interest, and who finally argued
that unless he supported it he simply couldn't win, he answered as
simply: "But I don't *have* to win." Since it is too much to expect such
forthrightness of politicians in a democracy, one might add that in
Stevenson it could seem perverse because of some disposition to
believe that the impolitic stand must be the right one; whereas the
arts of winning elections are a quite legitimate concern for men of
principle too. In any case his political courage was one of his chief
claims to distinction. It made him the first important national leader
to meet McCarthy head on.

He then asked moral courage of the American people too when he
dwelt on the crisis of our time, and told them that they had been
"called to greatness." In 1952 his eloquence on this subject was
tinged with a desperate sense of urgency because communism under
Stalin was a ruthless tyranny, much more dangerous and difficult to
deal with than it has become since the leaders of the Soviet have taken
to the theme of "peaceful coexistence." But Americans can still afford
to read what Stevenson said at that time, for he was confronting the
ultimate issues of the modern world, the fate of all mankind, and
there is no political voice in America today as eloquent as his. In
summoning Americans to greatness he amplified the main theme of
his speech of acceptance:

> The revolutions of our times are manifold revolutions; their flames
> burn from one end of the globe to the other. The intercontinental air-
> plane makes counties of continents; it makes lakes of oceans. In the
> words of the song, "There is no hiding place down there." Much of
> mankind is changing its entire outlook upon the world; whatever was,
> is cast out; whatever is, is questioned. Mankind and its hundreds of
> millions is on the march, toward what goal and with what destruction on
> the way no man can foretell. Whole nations have sunk out of sight be-
> hind iron curtains; whole peoples have disappeared from view. . . .
> The problems of a tortured, convulsive humanity stagger the nation.
> Unprecedented times demand of us unprecedented behavior. The task

that confronts us will try our souls. It will exact a high price in discipline of mind and in austerity of spirit. It will determine whether we are worthy of our high place in the world, whether we are worthy of our forefathers who converted a wilderness into a country, fair and free, and left to us all the riches, material and spiritual, that they wrought in pain.

Long ago we asserted a great principle on this continent: that men are, and of right ought to be, free. Now we are called upon to defend that right against the mightiest forces of evil ever assembled under the sun.

This is a time to think, a time to feel, a time to pray. We shall need all of the resources of the stubborn mind, the stout heart, the soul refreshed, in the task that confronts us. It is the most awesome task that any people has ever faced. . . .

Such blessings as God might give America, Stevenson went on, were still no guarantee of salvation. "Nature is indifferent to the survival of the human species, including Americans." But he could then add that their responsibility was also a privilege, no occasion for despair. In other speeches he reminded them that from George Washington on their great leaders had declared the high mission of America as the first great experiment in democracy. Today the very urgency of the call to greatness was heartening:

This invitation does not come to every generation. And it is our rare privilege to be born in an age of testing and decision. We are living in one of the great watershed periods of history, which may well fix the pattern of civilization for many generations to come.

Let us face our mission then, he concluded, in the spirit of Ralph Waldo Emerson, who wrote:

If there is any period one would desire to be born in—is it not the age of revolution when the old and the new stand side by side and admit of being compared; when the energies of all men are searched by fear and hope; when the historic glories of the old can be compensated by the rich possibilities of the new era? This time like all times is a very good one if one but knows what to do with it.

On what to do with it specifically Stevenson had much to say. He
did bring a fresh look to issues of foreign policy, which the cold war
has made the matrix of all national policy. In particular he was one of
the first statesmen to be much concerned with the problems of Asia.
True, his understanding was still limited. In Indochina, soon to
become Vietnam, he saw only the gallant war that "our French allies"
were waging against Communist guerrillas, not another revolt against
Western colonialism; in South Korea he overlooked the autocratic
rule of Syngman Rhee, one of the corrupt, undemocratic regimes that
our military would so often support. But he saw clearly the larger
problems that Americans were still blinded to because of their
obsession with the war in Korea and recriminations over the loss of
China to the Communists:

> Across the continent of Asia more than a billion of the world's peo-
> ples are churning in one of history's greatest upheavals. All the strug-
> gles of man over the centuries—economic, political, spiritual—have
> come together in Asia and now seem to be reaching a climax.
> The causes behind that upheaval are many and varied. But there is
> nothing complicated about what the people want. They want a decent
> living—and they want freedom.

Communism was posing as the champion of the Asian peoples,
attempting to direct the forces it had not created by identifying itself
with the deeply felt needs of these peoples. It was important for
Americans to understand the emotional basis of its strong appeal:

> When we think of Communism we think of what we are going to
> lose. When many of the Asiatics think of Communism they think of
> what they are going to gain—especially if they believe they have nothing
> to lose.

To combat this appeal called for both economic aid to the Asian
peoples and a respect for their culture and their aspirations to
independence, an assurance that "America will never seek to dominate their political and their economic development." Specifically, we
should do much more for India and Pakistan, which Republican
critics of our foreign policy were ignoring. But everywhere, Stevenson

warned, we must not permit our necessary concern for the urgent tasks of defense and development to obscure the end—"the widening and the deepening of freedom and respect for the dignity and the worth of man." To the usual objection that all this was visionary, he replied that "history has shown again and again that the self-styled realists are the real visionaries—for their eyes are fixed on a past that cannot be recaptured."

In the years that lay ahead, John Foster Dulles would display no such sympathetic understanding of Asian peoples and their aspirations when he made foreign policy for President Eisenhower. In the campaign he began contributing to the confusions and inconsistencies that from the outset gave the "great crusade" an appearance of hypocrisy. As Stevenson knew, the General basically agreed with the policy of the Truman administration, in which he had had some voice; but his problem was that as a crusader he felt obliged to find an issue, come up with something new and big. For his first major speech Dulles sold him the idea of a pledge to roll back Soviet power in Europe and "liberate" the satellite countries, a gesture that incidentally might also win the votes of the many Americans of East European descent. When signs of alarm made him realize that this would mean war, he at once backtracked, saying that he had not really meant what he said, or seemed to have said—he would help these unhappy peoples only by peaceful means and would never start a war. This he did mean, but the question always remained whether he really knew what he was saying, understood the implications of the sonorous promises his professional advisers and ghost writers put in his mouth. We are obliged to look into the Eisenhower campaign, not merely because it set off the much higher level of Stevenson's, but because it illustrated the common irresponsibility in American politics that Stevenson valiantly set himself against, and because it clearly foreshadowed the failings of his Presidency.

Now, simply to understand Dwight Eisenhower—not merely to be fair—it must be repeated that he was never a conscious hypocrite in this campaign. He radiated the qualities that had won him the respect of Stevenson—simple decency, modesty, good will, earnestness in seeking always to be good. He was genuinely a man of peace, never so arrogant and vain as General MacArthur; among his benefactions to the American people was helping the old soldier to fade away more quickly by never invoking his popularity, never seeking his company or his counsel. He was as genuinely resolved to retain most of the New Deal reforms on grounds of social justice or simple humanity. Hence many thoughtful, liberal people were attracted by his new look, believing that he could regenerate the Republican Party, put an end to its futile efforts to repeal the New Deal, and enable it to play a worthier role, immediately with more freedom than any Democratic administration could hope to enjoy. Among these people was Emmet John Hughes, the most gifted of his ghost writers, who when he joined his staff after the campaign had started made a point of dropping all talk about "liberation" and the "crusade." In *The Ordeal of Power* Hughes gives an intimate account of Eisenhower's kind of honesty and humility—his distrust of eloquence, his intense aversion to calculated rhetoric, his "almost fiercely stubborn resolve to respect the truth as he saw it." To those near him "it was unthinkable that he would willfully twist a fact, distort an issue, or delude with an empty pledge."

To many other people, including Stevenson, it nevertheless seemed clear that General Eisenhower doted on the rhetoric of platitude, distorted every serious issue, made many an empty pledge; so again it should first be said that he did not do so "willfully." One reason was superficially ironic: it was the experienced leader—not the visionary egghead—who was the awkward novice in politics, the innocent among the wolves. In his humility the General respected the judgment of the Republican leaders, the "experts," and he was more inclined to accept their advice because he was devoted to the interests of "the team." For much the same reasons he was dependent on his ghost writers and constantly indulged in the "campaign oratory" that he supposedly disdained. But the main reason for the low level of his campaign was his modest intellectual powers, about which he was not humble enough. General Eisenhower had no historical sense, little understanding of the modern world, and limited powers of understanding. More unfortunate, he was neither sensitive nor sophisticated enough to select wisely the men on whose understanding and judgment he had to depend. Hughes reports an example of his insensitivity that is especially pertinent for judgments of his campaign. The General thought Stevenson a quite decent fellow until he listened to his speech of acceptance, the words about wishing that this cup might pass; whereupon he snapped off the TV set saying, "I think he's a *bigger* faker than all the rest of them." Like most Americans, he prided himself on always insisting on the genuine article, but could never be trusted to distinguish it from the phony, all the fake that pervades American life.

The most disgraceful features of Eisenhower's campaign may be explained, if not condoned, by his naïveté and humility. Though he disliked Senators McCarthy and Jenner, he agreed to give them his hand because he believed he ought loyally to support the whole team. He permitted the Republican National Committee, the regulars on the team, to climax his campaign by a highly advertised national broadcast featuring McCarthy. He did not call the signals either for Nixon, another pro, who conducted his own campaign in his own imitable style. Since the General made a point of not getting into wrangles with his opponent, he ignored Stevenson's protests against the tactics of his team. In the midst of the Korean War Nixon went on charging President Truman with having "lost 600,000,000 people to the Communists." Stevenson he called "Adlai the appeaser," who hadn't had "even backbone training," folks, because he was a "Ph.D. graduate of Dean Acheson's cowardly college of Communist containment." I think it pardonable that Stevenson was never able to embrace Richard Nixon in his charity. Whatever twinges of conscience General Eisenhower felt were presumably allayed by the thought that politics was a rough game, and that he himself was playing it clean.

His own apparent irresponsibility—his refusal to get down to serious, meaningful debate with Stevenson—may be attributed to mixed motives. General Eisenhower wanted to play ball with his team, which was hardly bent on educating or elevating the American people, while at the same time he wanted to remain above partisan politics, in keeping with his role as a national hero. But again the plainest reason for his commonplace, unheroic campaign was his limited understanding of what it was all about. Sincerely believing that it was "time for a change," he could never understand Stevenson's observation that "change" was "about the most important word in the world today." He offered no new program because he had none, could not conceive the need of any basic change. His "stubborn resolve to respect the truth as he saw it" was made easier because this truth was usually simple and agreeable. He had only a few clear, strong convictions about national policy. And even so these led him into honest confusion.

When the General came to terms with Senator Taft, he was not actually surrendering. He endorsed in good faith the main theme of the manifesto that Taft drew up, "liberty against creeping socialism," and agreed with him that this called for a drastic reduction in government spending and taxation. Naturally fond of taking "strong" stands, he had already said that what the country needed was a $40 billion cut in the budget. He had then been embarrassed when even admirers asked how the country was going to build up its military power and continue to aid its allies—a problem that would plague him throughout his administration. He explained that he had not meant an immediate cut, only a gradual one over five years maybe; and in their manifesto Taft spelled out his pledge for him—a $10 billion cut the first year, $25 billion the next. This could still seem like the empty pledge it proved to be because Eisenhower was a sincere internationalist, who unlike Taft believed in spending on aid to foreigners, but anyway he believed too in the slogan about creeping socialism. For such reasons he was content to campaign chiefly on the official party slogan, "Corruption, Korea, and Communism"—popular issues connected only by alliteration, that were not really issues at all, since Stevenson was as opposed to communism and corruption, as much in favor of an honorable peace in Korea.

Eisenhower no doubt felt strongly about "the mess in Washington," which at first he said was the only issue in the campaign.

Stevenson made little impression when he commented that corruption was the only one on which the oddly assorted Republicans could agree, and that in Illinois he had had more experience than any of them in dealing with it. He tried to expose the roots of the problem, beginning with the simple truth that "behind every crooked tax collector is a crooked taxpayer." He pointed out some of the many forms of corruption in both political and civic life: the businessmen who initiated and throve on graft, the many swindlers in business, the politicians who voted favors for special interests, the respectable citizens who applauded his own move against the slot-machine racket in Illinois and went on playing the slot machines in their lodges and country clubs. Government, he summed up, was a fair reflection of "the intellect, the ethics and the morals of the people, no better, no worse." But for General Eisenhower the problem remained as simple as it seemed to most of the voters who blamed Truman for the corruption: there was only to root out the crooks in government. He had too much respect for business to worry over its connections with the mess. The American people were never at fault. In following the party line written into his script he sometimes implied little faith in the people, since they had put up with all the creeping socialism and appeared to be in danger of being duped by the creepy subversives in their midst; but at bottom he was sure Americans were naturally so good that they did not need to be elevated.

General Eisenhower also felt honest concern about the Communists in government, but on this issue he was more careless about the truth. At first blaming the Truman administration for loose security policies, he later implied that it had deliberately shielded the Communists. In playing up the issue and magnifying the harm done, he appeared to support the McCarthy-Nixon line that the chief danger to the country still came from within, not without, and that Stevenson could not be trusted to deal with it, nor could apparently even J. Edgar Hoover. He would naturally be embarrassed by the issue as Stevenson defined it: "The point is that we have got to fight communism, not just Communists." Eisenhower's resolve to respect the truth was not stubborn enough to make him acknowledge the plain truth that the Truman administration his party was accusing of being soft on communism had opposed most resolutely, and so far successfully, the aggression he himself had failed to foresee. The Republican platform he was supposed to be running on was most unequivocal about the administration's prompt response to the aggression in Korea: "We charge that they have plunged us into war in Korea without the consent of our citizens through their authorized representatives in the Congress, and have carried on that war without will to victory."

The least honest, responsible stand of General Eisenhower in the campaign was on the Korean War, one of the chief concerns of the voters. In the summer he admitted candidly that he did not believe there was "any clear-cut answer" to the Korean problem, since he was on record as opposing MacArthur's "dangerous" policy of bombing bases in China; the most we could do was stand firm and "try to get a decent armistice." As his crusade got under way, however, he rejected Stevenson's proposal to eliminate the war as a campaign issue, choosing to cash in on the popular concern. "There is a Korean War—and we are fighting it—for the simplest of reasons," he orated: "Because free leadership failed to check and to turn back Communist ambition before it savagely attacked us. . . . There is no other reason than this: We failed to read and to outwit the totalitarian mind." The Truman administration had demobilized too fast, allowed America to become weak, "abandoned China" to the Communists, and withdrawn our forces from Korea. As for what to do now, the General once proposed that the South Koreans take over the fighting: "If there must be a war there, let it be Asians against Asians." Another time he played loose with the truth by contradicting his statement in the summer: "I have always stood behind General MacArthur in bombing those bases."

Stevenson had no trouble pointing out that the General had scarcely proved his own ability at reading the totalitarian mind. As late as November 1945 Eisenhower had told a House committee: "Nothing guides Russian policy as much as a desire for friendship with the United States." He had been Chief of Staff of the Army when the Joint Chiefs recommended that American troops be withdrawn from South Korea, which they advised was of little strategic interest, and that we retire to a reasonable defense perimeter—one that General MacArthur had also approved; this was not just Dean Acheson's doing. As for the General's party, its record was worse, beginning with Governor Dewey's promise in 1944 that the Republicans would demobilize faster. In Congress the Republicans had not proposed that we send an army to China to prevent the victory of the Communists, the loss of 600 million people they were charging to Truman. Neither had they attacked the administration's policy in South Korea; they were always for reducing appropriations. Stevenson granted that mistakes had been made by both parties, but he suggested that instead of competing in denouncing each other they get on with our business. He recalled Winston Churchill's saying that if the present tried to sit in judgment on the past, it would lose the future. But he was indignant primarily for the obvious reasons—that while the nation was fighting a war, with the stakes life and death, the Republicans were splitting it by partisan politics. "Here is change indeed—frightening change." And Stevenson was no happier when Eisenhower finally made an honest pledge that mightily impressed the voters.

The General had been floundering on foreign policy until mid-October, when Emmet Hughes wrote for him a thoughtful speech on the Communist challenge, which swung the *New York Times* to his side. Hughes was then struck by an inspiration. All on his own he wrote a speech about Korea, which the General saw and approved just a day before giving it. Its climax was a proposal that he and his staff had never discussed:

Where will a new Administration begin?

It will begin with its President taking a simple, firm resolution. That resolution will be: to forego the diversions of politics and to concentrate on the job of ending the Korean War—until that job is honorably done.

That job requires a personal trip to Korea.

I shall make the trip. Only in that way could I learn how best to serve the American people in the cause of peace.

I shall go to Korea.

Hughes (formerly an editor of *Life* magazine) writes proudly about this speech in *The Ordeal of Power*. It was just like Eisenhower in both style and substance; it was unambiguous, yet did not commit him to any specific policy; and it was perfectly timed, coming some ten days before the election—late enough to wow the aroused voters, too late to permit effective rebuttal. He notes some "amusing" reactions to the speech, in particular because of the "curious fact" that months earlier Stevenson and his advisers had considered making precisely the same pledge, but had dropped it as pointless. Hughes seems untroubled by the indignant objection Stevenson raised to this slick politics—that the speech was empty of content, gave no idea what the General would or could do in Korea, and evaded the real problem, that the terms of peace would be decided not in Korea but in Moscow. "There is no greater cruelty," he said, "than the raising of false hopes—no greater arrogance than playing politics with peace and war."

At any rate, the speech was unquestionably the most effective one of Eisenhower's campaign. Stevenson had been drawing closer to him in the polls and conceivably might have won the election, or at least made it as close as most observers expected it to be; but his professional advisers at once felt what was soon made evident, that the Korea speech clinched the General's victory. This turned out to be a landslide. Eisenhower carried 39 states, with 442 electoral votes to Stevenson's 89, and won more than 55 percent of the popular vote. Hughes reports that in the week following the great speech the General showed no special interest in it, never mentioning it in their conversations. In retrospect one can see that it climaxed a fateful decision. As Stuart Gerry Brown observes, early in the campaign he decided to take the easy, popular course in Korea, telling the people what most of them wanted to hear about this and other issues; and once started on this career, "he might never again be able to check a popular tide, even when he deplored its course," but find himself "drifting on the waves of his own popularity." Immediately Eisenhower rejoiced in the success of his crusade, talking as if it were a victory of ideas and ideals instead of the personal victory it obviously was, inasmuch as his party ran far behind him in Congressional and gubernatorial elections. We are brought back to the issue of the mentality of American voters, who by so large a majority preferred a candidate who offered them so few ideas worth mentioning.

Some commentators, such as Elmer Davis, gloomily drew the obvious conclusion from Stevenson's defeat: it might be a long time before another candidate would run on a platform for talking sense. Any practical politician might have added that appealing to reason rather than emotion is of course a poor bet—the election only proved needlessly that emotion is always an odds-on favorite. I have already mentioned the close studies made of the election, which showed in depressing detail that voters in general were not only poorly informed about the issues but little interested in most of them, even unaware of the existence of some. Stevenson himself had particular reason to feel crushed because he had invested so much faith in the American people, and thought he sensed "a kind of driving desire in people to find a more exalted meaning in democracy." Although some of his friends said he knew in his heart that he could not beat the war hero, George Ball, a close associate during the campaign, writes that he never doubted he would win, if only because the whole organization and ritual of a campaign are calculated to bolster the confidence a candidate needs. Stevenson remembered too how he had come from far behind in Illinois.

When he formally conceded his defeat, he revealed his immediate feeling in the Lincolnian anecdote he told his heartbroken followers about the little boy who stubbed his toe in the dark: he was too old to cry, but it hurt too much to laugh. Stevenson was soon able to laugh, however, as he did in his talk to the Gridiron Club about the funny thing that happened to him on his way to the White House. "Did anyone starting from scratch ever enter our public life with such widespread approval, and then leave with such widespread approval —all in the space of four years?" More important, he proceeded by word and deed to reaffirm his faith in the American people. In the introduction to the volume of his campaign speeches he substantially repeated what he had said of the campaign as it ended: "It has been the most exhilarating and most heartwarming and most uplifting experience a man could have." He had seen a great deal more of the country and the people, and had learned much by listening as well as talking. One sobering thing he learned was the increasing power of the mass media to manipulate people and sell personalities, and he might have worried more over the "professionalized emotionalism, showmanship, and huckstering" that the managers of the Republican campaign were so proficient in; but he wrote, "I am not troubled by that danger." He was more impressed by the signs of "growing political maturity" in America. He concluded his introduction by quoting Thomas Jefferson: "No experiment can be more interesting than that we are now trying, and which we trust will end in establishing the fact, that man may be governed by reason and truth." Stevenson still trusted.

The truth about American voters appears to be somewhat more complex and confusing than he assumed—but also than politicians usually assume. The astute Nixon, for example, gambled heavily on the issue of domestic communism that had made McCarthy so famous and the whole Senate so afraid to attack him. Elmo Roper found from his polls that almost half the people said one of the most important things the next administration had to do was to keep Communists out of the government, but he wondered how many were convinced that there were enough of them in government to be a serious threat; when asked how they were going to vote, people almost never mentioned the subject. Likewise the more intensive studies of the election recorded in *The American Voter* revealed that in spite of the public commotion this issue rarely came up; voters mentioned more often even such esoteric subjects as Truman's Point Four program.[4] On the other hand, Roper found that the chief reason why people feared Stevenson was the transparently false idea that he was a "captive" of the party bosses who had hand-picked him. This idea reflected the low opinion of politics and politicians that distressed him; though it might have comforted him too, since it generated a widespread distrust of Nixon.

[4] This book, written by Angus Campbell and others (1960), covers the 1956 election as well, and so gives some perspective on the shifting attitudes in 1952.

Nevertheless I assume, as usual, that those who hope Stevenson was right had better look first into the reasons for believing that his faith in the people was too optimistic. It is unnecessary to present all the evidence for the familiar assumption that the average voter is not an intelligent, informed citizen, but it is worth some while to consider his attitudes toward change, a main theme in this campaign and the most imperious reality of a revolutionary age. While voters almost always welcome some specific changes, their attitudes are rarely coherent. Low-income groups who appear most likely to welcome new deals, and so to look "liberal," turn out to be basically more conservative or resistant to change in general than are more prosperous people. These terms mean nothing anyway to the great majority of voters. Americans are notoriously indifferent to ideology, but only a small minority know and think enough even to make an elementary, rough distinction between "liberal" and "conservative," and the smaller minority who call themselves by these names mostly do so in terms of stereotypes. American voters force another qualification of the common charges against the "indistinguishable" major parties. Candidates often express sharper differences than do most of their following, and take stands that mean nothing to many of them. Men who call for a "truly" liberal or "truly" conservative party, always on the assumption that a great many Americans are not being fairly represented, exaggerate the desire for such a choice—as Barry Goldwater would discover. Although some liberals complained that Stevenson was too moderate, he was actually far ahead of most Democrats.

Similarly most voters have little sense of American tradition. On election day Stevenson had a charming talk with a group of school-children in front of the polling place, in the course of which he told them he hoped they would study more in their history books about this business of voting, how it all came about, because the more they studied it, the more precious it would become to them and the better they would vote; but the chances are that few of the youngsters ever learned much about this precious business, even though they would take two or three courses in American history before they left high school. A recent study of the teaching of American history in the high schools of Indiana gives a dismal picture of indifferent students going through the motions in required courses taught by poorly prepared teachers, most of whom had not read a book on American history in the past year. The favorite topic in their courses is war, especially the Civil War—not its causes or consequences but its battles. Few of the students come out with a live sense of the meanings of the American past, its bearings on the problems of America and mankind today. They are rarely able to explain a single tenet of Jeffersonian or Jacksonian democracy, which meant so much to Stevenson. They know less about American history since the Civil War, and virtually nothing about the growth of industry and of cities, the keys to modern America. The schools avoid such topics as Woodrow Wilson's foreign policy and the New Deal, which presumably are too controversial.

American schooling accordingly helps to explain a more surprising and dismaying conclusion of some analysts about the "independent" voters, those who switch their votes and bring about political changes. It had been assumed that they were in general more thoughtful voters, more seriously interested in the issues. Under scrutiny it appears that they may be mostly among the least concerned and most poorly informed, voting merely by hearsay. They swell the unthinking mass movements, or what in elections are called "stampedes"— an unfortunately accurate term for many a political victory. Most standpatters have clearer reasons for their position, and many have firmer principles—as readers may realize from their own experience, no less if they think of themselves as independents.[5] On the other hand, the standpatters bring up the unseemly behavior of college-educated voters. If these provide the most thoughtful, enlightened of the independents or shifters, most of them can be depended upon to vote Republican, and not because they are better informed; they

[5] I am myself not in the least ashamed to say that I have voted Democratic in every Presidential election except 1948. Unenthusiastic about President Truman, who I thought had no chance anyway, and unable to stomach Thomas Dewey after hearing him talk like the "man on the wedding cake" he resembled, I switched for sentimental reasons to Norman Thomas; but I rejoiced no less in Truman's surprise victory. Adlai Stevenson was of course always a Democrat.

adhere to their class interests, or vote by the pocketbook, more consistently than do the workers many of them fear. When Goldwater ran for President, college-educated Republicans were more loyal to him than were the less educated.

Yet voters in general are less swayed by purely class interests or their pocketbook than is often assumed, else their behavior would be much more predictable and the Republican Party would never win. They are usually doing some thinking of sorts. The fairest estimate of their behavior that I know is *The Responsible Electorate* (1966), by the late Professor V. O. Key, Jr., a recognized authority on the subject. "The perverse and unorthodox argument of this little book," Key wrote, "is that voters are not fools." Granted much odd behavior, "in the large the electorate behaves about as rationally and responsibly as we should expect, given the clarity of the alternatives presented to it and the character of the information available to it." Specifically, they derive their preferences in policy from their experience since the last election, and their move to a different party is broadly consistent with these preferences—not so unthinking as other analysts believe. They are unlikely to be attracted by promises of the novel or unknown; they approve or reject what they have known.

This thesis is still not very comforting to those who would talk sense to the American people. Stevenson had much to say about the dangers and the promise of the unknown future, neither of which evidently impressed most of the voters. He was saddled with all the popular grievances against the Truman administration, which could mean that he was defeated before he started. He suffered the more unfairly because of another well-known tendency of voters, who are more likely to punish an administration for its mistakes than reward it for its achievements; hence many of them forgot "how good they had it" under Truman. One consequence of this behavior is that a minority party cannot hope to win the next election by offering a responsible, constructive opposition. In Key's words, "As a matter of practical politics, it must appear to be a common scold rather than a bold exponent of innovation." It follows that as a crusader Eisenhower won votes more by acting the scold than by giving democracy the "more exalted meaning" that Stevenson too thought Americans were seeking. Still, all this is not simply irrational. A party in power should properly be held responsible for its administration, not be approved merely for its promise of a new look. Limited as are the abilities of voters to decide on wise policy, they can better size up past performance than estimate future performance. Even all the mindless floaters in the current of public opinion help to keep government flexible, responsive to the people, and able to adjust more smoothly to change.

But the popular support of General Eisenhower was not, once more, by any means simply mindless. If his personal victory was due more to his personality than to his program, this was an engaging personality, the more attractive because of his eminence; to Republican party workers who taunted Stevenson with their slogan banners, he could say cheerfully, "I like Ike too!" At that the studies of the voters make it clear that he did not win by personality alone, any more than Franklin Roosevelt did in the great shift of 1932. His victory helped to inspire the once fashionable theory that the "father image" is all-important, but the analysts have now played this down. (It is pleasant to think that the politicians who were sold this idea by Madison Avenue men revealed that they can be as gullible as the businessmen who are sold on the experts in motivational research, the depth boys who gave Henry Ford the Edsel.) Like Stevenson, Eisenhower had a new look that inspired clubs of Volunteers, enthusiastic amateurs who enlisted in his campaign as in 1940 others had in the campaign of Wendell Willkie—a Republican who grew much like Stevenson. There remain the sound reasons for believing that it was time for a change, and that in some ways General Eisenhower was ideally suited to preside over a change. Frank Sorauf sums up the long debate over the proper function of the political party in America:

Does it make its most effective contribution to democracy by aggregating majorities, by compromising differences behind candidates, by suppressing disruptive conflict? Or does it better serve democracy by educating the electorate, by framing alternatives for it, by illuminating choice, and by affording a means to common goals?

These were essentially the alternatives represented by Eisenhower and Stevenson; and those of us who prefer the second one might grant that especially in 1952 there was much to be said for the first.

About the basic issues of the American electorate there remain other pertinent complications. The specialists in political behavior usually emphasize the behavior of the majority, or of the "average" voter, and in their studies he comes out looking the more ignorant and foolish because of their elaborate "methodology" and all the tables in which he is pinned down.[6] Key differed from most in that he was sensitive to the differences of individuals within the classifications of "group attitudes," and especially in that he was always interested in the exceptions—the many businessmen, college graduates, workers, and members of any specified group who do not vote like their fellows. I would stress more than he that the small minority of thoughtful, informed voters may have considerably more influence than can ever appear in statistics. I would add that his "perverse and unorthodox argument" makes better sense to those who have some historical sense, which too often seems wanting in the specialists. In pointing out how little most voters know and think, they may forget what Stevenson knew, that on these conditions American democracy had been operating for generations, after all with some success. On the record most voters have not been apathetic either, but have at least been groping for good leaders. In Stevenson's own lifetime they had made by and large a considerably better showing than their fathers, electing three of the greater Presidents—Theodore Roosevelt, Woodrow Wilson, and Franklin Roosevelt. Since the war they have

[6] Having mentioned *The American Voter,* which is a very thorough and often illuminating study, I should warn readers that much of it is written in the dreadful jargon fashionable in the behavioral sciences. Elementary ideas are often disguised as follows: "The property of being pro or anti, favorable or unfavorable, and so forth, is inevitably found in attitudes within a political system that is polarized by two parties." But the authors also suggest some caution about the methodology of their fellows: "Electoral research has invested a great deal of attention in explanatory factors that are vastly less efficient in predicting behaviour than the simple device of asking a person how he intends to vote."

been displaying more independence by splitting their ballots more than ever before. Half a million such voters had given Stevenson his landslide victory when he ran for Governor of Illinois, since President Truman barely carried the state.

Another complication is less heartening. The American electorate, wrote Key, "behaves about as rationally as we can expect, given the clarity of the alternatives presented to it and the character of the information available to it." This proviso brings up the behavior of the American press, sometimes called "the fourth branch of the government." In 1952 it was as usual overwhelmingly, automatically Republican. As Stevenson pointed out in a wry talk to newsmen, the big newspapers had begun committing themselves to Eisenhower "before they knew what that candidate stood for, or what his party platform would be, or who his opponent was, or what would be the issues of the campaign." He found it hard to share the worries of editors who argued that the election of Eisenhower was needed to assure the preservation of the two-party system, else the Republican Party might fade away; for a party that controlled 90 percent of the press might be expected to survive what appeared to be "one of the longest and loudest deathbed scenes in history."

In his criticism of the press Stevenson was not bitter, knowing that at least he was given much publicity and his campaign was reported in more detail than most voters demanded. He was popular with reporters, despite the troubles he gave them with his copy, since newsmen are rather different from their wealthy publishers. It was on the editorial page that the press was 90 percent Republican, and most readers pay little attention to this page. Franklin Roosevelt, also opposed by the great bulk of the press, had sufficiently demonstrated that it has less influence than publishers like to think.

Nevertheless Stevenson's complaints about a "one-party press" were clearly justified. It gave General Eisenhower more and better publicity, as did all the big mass-circulation magazines, and too many newspapers obviously slanted the news, a common practice not obvious enough to most readers. The Chicago *Tribune,* the worst offender in this respect, was somewhat handicapped because Colonel

McCormick disapproved of Eisenhower too as an internationalist; he fumed that both candidates "will do well by Britain and Europe," and could not bring himself to support the General until near the end of the campaign. But meanwhile the New York *Daily News,* the paper with the largest circulation in the country, had made up for his shortcomings by its wholehearted attacks on "Adelaide." It had at once spotted a generally unrecognized menace in Stevenson when he quoted the words of Christ about letting this cup pass: "When a man takes to likening himself to the Savior, it is logical to assume that he at least has delusions of grandeur, and may be a religious fanatic who would prove dangerous in high public office." This choice piece of logic may give us pause as another of the many forms of corruption in American life. Possibly the editor responsible for it was coarse and just as possibly stupid enough to believe what he wrote, but he was cynically doing a job for his publisher. It is well known that most of the editorial staff of the Chicago *Tribune* privately voted for Roosevelt while their employer did his best or worst to make out that the President was virtually a traitor. They belonged in that large company of professional men, including alleged "scientists" in attitude research, willing to sell their skills for uses often questionable when not strictly corrupt.

Or let me consider the treatment of the campaign by *Time* magazine, which makes a pretense of responsible, objective reporting of the news. On the whole it (meaning Henry Luce) treated Stevenson fairly, complaining chiefly that his party had "no dynamic approach to the future." From the beginning, however, it went all out for General Eisenhower, stressing how dynamic his approach was; it hailed the meaning he found in his nomination—"dedication to the shining promise of tomorrow." From then on it almost always gave him more space than Stevenson, and usually the lead article. Its main difficulty was that it could not help gagging now and then over his soporific speeches. In June it reported that he was in "top fighting form, and getting better," but a month later it intimated that tops for the General had meant no thought to speak of; it reported that he must now start thinking, admitting that his speeches were "marred by too many hollow notes, too many platitudes." Another month and it went into raptures over the speech he gave to the American Legion: "A great American soldier disclosed political greatness this week and rediscovered courage as a policy for the nation." The next week it complained that the great soldier was "running like a dry creek." But the main theme remained that he was getting better and better, hitting harder and harder, clicking like an old pro. In its pre-election issue *Time* gave him the cover and a laudatory story to go with it. Following the election it reported that the campaign had been "fought and won on transcendent issues of morality." It incidentally noted the "alarming fact" of a "wide and unhealthy gap between the American intellectuals and the people," but at once dropped the alarm. As for Richard Nixon's contribution to the transcendent issues, *Time* was somewhat uneasy over the disclosure of his secret fund, suggesting that he made a mistake in calling this a "smear" by "Communists and crooks in Government," but following his Checkers speech on TV it resumed the high praise it had given him from the beginning as a "forward-looking" type and a "progressive fighter against Communism and corruption." Amen.

In spite of all this, Stevenson himself was not alarmed by the gap between intellectuals and the people. The studies of the electorate would offer some evidence confirming his feelings about the people. Considering that the Democratic vote in Presidential elections had been declining steadily ever since 1936, it was not at all surprising that he was beaten, even so badly. For an egghead running against most popular Ike, starting with only a third of the people on his side, he had won remarkable support. He stirred up so much interest that many more Americans marched to the polls than ever before, giving more votes to him than any defeated candidate before him had got. In defeat he was immediately heartened by an unprecedented flood of almost a hundred thousand letters, including many from people who had voted for Eisenhower with misgivings. Many editors who had worked for his defeat now wrote of his virtues, suggesting (he told the Gridiron Club) "that it couldn't have happened to a nicer guy." The collection of his major campaign speeches became a best-seller, another tribute unknown to also-rans in the past. The statistical studies indicate that while the obvious personality of "Ike" was most appealing, the rare personality of Stevenson was also widely appreciated. Many ordinary people liked the novelty of being talked up to. During the campaign Richard Rovere reported overhearing a bus driver tell some passengers, "I don't suppose the average fellow's going to catch on to what he's saying. But I'm telling you, this is just what *I've* been waiting for." The driver, added Rovere, was about as close to average as anyone could hope to get.

Finally, however, I would emphasize important considerations that the analysts neglect, because they cannot measure them even with the help of computing machines. Stevenson knew that he had aroused much fervor among the young, especially college graduates, who joined the Volunteers for Stevenson teams that sprang up everywhere. Numerically these zealots were a very small minority, negligible in a statistical analysis, but for his purposes they were a significant minority. Richard Goodwin, who at the time was a senior in college, has told what Stevenson meant to his generation:

> He revealed a world we already sensed was there, bared challenges we were aching to undertake. The words were the words of sacrifice but the music sang of meaning and purpose to a young man. . . . As much as any, he was the end of post-war America and the beginning of a time still nameless. . . . And all these principles, and many more, he suffused with another welcome and shining truth: the pursuit of national self-interest was not inconsistent with the desire for justice and dignity and well-being for all the people of the world—that there was no basic unresolvable contradiction between realistic policies, and high ideals. He told us our sights were too low, the course we had charted too narrow. . . . He told an entire generation there was room for intelligence and idealism in public life, that politics was not just a way to live but a way to live greatly, that each of us might share in the passions of the age.

Another small group with an influence out of all proportion to its numbers was the intellectuals, in whom Stevenson kindled more enthusiasm even than Franklin Roosevelt had in the palmy days of the New Deal. Like his distinguished team of ghost writers, many were active in his campaign and some remained active in public life. More important, if still more immeasurable, were the changes in their attitudes. Since the New Deal and especially the world war they had been veering away from the common hostility to American culture, the assumption that there was no place for them in American society. In 1952 a symposium on "Our Country and Our Culture" in the *Partisan Review* confirmed that most of them no longer thought of themselves as rebels or exiles. The editors had posed a question: "Where in American life can artists and intellectuals find the basis of strength, renewal, and recognition, now that they can no longer depend fully on Europe as a cultural example and a source of vitality?" To Stevenson the question would have seemed silly and the answer obvious—they could find it in living American tradition, the idealism to which he had appealed and the many young Goodwins responded; he had never assumed that America was a land of barbarians in which thinkers and writers had perforce depended on Europe for their strength. Following his defeat some intellectuals inclined to despair again, some writers to believe that politics was none of their business; and they could easily find an excuse for such attitudes in the Eisenhower era. But most went on trying to realize their values in and for America. As for "recognition," they were getting more, to some extent because of Stevenson. The Eisenhower administration, which at first epitomized the popular distrust of eggheads, itself eventually paid them a tribute: the Republicans organized a movement to line intellectuals up on their side.

The most striking evidence of Stevenson's success in making politics more respectable I heard of from James Rowe, a professional who scheduled his campaigns in both 1952 and 1956. In 1960, when Rowe was helping to manage Lyndon Johnson's campaign for the nomination, he was struck by a change in the county chairmen he was meeting all over the Middle West. Many were younger men and of higher caliber than the general run he had dealt with ever since the days of Roosevelt. Upon inquiring how they happened to get into politics, he was given an almost invariable answer: they had done so during or after the campaign of 1952, at the urging of their wives. Stevenson deeply impressed many educated women, another group seldom dignified by a separate table in the statistics.

This chapter in his career may be concluded by a quotation from William James with which he prefaced the collection of his major campaign speeches:

> Reason is one of the very feeblest of Nature's forces, if you take it at any one spot and moment. It is only in the very long run that its effects become perceptible. Reason assumes to settle things by weighing them against one another without prejudice, partiality, or excitement; but what affairs in the concrete are settled by is and always will be just prejudices, partialities, cupidities, and excitements. Appealing to reason as we do, we are in a sort of forlorn hope situation, like a small sandbank in the midst of a hungry sea ready to wash it out of existence. But sandbanks grow when the conditions favor; and weak as reason is, it has the unique advantage over its antagonists that its activity never lets up and that it presses always in one direction, while men's prejudices vary, their passions ebb and flow, and their excitements are intermittent. Our sandbank, I absolutely believe, is bound to grow—bit by bit it will get dyked and break-watered.

In his introduction Stevenson wrote: "Well, I am not downhearted or even disappointed, and I believe more than ever that 'our sandbank' of reason in major political campaigns is bound to grow."

6

Interlude: The Eisenhower Era

For years I thought what was good for the country was good for General Motors, and vice versa.

—*Charles E. Wilson*

Some passages in President Eisenhower's Inaugural Address sounded almost like a vindication of Stevenson's campaign. "We are called as a people to give testimony, in the sight of the world, to our faith that the future shall belong to the free," he said predictably, but he went on to suggest that this faith might call for some sacrifice. "We must be ready to dare all for our country. For history does not long entrust the care of freedom to the weak or the timid. . . . No person, no home, no community can be beyond the reach of this call." Always America would seek peace, join all efforts to remove the causes of mutual fear among nations, but the peace we were dedicated to was "nothing less than the practice and fulfillment of our whole faith." The soldier-President concluded: "More than a haven for the weary, it is a hope for the brave." And his listeners had more reason to be heartened than his unquestioned earnestness about these best of intentions. In the exercise of the great powers of the Presidency he had the advantage of both high prestige abroad and of great popularity at home. Excepting Franklin Roosevelt in the early weeks of the New Deal, no President began his administration with a country so strongly behind him, and none had such favorable auspices for carrying out what Eisenhower was pleased to call a "mandate for change," the title he later gave to the first volume of his memoirs.

What followed in his first administration could appear to justify the slogan of his campaign for re-election—"Peace, Progress, and Prosperity." Peace was made in Korea as he sensibly accepted a limited victory, a truce that MacArthur and the Old Guard had denounced as "ignominious bartering with our enemies." On the home front he vindicated the shrewd prophecy of Samuel Lubell: "To solidify itself permanently in American life, the New Deal needs at least one Republican victory." President Eisenhower held the main line established by the New and Fair Deals. The country still suffered from unemployment, but it remained generally prosperous and rejoiced in the biggest tax cut in its history. Senator McCarthy was at last disgraced, deprived of the power to make headlines. Although there remained noisy irreconcilables, they were less numerous and powerful, and a bitterly divided nation returned to its senses. It is unlikely that any other man in the White House could have helped as much to restore sanity and peace at home.

Yet the bulk of this achievement was not directly President Eisenhower's doing. Although he dutifully went to Korea a month after the election, en route holding what was highly publicized as "the epic mid-Pacific conference," he made no important decisions either at this or in Korea, and he did not personally end the war. The most apparent reason for the truce was the opportune death of Stalin early in 1953; though it then took more months of haggling, an agreement was finally reached by the same team of negotiators who had started work under the Truman administration. The President labored no more to consolidate the gains of the New Deal; he merely left most of them intact, with the help of the Democrats in Congress. Likewise he inherited the prosperity he boasted of, perhaps stimulating business by the tax favors his administration granted it, but certainly not by any bold measures, nor by fulfilling pledges to stop inflation. On no front, foreign or domestic, did his administration make marked "progress." As for McCarthy, the President allowed him to run wild for two years until he attacked the Army, and even then he did not take firm action himself, or ever combat McCarthyism as vigorously as Stevenson had when it was dangerous to do so. Neither was it bold leadership that reunited the country—perhaps the best reason Americans have for remembering President Eisenhower with gratitude and affection. The return to sanity was due rather to his simple decency and his distaste for violent partisanship, an aloofness from the heat of battle that was also a source of his weaknesses as President.

The main theme of this chapter is a record of failure, at least by the standards he set in his Inaugural Address. In normal times Dwight Eisenhower might have made a quite respectable President, but for our times his good intentions were not enough. They could do positive harm because he always thought that the policies they led him to adopt must be just as good, and that critics of them were simply unreasonable or irresponsible. His failure was a personal failure for mixed reasons, not simply discreditable, but pertinent for the light they throw on the Presidency to which Stevenson aspired. It was also a failure of the Republican Party, whose leaders in Congress gave Eisenhower more trouble than help. And it was more significant because it reflected the state of the nation at this time: the failings of the American people, most of whom were in no mood to "dare all" or rise to "a hope for the brave," but wanted everything made easy and comfortable; and the failings of the American press, which was the most adulatory any President ever enjoyed. On all counts, the Eisenhower administration set the challenges to which Stevenson responded. It helped to define the measure of his growth as a statesman and a critic of America. It made clear his political importance, finally the measure of his political success.

This whole story may begin with the opening sentence of the President's Inaugural Address: "The world and we have passed the midway point of a century of continuing challenge." In *The Ordeal of Power* Emmet Hughes, author of the address, reports that in the margin of the manuscript Eisenhower had scribbled an angry comment: "I hate this sentence. *Who* challenges *whom? What about?*"[1]

---

[1] In citing Hughes so often, I do not think I am being unfair to Dwight Eisenhower. Although he became disillusioned with the President, Hughes left his

This might have been a legitimate protest against hackneyed rhetoric, but since he accepted the sentence and recited the later passages that amplified the challenge, it appears that once more he did not clearly understand what he was saying. Certainly the President did not proceed to request any sacrifices of the American people, instead making a point of reducing their taxes. On the home front he was all for "normalcy"—business as usual. He had already made this clear by the Cabinet he had assembled.

To clean up the mess in Washington, he writes in *Mandate for Change,* he was resolved to find men of the highest possible character, integrity, and ability, and he was gratified by his success. "I am certain that my Cabinet was as well prepared for future governmental duties as any such team that ever assembled on Inauguration Day in Washington." Irreverent commentators described his team as a dozen millionaires and a plumber. The plumber was Martin Durkin, an AFL man appointed Secretary of Labor, but he soon gave up and returned to his union. Eisenhower explains that Durkin was never able to understand his function, which was to help develop policies aimed at the welfare of the entire nation, not just of labor unions; he persisted in pleading the special interests of labor. It did not occur to the President that a similar objection might be raised against all the wealthy businessmen in his Cabinet. He kept on his Secretary of the Interior, Douglas McKay, who said candidly, "We are here in the saddle as an administration representing business and industry." In his awe of big business, Eisenhower substantially agreed with Charles E. Wilson, his Secretary of Defense, on the identity of the interests of General Motors and America. Hence his Cabinet was preponderantly conservative, to the right of center. Like the President, most of his

---

service in sadness, not bitterness, and his intimate accounts of him ring true. In particular he makes Eisenhower much more attractive than he appears in his own memoirs, conveying a livelier impression of both "the ordeal of power" in the Presidency and the basic honesty and humility he brought to it. The memoirs are not only dull but so complacent that they obscure his decency and kind of humility. In them it appears that his heavy responsibilities were eased because he always arrived promptly at wise and morally right decisions, he never made a serious mistake, and the only real ordeal was all the incomprehensible misunderstanding and irresponsible criticism he had to put up with from both foreign statesmen and Democrats.

assistants were confident that it would be easy to clean up the mess and, in the words of Hughes, install a businesslike administration by "common-sense, good-old-American, down-to-earth, shoulder-to-the wheel, feet-on-the-ground practices." The tone of his administration was set by the three most influential members of his Cabinet—Charles Wilson, George Humphrey, and John Foster Dulles.

Wilson, who had been head of General Motors, perfectly exemplified the basic complaint against the business class as a ruling class, that its main interests and experience tend to unfit it for political rule. Politically he was to the right of Senator Taft, who had at least learned that government had to provide some services, such as education and housing, when free private enterprise was unable to. He was not even efficient as an administrator of his Defense Department, since running a big government bureau is rather different from running a private corporation and requires some political sense.[2] His basic failing, however, was an engrained incapacity to grasp the larger interests of the nation. He was ignorant of world affairs, which set the needs of the Defense Department. He was as ignorant of science, the basic source of power in the modern world, and so refused to squander the taxpayers' money on basic research, which he defined as "when you don't know what you're doing." Having entrusted the American defense program to Wilson, President Eisenhower should not have been so dumfounded when the Soviet Union came out with the first Sputnik. At about the same time another auto magnate, Henry Ford, squandered a quarter of a billion dollars on a spectacular flop, the Edsel. Readers may recall the beaming lady in a *New Yorker* cartoon saying how nice and fair it all was—the Russians had the Sputnik and we had the Edsel.

George Humphrey, the Secretary of the Treasury, was a disciple of Taft. A man of great force, he impressed Eisenhower by his dedication to sound fiscal policy and became his most trusted adviser on domestic issues. His ideas about economics came straight out of the

[2] I have been told on good authority that Wilson was being eased out of his position in General Motors when Eisenhower tapped him, which would imply that what was not good enough for General Motors was good enough for the U.S.A. But at least he had been good enough to reach the top.

nineteenth century, if in a schoolboy text. Knowing and caring as little as Charles Wilson about world affairs, he did know that the main job was always to build up the economic strength of America, and that the means were quite simple—stimulating business initiative by reducing taxes, doing away with all government extravagance, and balancing the budget. Awed by his passion for economy, Eisenhower learned from him that the supreme challenge facing America was to keep its budget balanced.

The President was less troubled than he might have been by the thought that this made life more difficult for the other man in his Cabinet whom he most admired and trusted—his Secretary of State, John Foster Dulles. Humphrey was never happy about spending money on foreign aid programs, always in favor of cutting them to the bone. Dulles always needed money to bolster by military and economic aid the pacts he was making. His foreign policy also had to be tempered to the views of Charles Wilson, another economizer, who introduced a "new look" in defense policy. Since conventional weapons cost more than nuclear weapons, Wilson decided that we must concentrate on the latter, thereby getting "a bigger bang for a buck." Abetted by the Air Force, he announced that we could not afford to fight limited wars—"We can only afford to fight a big war." Dulles accordingly announced that the United States was abandoning its "traditional" policy of "meeting aggression by direct and local opposition," as it had in Korea. Henceforth we would operate on the principle of "massive retaliation," the biggest of bangs "by means and at places of our choosing." Actually, of course, the Eisenhower administration never dared to attempt such retaliation; but the new principle continued to govern its defense budget.

We are accordingly brought to the all-important issues of foreign policy, which from 1952 on most concerned and troubled Stevenson. Dulles, who Eisenhower said was the greatest Secretary of State he "knew anything about," impressed most informed observers as one of the least statesmanlike. There is no question that the prestige of the United States sank all over the world during the Eisenhower administration. Since Dulles was much more sure of himself than was the

President who entrusted him with foreign policy, it is harder to forgive him for all he did to alienate both neutrals and our allies, frighten them more than he frightened the Communists. But let us first try to be fair to him.

To begin with, he inherited from Truman and Acheson the policy of containment. However necessary at first, this was likely to become primarily negative, a matter of simple anticommunism—about all that most Americans knew or cared about in foreign affairs. With this hand-to-mouth policy came no alternative programs for the future. When Stalin died, Eisenhower was exasperated by the discovery that there were no plans in the government files for this contingency, even though the experts had been debating for years what might happen after his death. In the face of such difficulties, compounded by the provinciality of his business colleagues in the Cabinet, Dulles worked with indefatigable energy in a position he had long prepared himself for. He posted an all-time record by traveling more than 550,000 miles in taking personal charge of the nation's diplomacy. His energy was backed by a moral earnestness he shared with Stevenson, a complete dedication to his duty as he saw it. If not flexible enough, he was at least firm in the series of crises that came up, and managed to discourage the Communist countries from gambling as recklessly as Khrushchev would during the Kennedy administration by sending missiles to Cuba. If he had too simple and self-righteous a conception of his cause, this too could be called a legacy of American diplomacy, the long tradition of taking a high moral line.

Yet there is no real "if" about the self-righteousness of John Foster Dulles, which made him so different from Stevenson. He saw the cold war as essentially a simple conflict between good and evil, in which he and America were always right, the Communists totally wrong. In such a conflict there could be no compromise; he endeared himself to the super-patriots by his suspicion of all efforts to negotiate with the Communists, and of their "peace offensives." He antagonized the many neutral countries, especially India, by asserting that there could be no neutrals in this struggle, neutrality was simply "immoral"; he could appreciate neither their natural desire to stay out of war nor their obvious retort to his demands, that America itself had grown up on a policy of neutrality and in both world wars had tried hard to preserve it. Hence he went about building the flimsy alphabetic defenses in which he set great store, such as SEATO and the Baghdad Pact, later rechristened CENTO when the rulers of Baghdad repudiated it. In pursuing this course, he built up the American reputation for hypocrisy by his willingness to support Chiang Kai-shek, General Franco, or almost any dictator so long as he was against communism. An uncompromising war on this evil justified any other compromise on principle.

The worst in Dulles was brought out by his enlistment in the "great crusade" of General Eisenhower. Since this had to have a "dynamic" policy, he pledged the administration to an abandonment of the "negative, futile, and immoral" policy of mere containment. With his reckless campaign talk about "liberating" Eastern Europe, which was also calculated to liberate America from the Democrats, he coupled as wild talk about "unleashing" Chiang Kai-shek to attack mainland China, supporting the myth that Chiang would be welcomed by the Chinese people; whereas the actual problem was to protect him from the Communists. Dulles gladdened the hearts of the Old Guard by writing another promise for Eisenhower to recite in his first State of the Union message: "I shall ask Congress at a later date to join me in an appropriate resolution making clear that this Government recognized no kind of commitment contained in secret understandings of the past with foreign governments which permit . . . enslavement [of any people]." Emmet Hughes thinks the Secretary actually believed there were such secret agreements buried somewhere in the vaults of the State Department, and the wild applause that greeted the President's promise suggested more plainly that many Republicans had been taken in by their own campaign nonsense about Dean Acheson's being soft on communism. In any case Dulles gave comfort to the many who followed the McCarthy-Nixon line, and who made it more difficult to pursue a reasonable diplomacy.

The high moral line he took was most dangerous because he

coupled it with the power politics made necessary by the cold war, which was encouraging a shortsighted realism that banked solely on power. After one crisis, Dulles published an article in *Life* magazine boasting about his mastery of the art of "brinkmanship," gambling most coolly when the stakes were highest. The allies of America were irritated by his bluster, as by his threats of "agonized reappraisal" of our policy if they didn't behave themselves in Western Europe, but they were also worried because they could never be confident that he wouldn't go over the brink, taking them along. At home Senator Jackson perhaps minimized the danger when he described Dulles as the "original misguided missile, traveling fast, making lots of noise, and never hitting the target." The trouble remained his influence on public opinion. He confirmed not only the national self-righteousness but what Dennis Brogan has called "the illusion of American omnipotence." He made this illusion more dangerous by making it more comfortable, pointing out that his policy of massive retaliation demanded no financial sacrifice but was cheaper.

Otherwise the consequences of his stewardship were thoroughly anomalous. His arrogance was to some extent offset by the influence of President Eisenhower, who in spite of his great admiration for Dulles was a quite different type: never so passionately dedicated as his apparently logical, legalistic Secretary, and always more willing to seek peace by compromise. The President won most popularity by the peace in Korea and later "the spirit of Geneva," when he met Soviet leaders at a summit conference. The principal achievement of his administration, indeed, was that it maintained peace by not fulfilling its pledges or carrying out its threats. When Russian troops ruthlessly crushed the Hungarian Revolution, for instance, it did nothing to help "liberate" the unfortunate Hungarians, even assuring the Soviet that it would not intervene. Previously the administration had failed to pass another test of its policy. When in 1954 it became clear that the French were losing their long, futile war in Indochina and could be saved only by American military intervention, President Eisenhower was under more pressure to send in our military because the United States had been paying most of the costs of the war, and he had said that the fall of Indochina would be "of a most terrible significance." He and Dulles therefore warned China against intervening directly or indirectly, threatening massive retaliation. The Chinese ignored the warning, rightly guessing that it was a bluff. One reason why the administration did nothing was that the Army Chief of Staff advised against intervention, since the "new look" had already left the Army unprepared to fight a limited war.

This anticipated the most incongruous result of the aggressive new policy of Dulles. In effect it paralyzed American diplomacy. As the Soviet too kept making bigger and better nuclear bombs, the United States would never risk massive retaliation except in case of a direct threat to its most vital interests, such as an attack on its European allies. It was reduced to the policy of containment that Dulles had spurned, only now it had less success. The Russians grew more aggressive in the Middle East as the Chinese did in Asia. Since they only had to be careful to leave Western Europe alone, the Communists were freer to stir up trouble everywhere else in the world by conspiracies and *coups d'état,* guerrilla wars of "liberation," satellite "volunteers," and other such forms of aggression that could be contained only by a limited war the United States was no longer prepared to fight. As Stevenson put it, the administration seemed to be saying to the Communists, "One false move by you guys and we'll cut the national defense budget by another billion dollars."

The self-confidence of Dulles also assured more fumbling than usual in the conduct of foreign affairs by making him an exceptionally poor administrator. He trusted no one but himself to carry out important diplomatic tasks, paying little heed to his Department and the dispatches of ambassadors, and since there was always enough crisis to keep him on the run, many matters suffered from neglect. In eight years the agency in charge of foreign aid had as many different chiefs, one of them an ex-Congressman who had voted against foreign aid. The Foreign Service was encumbered with a number of inexperienced ambassadors, businessmen whom Eisenhower obediently appointed at the behest of his political advisers, and whose only apparent qualification was that they had contributed money to the Republican campaign. One such duckling he rewarded with Cuba publicly embraced its brutal dictator Batista, helping to explain why the supporters of Castro might trust the Soviet more than the United States.

Latin America in particular suffered because Dulles saw no serious Communist menace there, but also because he subscribed to the basic policy of the businesslike Eisenhower administration. This was to confine American aid to military and technical assistance, to trust private investment to take care of all other problems, and to favor governments that were hospitable to American businessmen. Since rightist dictators were usually most hospitable, Vice-President Nixon went to Cuba to praise the "stability" of Batista's government, and the President awarded the Legion of Merit to the notoriously corrupt Jiménez of Venezuela, whose merits included "sound foreign-investment policies." In 1953 an Assistant Secretary of State for Inter-American Affairs did try to launch a hemisphere program of economic aid and social reform, but he resigned when George Humphrey attacked so un-American an idea. Although most of Latin America remained nominally safe for American businessmen, its people grew more hospitable to supporters of Castro.

One more typical incident leads to the failings of the Eisenhower administration on the domestic front. Early in 1953 Emmet Hughes worked long and hard on drafts of a speech, "The Chance for Peace," enlisting the help of Paul H. Nitze, chief of the State Department's policy planning staff. A key passage read: "This Government is ready to ask its people to join with all nations in devoting a substantial percentage of the savings achieved by disarmament to a fund for world aid and reconstruction." Although Eisenhower liked the main idea, Hughes had trouble persuading him to give the speech because Dulles was cool to it. When he did give it, he was rewarded by unusually enthusiastic praise; commentators hailed the speech as "America's voice at its best," especially welcome because the President had "obviously undertaken to seize the peace initiative from the Soviets." The next day, however, the President went off to his golf course in Georgia. His Cabinet met in a "special" session presided over by the Vice-President; Nixon outlined the main business of the day—the time to start winning the 1954 elections was right now. The Cabinet never got around to discussing the speech. Nothing came of it, except a darker cloud over the reputation of Paul Nitze. Unpopular with Republican leaders in the Senate and suspect to Dulles because he had served in the State Department under the Truman administration, he was eventually eased out of his position. The President deplored the pressures against Nitze, when he was informed about them too late, but he did nothing about either them or his peace initiative.

What was on Vice-President Nixon's mind during that unhistoric session of the Cabinet was the "dangerous" idea getting around that much of Eisenhower's program was getting more support from Democrats than from Republicans. This idea was more dangerous for a reason he did not go into, that it was substantially true. The strongest opposition to both the President's internationalism and his maintenance of the New Deal came from Republicans in Congress, when not from within his own Cabinet. Among Nitze's enemies was Senator Knowland, who succeeded Robert Taft as Republican leader of the Senate when Taft died. Although he was a right-winger known to be hostile to most of Eisenhower's program, and as a leader might have decisive influence, the President made a point of remaining strictly neutral when the Republican Senators were debating his selection. On principle he was committed to the methods that made him a weak leader, among the least effective men who had occupied the White House.

Needless to repeat, the Presidency has become an appallingly difficult position, calling for an exceptional combination of abilities as statesman, executive, politician, and leader of the people. The sheer size and sprawl of the government defies the simple businesslike methods in which Eisenhower trusted. But the primary difficulty was that first and last he wanted to preserve his "public image" as a hero who was above politics and partisanship. He naturally disliked politics anyway, considering it a rather dirty game, and disliked still more any brawling with the leaders of his party. Trusting to his experience as a war leader, he depended on efforts at persuasion and conciliation, in which his vaunted personality never sufficed in Washington; he knew too little about government or politics. His creditable motives blinded him to the vulgar truth that only as a politician could he have hoped to control his own party, still dominated by the Old Guard. As it was, his obvious popularity assured his failure to develop not only the skill but the will to employ effectively the powers and natural advantages of the President.

Other motives were less creditable. However sincere in his role as national hero, Eisenhower was too pleased with it. As Marquis Childs commented, "His view of himself was the official view of the Eisenhower personality, the view seen through channels." Never inclined to be self-critical, he grew more uncritical because of his great popularity and the adulation of the press, which made him almost immune to sharp criticism even for his obvious failures. He was too content with the clichés about his lofty ends, too indifferent to practical means, and often failed to carry through with his declared purposes, just as he failed with his peace initiative. And his incompetence was fortified by an illusion he had become wedded to in the heat of his partisan campaign. The Republicans had long charged that Franklin Roosevelt had "usurped" the powers of Congress, reduced it to subservience, and made the Presidency a grave threat to the Constitution and the liberties of the American people. Actually, since 1938 neither Roosevelt nor Truman had been a match for the coalition of Republicans and Southern Democrats that controlled Congress; a single chairman of one of its powerful committees could hold up an administration bill; and a jealous Congress was encroaching on the President's rightful powers to conduct foreign affairs, as Eisenhower would discover when the Bricker Amendment limiting these powers was almost passed because of strong Republican support. A vigorous President was needed to represent the national interest if only because Congressmen were so often more devoted to local or special interests. Eisenhower's policy of dignified neutrality could frustrate his own intention of acting for the nation.

Still another source of his weak leadership was the staff system he set up out of his military experience. On the surface it looked very neat, orderly, and efficient, with Cabinet members like generals, each with his clearly defined province and powers, all passing up to the Commander in Chief the information and Counsel he needed. It could never in fact be so orderly, of course, but it looked neater because Eisenhower disliked any appearance of disorder and got depressed or angry when his Cabinet-generals quarreled or failed him. At best, his staff system made him too dependent on his undistinguished Cabinet; he was presented with nothing like the breadth of information and diversity of opinion he needed for perspective and understanding. His White House staff, the palace guard headed by Sherman Adams, did its best to ease his duties, often by shielding him from disagreeable news, while he himself was proud that he didn't waste time reading the newspapers and their finicky columnists. As a result, he was often woefully ignorant of what was going on both in his administration and in Congress. At press conferences he repeatedly betrayed how ill-informed he was: "I have never heard . . . If that is true, why you are telling me something I never heard." The conferences also betrayed his dependence on ghost writers because of his difficulties in expressing himself clearly or coherently.[3] On all counts, President Eisenhower could not readily go to the people on his own or do much to educate them.

Shortly after his re-election he gave perhaps the most spectacular demonstration of the indecisiveness Stevenson was charged with. On the same day he sent his budget to Congress, Secretary of the Treasury Humphrey made unprecedented history by holding a press conference at which he attacked his Commander in Chief's budget, predicting that unless it was drastically cut "you will have a depression that will curl your hair." At his own press conference a few days later the President answered, Well, he didn't think the economy was in such a

[3] Oliver Jensen translated the Gettysburg Address into his kind of English: "I haven't checked these figures, but 87 years ago, I think it was, a number of individuals organized a governmental set-up here in this country, I believe it covered certain Eastern areas, with this idea they were following up based on a sort of national independence arrangement and the program that every individual is just as good as every other individual."

bad way, but he completely agreed with "the thought behind the Secretary's statements," the budget ought to be examined very closely, and it was the duty of Congress to save every dollar it could. He hemmed and hawed for the next few months, now defending his budget, now defending the good Republicans who wanted to slash it and saying how gratified he was by all the good citizens who were calling for less government spending. As a result, his budget was slashed by $4 billion. The ultimate consequences of such leadership was summed up in an incident recounted by Richard Neustadt in his *Presidential Power*. When a Bureau of the Budget man, testifying on a later bill before a House committee, clinched his case by emphasizing that it was essential "to the program of the President," everybody laughed, Republicans and Democrats alike.[4]

All this provides some substance for the speculation about whether Stevenson would have made a great President. In some ways he resembled Eisenhower, most plainly by his appeal as a man above ordinary politics. Like him, he had no love of power and was not a close student of the problem how best to achieve it and exert it. He too depended on methods of persuasion and conciliation, which in view of Eisenhower's intellectual limitations one may forget amounted to an appeal to reason. Hence one may doubt that Stevenson would have dealt effectively with the conservative coalition, especially because the Republican Old Guard would most likely have been more embittered and irreconcilable had Eisenhower been defeated. Most important, however, were his obviously superior qualifications. No amateur in government, he had no such disdain of politics nor such lofty illusions about the role of a President. He could have been trusted to select a more enlightened Cabinet and to keep far better informed. Surely he would have fought much harder for his program, done his best to carry through on all matters he considered important. Having a clearer idea of what he wanted to accomplish and why, he would have done more to educate the people and could have appealed to them more effectively. How Congress and the people would have responded to his leadership remains anybody's

[4] Who remembers reading an editorial about this in the Eisenhower press?

guess; but I think there is no question Stevenson would have offered more intelligent, responsible, and firm leadership than Eisenhower did.

Hence I would qualify the common opinion that Eisenhower was better able to dispose of the dangerous McCarthy. His more thoughtful supporters had argued that his election would silence the Senator from Wisconsin, but the event proved McCarthy's argument that it would give him more power in the Senate. For two more years he went on making headlines by baseless charges while the President said and did nothing about it. He intensified his assault on the State Department by sending abroad his young vaudeville team, Cohn and Schine, to investigate waste and loyalty in the American missions, and by denouncing the United States Information Service for having subversive books in its libraries. Writers, educators, churchmen, judges up to the Chief Justice himself—anyone who showed a decent respect for civil liberties he vilified for "coddling Communists" and "shielding traitors." The tactics that kept him popular even though he turned up no live Communists were described by Senator Ralph Flanders, the first Republican to summon the courage to denounce him on the floor of the Senate: "He dons his war paint. He goes into his war dance. He emits his war whoops. He goes forth to battle and proudly returns with the scalp of a pink Army dentist. We may assume that this represents the depth of the seriousness of Communist penetration at this time."

In *Mandate for Change* Eisenhower explained why he remained aloof all this time. Early in his campaign he had stated plainly his disapproval of un-American procedures, and thereafter he declined to be drawn into any public arguments with or about McCarthy because they would only enhance his publicity; he was sure that in time the Senator would destroy himself. He added that lashing back at one man "was not as important to me as the long-term value of restraint, the due process of law, and the basic rights of free men." Eisenhower completely ignored, however, all the havoc McCarthy wrought during his dignified restraint, in particular the outrages on due process and the basic rights of free men. The Senator succeeded in demoralizing the State Department, the more thoroughly because Secretary Dulles lacked the courage to defend his Foreign Service officers against the Senator's abuse. The Department became so cowed that it burned books on its own. Scott McLeod, a disciple of McCarthy who was made its security chief, boasted that 534 employees had been dropped for security reasons by 1954; inquiry then forced the admission that only eleven had been dropped for loyalty reasons and no Communist had been found. The White House itself joined in what Stevenson called the "numbers racket," the President announcing the removal of 2,427 security risks, whom his Attorney General Herbert Brownell described as mostly subversives, spies, and Communists; though again an administration spokesman later had to admit that only one alleged active Communist had been found among more than two million government employees. Meanwhile the Republican leaders in Congress were backing McCarthy. Although most no doubt did so in the spirit of Senator Taft, who did not believe his slander but welcomed him as a help in defeating New Dealers, they took up his war whoops. In 1954 the Republican National Committee commemorated the birthday of Abraham Lincoln by adopting the slogan "Twenty Years of Treason" to describe the Roosevelt-Truman administrations that had won the war and assumed the leadership of the free world. Itself the most treasonous campaign slogan ever employed by a major party in America, it warranted Stevenson's charge that Eisenhower's lieutenants had ended the great moral crusade by taking McCarthyism away from McCarthy.

Above all, Eisenhower in his memoirs still seemed quite blind to the deeper, frightening significance of the four-year reign of McCarthy that always troubled Stevenson. It made the foreign policy of Dulles more aggressive and uncompromising because he was afraid of being accused of softness on communism. It both shocked and alarmed our European allies; they could see that it made a travesty of the democratic principles the United States was supposedly defending. It betrayed a lack of self-confidence, making Americans seem much more fearful of communism than any other people. At its worst suggesting the thought control of communism, it was the ugliest symptom of the conformism that was growing more marked during Eisenhower's administration. The Four Freedoms, Stevenson observed, had been replaced by the "four fears"—of depression, of communism, of ourselves, and of freedom itself.

At any rate, the President did very little to dispose of McCarthy, still less of McCarthyism. The Army hearings that exposed on television the sliminess and cruelty of the Senator embarrassed him because it was mostly Republicans who were being hurt. The Senate committee that investigated the charges against him included respectable Republicans, but Eisenhower was again embarrassed when Senator Flanders' resolution censuring McCarthy was opposed by Knowland. Asked whether Knowland spoke for the administration, he answered characteristically, "They hadn't even asked him about it, they hadn't even asked him a thing about it. He had taken no stand whatsoever." (At that time his press conferences were still being reported in the third person.) The large majority that at the end of 1954 finally voted for censure did not include the principal Republican leaders in the Senate. The chief contribution of Eisenhower to the tardy proceedings was the selection of Vice-President Nixon to formally repudiate McCarthy on behalf of his administration. McCarthy turned viciously on the President, but even he could not accuse Nixon of coddling Communists. Only this brings up another failing in leadership.

In the Congressional elections of 1954 the Vice-President campaigned arduously, but still in his old style. Although Eisenhower publicly rejected communism as a campaign issue, saying the real issue was his legislative record and program, Nixon again chose communism. This should not be a political issue, he would begin his usual double-talk, because both Democrats and Republicans were loyal Americans, "but—." Thereupon he dredged up again all the mud about Truman and Acheson. "And isn't it wonderful, folks, to have a Secretary of State who will stand up to the Russians?" Somehow he managed to blame the Democrats for the defeat of the French in Indochina. Stevenson came in for his full share of innuendo just short of outright falsehood: "Mr. Stevenson has been guilty, probably [*sic*] without being aware that he was doing so, of spreading pro-Communist propaganda as he has attacked with violent fury the economic system of the United States and has praised the Soviet economy." And so on, *ad nauseam*. When Eisenhower was asked whether he had approved this shift by Nixon and other Republican campaigners, he answered that none of them had come to him about the details of their talks, they were just "going out doing their best in their own way," but he "couldn't possibly comment in detail on the whole generally." To Nixon he wrote more positively: "Whenever my burdens tend to feel unduly heavy, I admire all the more the tremendous job you have done since the opening of the present campaign." As the campaign drew to a close he himself shifted to the Nixon line.

Even so the Republicans lost both houses of Congress. While the President himself grew more popular, they did steadily worse in succeeding Congressional elections. In 1958, when they lost by a margin of 57 to 43 percent, they set a historic record: for the first time a President had had three Congresses controlled by the opposition party. All along most Americans had continued to call themselves Democrats. Briefly, Eisenhower had failed to convert his immense personal following into a rebuilt, reinvigorated party. Like his fellow Kansan William Allen White, he had failed first of all to convert the leaders of the Republican Party he nominally led. Unlike Stevenson in Illinois, he had found no place in his administration for the enthusiastic young Volunteers who had campaigned for him, nor did his party organization find room for them.

In *Mandate for Change* Eisenhower confesses to his astonishment and dismay when a few days after his inauguration he had his first meeting with the Republican leaders of the Senate and the House. He discovered that some of them were astonished when he began by announcing his intention of redeeming his campaign pledges; they were mostly not only more interested in new jobs than new challenges but opposed to many of his policies, just as Stevenson had tried to make him see by harping on the "two-headed elephant." To be sure, few of them had ever known the responsibilities of power, only one

Senator having served under a Republican President, but with experience they remained stubborn enough to make him despair from time to time; insiders have said that he toyed with the idea of starting a third party. In his memoirs, however, Eisenhower forgets that he was a hero above politics and defends the record of his party. He had some justification in that quite a few Republicans in Congress were gradually learning to disown their political record, support policies they had long denounced as socialistic or internationalistic. Yet by and large his party remained unregenerate, devoted to its stereotypes. Its real leaders gave the President little help in what he repeatedly said was his task and the task of the party, "to produce a program that was so dynamic, so forward-looking, and so adapted to the needs of the United States that anyone running as a supporter of the program would have a distinct advantage." And they could give him such support as they did chiefly because of another of his limitations. His program was essentially conservative, not at all dynamic; it was forward-looking to the point of George Humphrey's nose for extravagance; and it was adapted mostly to the interests of the many Americans who were in no mood for sacrifice, exertion, hard thinking, or anything but the easy solutions he had promised them in his campaign.

The basic conservatism of the President became plainer when the disastrous elections of 1958 at last jolted him into a real effort to lead both his party and the nation. A "new" Eisenhower now fought hard for his program, with an emphatic use of the veto. But now more than ever the heart of his program was fiscal responsibility, specifically an insistence on the sovereign need of balancing the budget. Perhaps anticipating that his administration was about to run up the largest peacetime deficit in history, he resolutely opposed the efforts of Congress to add the kind of new programs he had once urged. And his obsession with the economy was more significant than he could realize. It reflected the national preoccupation with economic interests and values, for which the harsh word was "materialism." This in turn threw light on the moral, spiritual state of the nation, which the President was more pleased with since he had cleaned up all the "corruption," but which disturbed Stevenson for reasons he could never appreciate.

Eisenhower always liked to think of himself as a conservative in fiscal matters and a liberal in human relations. His genuine concern for human welfare had led him to extend Social Security, and he succeeded in raising the Federal Security Agency into his Cabinet as the Department of Health, Education and Welfare, even though to many Republicans in Congress "welfare" was still a frightening word. Yet the President was always more dedicated to his notions of fiscal responsibility, which he would never knowingly permit to be jeopardized for other public purposes. In *Mandate for Change* he told proudly how he had resisted pressure for some kind of federal program when unemployment rose to 3.6 million in the first of the recessions during his administrations. His fear of "creeping socialism" likewise restricted his liberality in providing for human relations, and there was always the most respected George Humphrey to warn him that the United States could not afford to spend as much on such things as education and public health as the Soviet Union did, else the richest nation on earth would be plunged into a depression that would curl his hair. During the prosperity Eisenhower boasted of, accordingly, his administration kept reducing the share of the national income spent on public services.

On the world scene the result, as Walter Lippmann pointed out, was a decline in American power and influence. The United States fell behind the Soviet Union in the pioneering outer space program, in the comparative rate of economic growth, and in education. Lippmann asked why it was being pressed so hard by a country whose gross national product was less than half of ours, and he gave a blunt answer:

> The reason, at bottom, is that in this period of cold war, the President has adhered to a principle which would probably no longer be suitable even in a time of total peace. He has adhered to a principle which puts private comfort and private consumption ahead of national need. . . . The challenge of the Soviet Union has been demanding an increase, not a reduction, of the share of national income devoted to

public purposes. We are falling behind in the race because we are not allowed to run.

On the home front this meant that Americans were wallowing in more and more consumer goods. According to the Humphrey-Eisenhower school of economics, federal money spent on education was an extravagance, a threat to not only the budget but the health of the economy; whereas billions spent on advertising eyewash and incessantly exhorting Americans to indulge in private extravagance helped to assure a healthy economy and so kept America strong. At the same time, President Eisenhower was always especially fond of the word "spiritual." He rejoiced in the unfailing applause when he celebrated the "spiritual strength" of America and condemned the "materialism" of the Soviet Union. Off the platform he had displayed at most a casual interest in spiritual concerns, but he began cultivating a religiosity that made him still more popular. Like most Americans, he felt edified by a comfortable religion that assured the country that God was on its side but demanded no sacrifice to speak of, least of all in the consumption of material goods. It made him still less disposed to ask how the increasing attention to private comfort and consumption was building the spiritual strength of America.

Stevenson was concerned about such questions just because of his more reasoned faith in the American people, and his deeper awareness of the astonishing progress that had been made in the last generation. He was concerned too over "government by merchandising" for more than the obvious reasons. Republican propaganda, echoed by a complaisant press, met all criticism of Eisenhower's blunders or failures by the refrain "Just have faith in Ike." Worse, a party that for years had been acting more irresponsibly than a "common scold" was branding serious criticism as un-American; Vice-President Nixon habitually described it as "spreading pro-Communist propaganda." Behind such conventional politicking were the pervasive tendencies to conformity, flourishing on the growth of an affluent mass society. The ever bigger advertising industry was selling the values of conformity, or of wanting and thinking what everybody else did. The big networks were shying away from "controversial" issues, or in other words the most important ones. (Edward R. Murrow stood out for his courage because he dared to take on McCarthyism.) Popular comedians confined themselves to innocuous subjects, bland satire. With the man on the street complacence was tempered by as easy a cynicism. True, there were still plenty of vigorous critics; Stevenson never sounded like a voice crying in the wilderness, and he always had a large audience. But one should not be surprised that his wit suffered somewhat from the strain of contending against the seemingly invincible popularity of Ike, in what now looks like about the most humorless decade in the nation's history.

7

The Education of a Statesman

Great movements and forces, springing from deep wells, have converged at this mid-century point, and I suspect we have barely begun to comprehend what has happened and why. In the foreground is the mortal contest with world communism, which is apparent, if the means of dealing with it are not always apparent. But in the background are the opaque, moving forms and shadows of a world revolution, of which communism is more the scavenger than the inspiration; a world in transition from an age with which we are familiar to an age shrouded in mist. We Americans have to deal with both the foreground and the background of this troubled, anxious age.

—*Adlai Stevenson*, Godkin Lectures, 1954

As for his future, Stevenson told the Gridiron Club a month after his first defeat by Eisenhower, several possibilities were being thrust upon him:

There are those . . . who feel that I should devote my classic talents to the welfare of mankind by frequent talking. There is another smaller group who insist that God, and/or the electorate, has appointed me as the scourge of the Republican Party. And finally there is a much smaller group that feels that it is not wholly unworthy or improper to earn a living. My sons are numbered in the latter group.

This period of indecision, however, was brief and relatively painless. Having been so richly rewarded by his four years as Governor and the exhilarating experience of his campaign for the Presidency, he evidently had no real yearning to return to the practice of law. But what decided him to remain in public life, he later wrote, was an automatic consequence of his defeat—it made him a "titular leader" of the Democratic Party.

Someone has defined such a leader as one who lives at the wrong address. Stevenson himself observed that in the American political system this role is "very ambiguous," inasmuch as the supposed leader has no office, no staff, no funds, no clear authority, no regular means of helping to shape policy—or in effect *no* political address. Also on the scene was another titular leader, ex-President Truman, who was inclined to think that he was the real head of the party. Even so Stevenson decided to assume the responsibilities of leadership as best he could. He felt an immediate obligation to his party because his campaign had left the Democratic National Committee with a deficit of close to a million dollars; so he began giving addresses at fund-raising dinners around the country. And another characteristic reason for Stevenson's decision was a feeling of obligation to go on trying to talk sense to the American people.

In this role, however, he refused to be merely a "scourge," still less a common scold. His defeat had made him feel more strongly the need of a loyal, responsible opposition. What united Americans was much more important than what divided them, he said repeatedly, and politics should be a means of consolidating our strength, "not of compounding our weaknesses"; but the McCarthys and Nixons were still working to divide the country, compound its weaknesses—carrying on what he saw as a corruption of democratic processes more dangerous than mere graft. As the Eisenhower era got under way, Stevenson accordingly settled down to the serious business of somewhat monotonous but basically responsible criticism. The American people had particular need of it because they were being told that criticism was more dangerous even than Rotarians had made out in the Coolidge era with their motto "Boost, don't knock." Too many were forgetting that free, open criticism of rulers and authorities is the hallmark of a free society, and essential to its health.

For such purposes Stevenson had some advantages in his role as merely titular leader with no political address. He was no slave to his popularity as was President Eisenhower, having won it by candor and courage, and now having nothing to lose. He could speak out more freely for himself, with still less thought of immediate political advantage. If he was bound to sound partisan in fund-raising and campaign speeches, he could be dispassionate in his many other addresses and articles, and for the most part was less partisan than Eisenhower. An "unemployed politician," as he liked to call himself, he had more time to study, reconsider his views, and explore new ideas. And Stevenson quite deliberately set out on a course of self-education.

Early in 1953 he went off on a six-month tour abroad, the first of his many journeys all over the world. His traveling companions, none of them officials, were his long-time assistant William Blair, the historian Walter Johnson, Barry Bingham of the Louisville *Courier-Journal,* and William Attwood of *Look* magazine, which had commissioned a series of articles by Stevenson, enabling him to finance his education. The tour took him all around the edges of the Communist world, from Asia through the Middle East to Western Europe. It proved to be almost as arduous as his campaign for the Presidency. He had set off as a private citizen, eager to find out what ordinary people were doing and thinking, but his first stop, Tokyo, signaled his fate for the rest of his life—never again would he enjoy the simple pleasure of leisurely, informal travel. A crowd was on hand to greet him at the airport. Everywhere he ran into admirers, and into official receptions arranged by the American missions, with such duties as laying wreaths. He managed to escape a few invitations but never the major consequences of his fame abroad, which was much greater than he had known.[1] He learned that he was "several

[1] One invitation he ducked was from Ambassador Clare Luce in Italy, who was making an undiplomatic name for herself by her all-out support of the Christian Democrats and the Vatican. Her regime, he was told, was known as Arsenic and Old Luce.

lengths behind McCarthy, but right up close to Eisenhower." Stevenson was perforce serving as an unofficial or "titular" ambassador.

This role had some plainer advantages. In all countries he enjoyed the privilege of talks with leaders—Emperor Hirohito, Syngman Rhee, Nehru, Sukarno, King Ibn Saud, Ben-Gurion, Tito, Pope Pius, Adenauer, Churchill—as well as many lesser diplomats and politicians. He wrote that he was "touched and astonished" by the eagerness of officials everywhere to talk, and by their candor. But he also managed to talk with plain people, from students and labor leaders to soldiers, porters, and peasants. After the ordeal of state banquets long into the night he would get up early of a morning to wander through markets, which he always loved. (Barbara Ward writes that on a later trip to Africa he delighted market women, who recognized in him the special gift of *Nommo*—"the man who, simply passing by, could make the day ten times more fun.") Hence he carried home vivid impressions of the life of the billion people along his route, too often unobserved or unfelt by official ambassadors. He realized more keenly the poverty of the great majority who live in the East, including "millions of refugees huddled in squalid camps and hovels stretching from Korea across Asia to western Europe—remnants of many more victims of the wars, revolutions, intolerance and savagery that have cursed our time on earth." He could appreciate the observation that Asians wanted above all other things "respect and rice"—in that order.

From all reports Stevenson made an excellent ambassador, by not only his obvious good will but his more uncommon graciousness and tact.[2] Always unassuming, he got along well alike with leaders,

---

[2] William Attwood has kindly allowed me to read the journal he kept throughout the tour. It pays tribute to the remarkable vitality of Stevenson, who stood up under the ordeal better than his younger companions. (*Time* magazine, incidentally, reported his grueling tour as if it were a jaunt, while poor Eisenhower labored away at his Presidential desk.) Attwood's notes also suggest that Stevenson was not always so keen and perceptive as one gathers from other accounts of his travels. His companions were more immediately impressed, for example, by the serious damage being done abroad by Senator McCarthy and urged him to make an issue of it. Similarly Attwood qualifies somewhat the usual enthusiastic accounts of how favorable an impression Stevenson always made on foreigners; thus his efforts at humor

officials, and the common people because of his readiness to listen to them. He had an advantage in that he had been preceded by Governor Dewey, who traveled with a bodyguard and had some tendency to lecture his hosts on American generosity and know-how, but Stevenson had need of uncommon resources of patience and urbanity. He soon learned why Asians are not easy to deal with.

In Japan Communist students with toothy smiles pressed him with questions betraying their ignorance of America and their gullibility, parroting the crude stereotypes of Russian propaganda; they ignored his questions about the tyranny in the Soviet Union. In his talk with Nehru, who was typically high-minded and misty, he got no satisfactory answer to his question why Nehru had praised Stalin as a man of peace after the dictator's death. An Indian newspaper charged that Stevenson's oratory was designed to cover up "all the sinister assignments that he undertakes for Wall Street"; here as elsewhere he encountered misunderstanding of America, especially the feeling that we wanted war. In the Philippines he was told of the appalling corruption, another commonplace in Asia that made it difficult to aid the new nations. And everywhere except Japan he encountered the xenophobia that intensified the difficulty.

At the same time Stevenson was kept aware of the failings of the Eisenhower administration. He learned of how much harm the General had done by the cheap campaign solution of the Korean problem he had first suggested—let Asians fight Asians. He saw more clearly the folly of our preaching capitalism to these wretchedly poor peoples, demanding that they be anti-Communist, and acting as if America would be hurt by their neutrality. He ran into the havoc wrought by McCarthy in both demoralizing American missions and shocking foreigners; in Europe he was told that the Senator and his boys, Cohn and Schine, had done more to hurt America in eight months than Russian propaganda had in eight years. Yet Stevenson made a point of never criticizing the Eisenhower administration. In

were seldom appreciated by Asians, who expect solemnity from statesmen. But in general the journal supports the common report that Stevenson was an admirable ambassador of good will, under unusually trying conditions.

parrying the inevitable questions about McCarthyism at every press conference, he stressed all the good in America that outweighed the undeniable evils. Singlehanded he could hardly remove the stains on the image of America abroad, and in his diplomatic efforts to brighten it he had to suppress or tone down some of the opinions he freely expressed at home; but essentially he was trying to convey to foreigners the faith that had survived his own defeat.

To Americans he naturally spoke with a somewhat different emphasis. In writing his series of articles for *Look* he had misgivings over his possibly too superficial impressions, since he spent only a few days in each country, much of the time in company not of his own choosing. (William Attwood, who edited the articles, had much the same nerve-racking experience that as a perfectionist Stevenson gave newsmen during his campaign.) His lasting impressions, however, appeared in the themes he developed in the next few years. They were largely summed up in a "Traveler's Report" he gave to a Chicago audience, which he included in a volume published later, *What I Think* (1956). Although he thought we were still winning the cold war, having encountered less hostility than admiration for America, he had learned that our influence was sagging because of worries over President Eisenhower's leadership; and he concluded, "We must now think afresh." His own efforts to do so may no longer seem very fresh, partly because he was not a brilliant thinker, but chiefly because ideas that in the Eisenhower era were daring and unpopular have since become commonplaces of serious thought. It is not generally realized, I believe, how far Stevenson often was in advance of his day (as time goes these days), and how much influence he may have had through his popular articles and some widely publicized addresses.[3] And since he got down to fundamentals, most of what he had to say is still pertinent.

While Secretary Dulles was saying that it was premature to nego-

[3] I was myself surprised when I read John Spanier's *American Foreign Policy Since World War II* (1965), a book that is highly regarded and in my opinion rightly so. In Spanier's thought about the crises of our foreign policy and "the challenges of the 1960's" there is little that Stevenson had not said a decade earlier. He never mentions Stevenson, I assume because he is unaware of any direct influence.

tiate with the Communists, Stevenson maintained that we must always be ready to do so, as we had in Korea. What was our objective, he asked: was it coexistence or extermination of Communist power? "We owe it to ourselves and our anxious, weary friends to expose Communist intentions if we can; to confer when we can; to reduce tensions and restore hope when we can." Now that we had the hydrogen bomb, Stevenson urged specifically that we again take the 'initiative in re-exploring the possibility of disarmament, make more than the perfunctory gestures we were growing accustomed to. When Dulles came out proudly with his doctrine of "massive retaliation," he at once raised what now seem the obvious objections to it. Our allies were appalled by it because any massive retaliation would call out as massive counterretaliation, of which they would be the first victims; there was no longer any real security in a superiority of nuclear weapons, since the Russians had enough of them to produce an "effectual atomic stalemate"; we were leaving ourselves "the grim choice of inaction or a thermonuclear holocaust"; and there could be no victors in a total war, "only survivors." Not to mention the inconsistency of an administration that kept on talking tough, complaining that neutrals and allies were not worrying enough about the Communists, while it cut its defense budget and reduced taxes.

In his "Traveler's Report" Stevenson anticipated increasing difficulties with our European allies, whose independence and criticism of our policies would exasperate Americans to this day. He remarked what many have yet to realize, that their talking back to us was a healthy sign: it proved that our policy of aiding Western Europe had been a great success, making our allies stronger and more self-reliant. Nevertheless he was troubled by his prophecy that it was going to be harder to hold them together, for we still had to learn we could never "go it alone," and that demands for unilateral action were only "the new face of isolationism." Similarly we had to learn that "we can't remake the world in our image and likeness." Stevenson directly attacked the illusion of omnipotence that Dulles was confirming, and that would also continue to affect our foreign policy to this day. Later he quoted Averell Harriman's warning that it was not only illogical but deadly dangerous "to arrogate to ourselves the sole responsibility for decisions which involve the future of many people"—as we were doing in our decisions about China, and later would do about Cuba and Vietnam.

The chief concerns that Stevenson brought back from his travels sprang from a livelier, fuller awareness of the revolution of rising expectations, the need of understanding and sympathizing with it, and the increasing danger of the immense gulf between the wealthy Western democracies and the impoverished non-Western peoples. He tried to drive home the elementary truths that the world's ills were not all caused by aggressive communism, and that we lacked the resources to remedy them all. Immediately we needed to think afresh about our policy regarding China. While expressing skepticism about the intentions of Red China, Stevenson did not pretend to know just what we ought to do about it. (And let me add as one who has always been unhappy about our policy that I have never known either—I am happy not to be Secretary of State.) His point was merely that we ought at least try to find out its intentions, seek a possible settlement, and have "something to negotiate *with* as well as *for*." Even this modest proposal would long remain courageous because of domestic politics. For years almost no prominent officials (including President Kennedy) would dare to suggest publicly that perhaps we ought to consider recognizing Red China, admitting it to the United Nations, or at least holding public debate on the issue. We remained wedded to Chiang Kai-shek, who was as unpopular with our allies and Asians as he was with the Formosans, on whom he had imposed his dictatorship without their consent. Everywhere in Asia Stevenson had heard of his unpopularity—a commonplace that was studiously ignored in Washington.

Let us therefore review a bit of ancient history that conceivably might be repeated—the affair of the Quemoy and Matsu islands early in 1955. Having announced with fanfare at the beginning of his administration that he was "unleashing" Chiang, President Eisenhower was now facing the real problem of protecting him; the Red Chinese were threatening an assault on these islands, recently reinforced by Chiang, because they were almost as close to mainland

China as Staten Island is to New York. The American Fleet was put in readiness to defend them, and the President asked for and got from Congress the sole responsibility for deciding whether an attack on them was a threat to Formosa that had to be repelled. As always in such emergencies, the people were called on to rally around the President whatever he did; Nixon led a chorus that denounced any questioning of his judgment as virtual treason, while Knowland, the "Senator from Formosa," called for a pledge to defend the islands at any cost. This time the possible bluff worked: the Communists did not launch an invasion, and Dulles congratulated himself on what he later called his most "brilliant" accomplishment.

Meanwhile Stevenson again had the courage to raise the obvious questions in a radio speech to the nation. While he granted that there was something to be said for averting a blow to the morale of Chiang's forces, was it worth risking a world war over little islands to which Chiang had a doubtful legal claim and we none whatsoever? Above all, were we prepared to alienate both our allies and the major Asian nations, none of which was supporting our policy? Stevenson called for consultation with both in an effort to reach some agreement on condemning any aggression in the Formosa Strait, pending a final settlement of the status of Formosa in which the United Nations Assembly might participate. If the Red Chinese rejected any peaceful solution, then at least it would be clear who the aggressors were, and in using force we would have our allies on our side. Stevenson ended with an appeal that we dedicate ourselves once more to the welfare of all mankind, "demanding nothing except a chance for all to live and let live," free from interference, intimidation, and fear:

> Let this be the American mission in the Hydrogen Age. Let us stop slandering ourselves and appear before the world once again—as we really are—as friends, not as masters; as apostles of principle, not of power; in humility, not arrogance; as champions of peace, not as harbingers of war. For our strength lies, not alone in our proving grounds and our stockpiles, but in our ideals, our goals, and their universal appeal to all men who are struggling to breathe free.

Perhaps the highest tribute to this speech was a comment on it the next day by Secretary Dulles. Forgetting that he had suggested military intervention in Quemoy and Matsu, he said that Stevenson's proposals merely "copied" those of the administration. It may have helped that Stevenson anticipated the objections of the rugged realists by quoting Napoleon: "In war, moral considerations are three-quarters of the battle." At any rate, his concern over Asia led him to emphasize these considerations more than ever. American muscle and money alone could never capture or control the revolution of the Asian peoples, whose grievances real or fancied the Communists were exploiting by appealing to ideals of national independence and social justice. Stevenson's travels had convinced him that American idealism had built up more admiration and good will abroad than most Americans realized, because of their sensitivity to the criticisms of the apparently ungrateful foreigners they had aided. He concluded *What I Think* with a wholly nonpartisan Armistice Day speech devoted to the vision of Woodrow Wilson, as still the best hope of America and mankind. One who suspects that he considerably exaggerated the admiration of America because of the warm reception he won by his own personal charm and good will may still subscribe to his basic thesis, and regret that he was never consulted by Eisenhower or Dulles during their first administration.

The most thoughtful work to come out of his "self-education" was *Call to Greatness,* a little book made up of the Godkin Lectures he gave at Harvard University in 1954. Here his main theme was the challenge of world-wide revolutionary change. The Eisenhower administration was doing its best to resist change outside the Communist world, maintain stability through governments favorable to us, and it attributed all its difficulties—the changes that nevertheless kept going on in the non-Western world—to the machinations of Communists. Stevenson argued modestly that we first needed to comprehend what has happened and why, and that we then had to offer the world something more positive and creative than mere anticommunism. Elementary as this wisdom is, his little book is still distinctly worth reading.

Stevenson began by offering a historical perspective, neither original nor profound in its insights, but helpful in an age obsessed with crisis, on lower levels with brash essays in brinkmanship. He cited the prophetic remarks of De Tocqueville and Henry Adams long before the advent of communism, about the potential mightiness of Russia and its fundamental differences from the United States. Czarist Russia too had been aggressive and imperialistic, but with some excuse, having been invaded five times from the West since 1610; the West could be blamed for its own imperialism. Now it had to deal as well with the hundreds of millions of newly independent peoples in the East whose resentments, enflamed by Communists, were potentially a much greater peril than the past invasions of Europe by Arabs, Mongols, and Turks. As someone said, the world had become like a drum—"Strike it anywhere and it resounds everywhere." It was easy to state our goals, the ends of peace and security, but the problem was how "with limited means to achieve these unlimited ends." Never before had "a government and a people had to learn so much so quickly" as America had in the few years since the world war.

All through the lectures ran a critique of current foreign policy, though without mention of Secretary Dulles by name. We could not cope with our difficulties "in absolutes of right or wrong," nor by promises of simple, inexpensive solutions. We had to live in not one but three worlds, the Communist, the allied, and the uncommitted, the many neutrals whose independent interests and ambitions we were vainly trying to deny. Diplomacy is "not the art of asserting ever more emphatically that attitudes should not be what they clearly are." Although we had made so many pacts that "the sun never sets on an American commitment," we could not afford the fantasies about "dictating our terms or philosophy through a preponderant power which doesn't exist," nor afford either to regard negotiation as a synonym for appeasement. We would never be able to face our problems realistically so long as "the future sits in judgment on the past and officials are held accountable as dupes, fools or traitors for anything that goes wrong." We had to realize that many of the hard problems of international life might never be "solved" at all, any more than was the long conflict between Moslems and Christians, and later between Catholics and Protestants. These differences were logically irreconcilable, as are the differences between democracy and communism today; but in Christian humility we should recognize that we "will simply have to learn to live with them," as eventually the embattled zealots did in the past.

Unfortunately, Stevenson acknowledged, our national tradition makes it hard for Americans to learn these elementary lessons. Our "idealistic and moralistic dogmas of international behavior" make them liable not only to self-righteousness but to illusions that end in excessive outrage and fear. Politicians play on these feelings more easily because of our tradition of immoral politics, which now makes us look worse to foreigners. "After a century and a half we have developed some immunity to vilification, abuse and misrepresentation in our domestic public dialogue"; but today what the vote-seekers say to the folks back home for effect "echoes and re-echoes around the world." Irresponsibility thrives as well on the self-confidence of Americans, the traditional assumption that all problems can be solved, every story should have a happy ending:

> So when we encounter a problem in foreign policy we naturally assume that it can be solved pretty quick, with enough drive, determination and red corpuscles. "The difficult we do immediately, the impossible takes a little longer." Just pour in enough manpower, money and bulldozers, and we can lick it. If one diplomat can't come up with the answer, fire him and hire another—or better yet, hire ten. And if that doesn't solve it, some Americans conclude that there can be only one explanation: treason.

Hence too many Americans believed that this was the explanation of why we lost China, "abandoned" to the Communists, whereas they had defeated the larger, better-equipped armies of Chiang Kai-shek. Stevenson did not go into the plainest reason for the collapse of Chiang, the inefficiency and corruption of a dictatorial regime we had spent more than a billion dollars to prop up, but he did insist that we "face the fact that throughout the East the central problem is the attraction and growing power of Communist China." He again maintained that the United States would soon have to formulate a reasoned policy toward it, the minimum conditions on which we were willing to live and let live with it. Again he did not specify this policy, nor go either into the "many interesting possibilities" about future Soviet-Chinese relations that he mentioned in passing, since the relations still appeared to be cordial. His point remained that our uncompromising refusal to negotiate, or to consider the concessions needed to give us something to negotiate "with," was a self-defeating policy. Nevertheless this would for years remain our policy, on the apparent assumption that somehow, without either war or diplomacy, Red China would cease to exist and so justify our refusal to recognize its existence.

Likewise Stevenson repeated that we must give more attention to "enormous India with its enormous problems," and to all the other non-Western countries. This world revolution would make as enormous demands on our patience, forbearance, and humility, qualities that our tradition had not engrained in American attitudes. At Indochina, however, he had taken a fresh look. It had not been a hard enough look to make him see that the French were doomed there (as his traveling companions realized), but at least it enabled him to understand their defeat.

At the conclusion of his tour Stevenson wrote in *Look:* "Southeast Asia's security hinges on war in Indo-China." In France he had disagreed with Mendès-France, who felt that Indochina should be written off; he maintained that the whole area would fall to the Communists if the French gave up. It appears that on his travels he was often too much impressed by the French and British colonial officials who entertained him. Still, his visit to Indochina had given him some second thoughts about "our gallant allies." The native government the French had set up was a puppet government, with no real freedom. Similarly the press was kept under tight censorship, allowed to print criticisms of America but never of the French. Stevenson caught glimpses of the terrible poverty of the people, the worse by contrast with the luxury in which the French lived. On all counts he recognized the futility of expecting these people to fight for

"democracy," as they were supposedly doing. He began to realize that
the only hope of their doing so was to grant them, or at least promise
them, full independence. Hence by the time he gave the Godkin
Lectures he knew that the French defeat was due not simply to
Communist aggression, but primarily to Vietnamese nationalism and
anticolonialism—the sentiments that were firing all Asia. He saw too
that military or even economic aid would not suffice unless the
governments we supported were supported by their people. Without
specific reference to the Vietnamese, he made a simple observation
that required no uncommon prophetic sense, but that most Americans
have only begun to ponder: "It is hard and futile to defend a
government whose people won't defend it." As for the Eisenhower
administration, one may now add, its immediate response to the
defeat in Vietnam was to build up neighboring Laos into "a bulwark
against communism" and "bastion of freedom" by installing an unpopular, right-wing military government and pouring in more money
per capita than it gave any other country, to little effect beyond
fantastic corruption.

Hence Stevenson spelled out some of the plain advantages of the
Russians, not yet plain to most Americans, in the ideological struggle
to win a world revolution that Communists had not started. They
could easily exploit the hatred of colonialism, which everywhere was
associated with the West; they understood Orientals better than did
Americans, who typically expected all other peoples to think and act
like themselves; they were much more patient, not insisting on quick
results; they were not at all "suicidally romantic and naïvely irrational" like the Nazis, but cool and calculating, always willing to
liquidate unprofitable ventures; and always they could show off their
achievement in making Russia a great industrial power in a generation, a feat most impressive to peoples who wanted to change quickly
a world that had not changed for centuries. Stevenson might have
added that our private enterprise system, the efficiency of which was
possibly overrated, was at best not clearly suited to countries lacking
capital, ample resources, or a tradition of capitalistic enterprise. He
also seemed too little aware of the liability of the undemocratic,

unpopular regimes we were supporting, such as that of Syngman Rhee in South Korea. But on the whole he gave a clear, emphatic statement of what the United States was up against, and why it could not hope to win the non-Western world merely by standing firm against Communist aggression.

Then Stevenson could add that outside of China communism was not clearly winning this world, and state as emphatically his belief— so far borne out by the event—that it was not the wave of the future, its present expansion "not another great historical movement with the durable qualities of its predecessors." If his hatred of its tyranny led him to minimize the spiritual appeal of "Marxist materialism" (for example in his statement that "it has no basic moral, spiritual or cultural content"), he was on firm ground when he observed that Communist imperialism was running against the great force it was trying to exploit, the revolutionary spirit of national independence. He could therefore ask calmly the critical question: "After seven years of ceaseless effort, enormous expenditure, burdensome taxes and the loss of many lives, where are we?" The answer was that we had come an astonishingly long way, by an unprecedented exertion that was itself heartening evidence of "democracy's will to survive." If we fell short of the absolute preponderance of power that our policy-makers foolishly assumed, we had at least succeeded in establishing a *balance* of power, which made our European allies no longer fearful of direct attack. Stevenson dwelt again on the growing strength and self-reliance of Western Europe. American worries over all the Communists in these countries were aggravated by the hysteria of McCarthyism. Americans had been taught to think of a Communist as a conspirator dedicated to the overthrow of our government, whereas most Europeans thought of "a neighbor, friend, fellow worker or even relative who votes Communist not to express his approval or preference for the Soviet system, but to express his disapproval of the conditions in which he lives and works." Stevenson would not be surprised when the big Communist parties in France and Italy settled down as respectable political parties, muffling the traditional summons to revolution and the dictatorship of the proletariat.

Finally, however, he emphasized the abiding challenges. America had a longer way to go, and would have to keep going indefinitely. It needed to understand much better the world revolutions, to learn more sympathy for the rising expectations of the poor peoples, and to give them a clearer idea of what we are for, not just what we are against. At the same time it had to maintain or better the balance of power, against an enemy that respected only power. "And here we encounter our greatest danger and our final task." We could maintain our power only by a coalition, but never for long by a coalition based on mere expedience or our own self-interest, only by one resting on an enduring community of interest, which required a decent respect for the opinions of our partners—not wards. Stevenson suggested that perhaps what America needed more than anything else was a hearing aid. But surely it needed a clear, deep dedication to its historic ideals, "the moral sentiments of human liberty and human welfare embodied in the Declaration of Independence and the Bill of Rights," which constitute its "greatest contribution to human society." Once more Stevenson ended by stressing moral considerations, what could be called platitudes, but what to him were always living truths, and truths he could utter without pompousness or self-righteousness.

Such considerations remained in the fore when Stevenson sought to "think afresh" about domestic problems too. In setting up his program of self-education in 1953, he arranged for a systematic review of these problems. He enlisted a staff of aides to make critical studies of all major public policies. It was again a most distinguished staff, including Kenneth Galbraith, Arthur Schlesinger, Jr., Seymour Harris, Thomas Finletter, George Ball, and Willard Wirtz, all of whom would serve under the administrations to come. Schlesinger in particular had argued that Stevenson made a mistake in campaigning so much on the early New Deal, which had perforce concentrated on the quantitative problems of food, shelter, and unemployment. Now, in a society growing affluent, the important issues were the challenges of abundance—the quality of American life, the cultivation of the mind and spirit, the opportunities for self-realization, or specifically such problems as civil rights and liberties, education, medical care, and the increasing millions of idle old people. This shift of interest was naturally congenial to Stevenson. He would draw on the studies made by his staff in his campaign of 1956, centered on the theme of the "New America."

Meanwhile, however, he made little use of most of them. Stevenson was never deeply interested in problems of the national economy. Members of his staff report that after they had done their homework they had a hard time getting him to read all their papers, having almost to hold him down and force his nose into them. Had he been elected President, he no doubt would have done his homework much more carefully, just as he had taken great pains to master all the problems of state government in Illinois. As it was, his main concerns in the interim are indicated in *What I Think,* a collection of thirty-odd articles and addresses. The most conventional of these is a "Farewell Report to the Citizens of Illinois," in which he put "foremost" on the list of unfinished business the highway program, no doubt the chief interest of the citizens; then came the needs of public schools and welfare services, matters actually closer to his heart. In other papers he ranged over many subjects, not including highways, but only about half a dozen are focused on economic issues.

Heading the list of contents is "My Faith in Democratic Capitalism," the core of his economic beliefs, originally published in *Fortune* magazine. In this Stevenson attacked all the talk about a basic antagonism between American business and government, the "two cornerstones of democratic capitalism." He deplored the New Deal ritual of castigating a business system that he, like almost all Americans, considered the permanent source of our prosperity. He gave more attention, however, to the attitudes of businessmen, since they were now in the saddle again and always had the press whooping for their cause. There was still too much adolescent clamor about the federal government as "a childishly operated nuisance, which hampers business, which intrudes, which confiscates or expropriates profits, and in a thousand ways spoils all the fun and is constantly threaten-

ing to 'socialize' all America by creeping"—this at a time when
business was making record profits.[4] Stevenson spelled out the
simple truths that government and private enterprise had always
collaborated, business alone had not created modern America, and
those who talked of "getting government out of business" welcomed
the billions of dollars' worth of business being done on government
military orders. In reminding businessmen of their social responsibilities, the greater because they had such prestige and influence in
America, he cited a big manufacturer who said of the oncoming
problems of automation, "I don't think it is the part, nor can it be the
part, of industry to try to plan the social aspects of this thing."
Stevenson pointed out that the government would inevitably have to
deal with the social consequences of these ever more rapid technological advances, and he saw "no reason why American industry should
not participate fully and freely in this enterprise."

Others might see more reason to doubt that it would, and to
complain of the common social irresponsibility of big business. In
any case, Stevenson was clearly more interested in the "social aspects"
than the purely economic; or more precisely, he was saying that they
could not be separated. Thus he questioned the "high government
spokesmen," in a businessman's government, who talked about
being conservative in economic affairs and liberal in human affairs.
What was social security—an economic or a human affair? What
was unemployment? The division seemed to him especially unrealistic
in our complex society. When in the Congressional campaign of 1954
he attacked the policies of the Eisenhower administration, including
the archaic economics of George Humphrey, it was not because they
were poor economics but because they favored the interests of the
few, who had been the chief beneficiaries of the big tax reduction.
Stevenson still had little idea of how best to promote steady economic
growth, little interest in this theme of the future. He was much more
concerned about human needs, the welfare of the many.

[4] The reader might be reminded of Nixon's charge that Stevenson was spreading
Communist propaganda by the "violent fury" of his attacks on our economic system (pp. 143–44).

Hence he introduced a seemingly incongruous theme early in his expression of faith in democratic capitalism. He warned against another "creeping" enemy—"the army of mass mediocrity, with banners flying." Like John Stuart Mill a century ago, he worried over what was happening to the individual, the supposed beneficiary but possible victim of an advancing technology in a society ever more organized, institutionalized, standardized. It appeared that in our century mass manipulation was a greater danger to the individual than economic exploitation had been in the past century. "Surely," Stevenson wrote, government and industry must seek "new and better ways of restoring scope to that strange eccentric, the individual." Again others might comment that it was not at all sure that industry would cooperate in this enterprise, since through advertising and the mass media it was the primary agent of mass manipulation, but again Stevenson was more interested in this problem than he was in the economic virtues of free private enterprise, which supposedly promoted individualism. In the preface to *What I Think* he made his main theme the necessity of criticism, and the value of the distinctive Western tradition of free critical inquiry and discussion, in particular because mass communications were making conformity "the easy option." Unthinking conformity "breeds the most insidious and permanent tyranny of all, in that its subjects are unconscious of their slavery."

No less characteristic was another qualification of his faith in democratic capitalism. "Materially we can—and will—do better still. But spiritually, morally, and politically, I don't think we are doing so well." Stevenson accordingly concluded that both industry and government "must become increasingly aware of their moral and spiritual responsibilities." In other words, the important question was always the ends of the material means provided so abundantly by our economy. This he took up in a lecture to a university audience, "America, the Economic Colossus."

Stevenson spoke proudly of the Colossus. We not only were without equal or precedent in our material power and well-being, but did not need to feel guilty over our good fortune, for we had not

raised our living standards by impoverishing others. He also saw
hope for the individual in spite of the development of mass production, through which machines, routine, and organization have taken
over; he thought we were finding the answers "by replacing the old
concept of freedom *versus* organization with a new concept of
freedom *through* organization." He could still sound optimistic when
he raised the critical question: How have we *used* our abundance? In
this respect he thought our record in recent years was best of all,
having in mind the billions we had spent on foreign aid.

As usual, however, Stevenson then dwelt on the reasons why we
should never be complacent. Congressmen had protested loudly
against the shipment of wheat to starving India because it was
neutral, others were denouncing aid to Britain because it had a
Socialist government, and always there were many to lecture our allies
on the error of their economic ways:

> Indeed, from our fertile fields or possibly from our less fertile minds,
> we seem to produce two kinds of economics. One is a highly refined,
> triple-distilled product which is roughly 200 proof *laissez faire.* This is
> bottled exclusively for export. We never drink it at home. For home
> consumption we have a much milder drink, a mixture of many ingredi-
> ents, which isn't so easily described but doesn't give such a shock to the
> system as we prescribe for others whose systems are much weaker.

One example was the pleasure economic conservatives took in the
imported slogan "trade not aid," which to them meant no more
handouts; then they discouraged the trade our allies wanted by raising
tariffs or imposing quotas, to protect American business from the
competition it supposedly doted and throve on. Still meaner were the
constant complaints that we were wasting our substance by playing a
global Santa Claus, whereas we were spending only a fraction of one
percent of our national income on aid to underdeveloped countries.
Speaking as a politician, Stevenson added parenthetically, he could
never understand this attack on Santa Claus as a presumably softheaded, subversive type; he remembered him as a good fellow and a
very welcome visitor. At the end he said our proper mood was a

"sober" pride in our achievements, tempered by awareness that our material power was a moral commitment and could be an inward corruption.

These themes recur throughout the volume. Most often Stevenson took up the threats to civil liberties, the miasma of McCarthyism, which was weakening us both at home and abroad. He coupled it with the popular sneers at intellectuals, suggesting an intentness on blowing out our brains. Substantially he repeated what he had said earlier, or what many others have said about the values of freedom of thought, speech, and conscience; but it should be remembered that Stevenson was the first to make McCarthyism a campaign issue, stressing it again in the elections of 1954 against the advice of other party leaders. Similarly with his concern over the pressures to conformity, the growing emphasis on being or becoming "well adjusted." These too were familiar ideas, soon due to become commonplaces; but Stevenson was the first Presidential candidate to make much of them. Recognizing that moderation, symbolized by Eisenhower, was the spirit of the times, he could see that it was being confused with mediocrity.

A related theme that he often returned to was education, its primary importance in a democracy, and now the need for federal aid. This was so plain that President Eisenhower himself told Congress that the nation needed $7 billion worth of new schools. Thereupon he recommended, in Stevenson's words, that it "pass not a law but a miracle"; to meet this whopping need he proposed grants of $66 million a year for three years, or about 2 percent of the federal grants he proposed for new highways. His Republican Congress buried the bill. He could not see either what Stevenson defined as the serious question—not merely "What will an adequate education program cost?" but "What is the cost of not having such a program?" When the Soviet Union forged ahead of us in Sputniks, an alarmed Congress would at last authorize federal aid to education, first of all to turn out more scientists and engineers to catch up with the Russians; but then the cry went up that resounds to this day: we needed more education to serve the "national interest." Stevenson maintained from the beginning that "education can serve the ends of democratic society only as it meets those of the individual human being." A free society needed many different kinds of people—informed people, yet "unique, different, unpatterned individuals." Its students should be taught above all to inquire, think for themselves. Another alarming consequence of McCarthyism stressed by Stevenson, but ignored by President Eisenhower, was that it made teachers everywhere still more fearful of "controversial" subjects.

Still another basic but neglected task of education was to preserve the intellectual, moral, and spiritual values at the heart of Western civilization. This Stevenson dealt with most pleasantly at a Smith College Commencement (1955), where he joined the speakers all over the land who were telling "thousands of helpless young captives how important they are—as citizens in a free society, as educated, rational, privileged participants in a great historic crisis." A brief review of our heritage, beginning with the ancient Greeks and Jews, led to the principal complaint about higher education today. It was turning out chiefly specialists, individuals who became absorbed in their particular function, who typically operated well in the realm of means but poorly if at all in the realm of ends, and who by neglecting mature values might lead profitable but purposeless lives. "You may be hitched to one of these creatures we call 'Western man,' " he told the seniors, "and I think part of your job is to keep him Western, to keep him truly purposeful, to keep him whole." By helping to counteract "the crushing and corrupting effects of specialization," they might do their share to meet this "crisis" we were forever talking about, which "will be won at last not on the battlefield but in the head and heart." And since he had "some rather large notions about you young ladies," he ventured to make some suggestions about their children too. As mothers they might help to form real personalities instead of more well-adjusted ones—contemplating, say, "the possibility of a Shakespeare perfectly adjusted to bourgeois life in Stratford." Stevenson recognized the frustrations that were often the price of the unprecedented opportunities young women now enjoyed: "Once they read Baudelaire. Now it is the *Consumers' Guide. . . .*

They had hoped to play their part in the crisis of the age. But what they do is wash the diapers." Always they may wonder whether they could not have fulfilled these homely functions as well without years of study in college. Still, in modern America they are not confined to the home—there are plenty of outside activities. Above all, "What you have learned here can fit you as nothing else can for the primary task of making homes and whole human beings in whom the rational values of freedom, tolerance, charity, and free inquiry can take root."

Other matters discussed in *What I Think* included medicine, the responsibilities of labor unions, the typical proposal of the Eisenhower administration to turn over to a few big corporations the $12 billion national investment in atomic energy, and "the embarrassment of riches we call the 'farm problem,' " since farmers were earning lower incomes by producing too abundantly. On all these domestic issues, however, Stevenson had more to say in the campaign of 1956. Since as a still "unemployed politician" he was freer to discuss philosophical issues, viewed in some historical perspective, this chapter in his career may be concluded by a review of an address he gave on "The American Vision" at the Columbia Bicentennial Conference in 1954.

"I am a great believer in national humility, modesty, self-examination, and self-criticism," he began, "and I have preached these virtues vigorously, although, of course, I haven't practiced them very diligently." Usually at his best when addressing university audiences, Stevenson may have startled this one by proceeding at once to a vigorous defense of America against "the new fashion of being cynical, sarcastic, skeptical, deprecating about America or fellow Americans," as if we were simply materialists, unequal to the task of resisting communism. If this fashion was hardly new, Stevenson's tone was certainly unfashionable in what writers were beginning to call our Age of Anxiety:

> To view our present and our future with such sickly anxiety is to ignore the lessons and the achievements of our past. For the plain truth is that we here in America have written the greatest success story in human history. The plain truth is that on the record of performance,

we here in America have in a few years made Socialism obsolete, shown that Communism is nothing but a noisome stagnant pool of reaction.

He reviewed the record in this century, not only the miracles of mass production but the diffusion of wealth, the rising standard of living of the many, and the plain refutation of Karl Marx's confident predictions about capitalism. "We have created a free society that promotes the general welfare of all far better, far more successfully than it has ever been promoted by any other system or social organization." With our domestic policy we have completely transformed our foreign policy. "Since the turn of the century we have successively and emphatically renounced, first imperialism, then isolation, and finally our historical neutrality." In the process of changing to a policy of total involvement, "America has fathered three unprecedented ideas: Lend-lease for Hitler's intended victims in war, the Marshall Plan for Stalin's intended victims in peace, and Point 4 to help undeveloped areas." I assume that intellectuals still need to be reminded of this literally extraordinary record.

But having given his three cheers for America, Stevenson brought up his usual misgivings, more congenial to his audience. "What's the matter with us anyhow?" His answer was not startling: the trouble was an ignorance that makes of material progress an end rather than a means, and constitutes "the peril of our hardheaded, pragmatic attitude that has helped us so much to achieve our vast social and economic transformation"; and an ignorance that begets fear, "the most subversive force of all." Stevenson wondered whether these might not be surface symptoms of something deeper, "a moral and human crisis in the Western world" comparable to the crisis of the crumbling Roman Empire. He wondered about a more obvious danger, "a spirit of materialism in which the aim of life is a never-ending increase of material comfort, and the result a moral and religious vacuum." He remarked again the danger that mass manipulation might be making robots of Americans. All this was all too familiar to intellectuals, but again novel for a Presidential candidate.

Stevenson ended with one cheer, a sober restatement of his faith in the American people that still might be too optimistic, but that in any case stated the necessary conditions for hopes of the future. He believed there were millions of people who saw or at least dimly sensed the dangers, wanted to live a truly human life, wanted to be independent persons. He believed there was "a hunger to hear a word of truth, a longing for an ideal, a readiness for sacrifice." As evidence he cited not only the famous speech of Winston Churchill early in the war but the appeal of the dictators to emotional forces rather than material interests. Even so there remained "the horror of our time in history," that "things are worse than ever before." Perhaps we were passing through another of the great crises of history when man had to make a mighty choice; and where, then, should we look?

> We look to ourselves—and we are not ashamed. We are proud of what freedom has wrought—the freedom to experiment, to inquire, to change, to invent. And we shall have to look exactly in the same directions to solve our problems now—to individual Americans, to their institutions, to their churches, to their governments, to their multifarious associations—and to all the free participants in the free life of a free people.
>
> And we look, finally, to the free university whose function is the search for truth and its communication to succeeding generations. Men may be born free; they cannot be born wise; and it is the duty of the university to make the free wise.

In his concluding sentences Stevenson was wondering again how many Americans cherished a free mind. His next campaign would give him reason for doubts.

8

~~~~~~~~~~~

The Campaign of 1956

I'm not an old experienced hand at politics. But I am now
seasoned enough to have learned that the hardest thing
about any political campaign is how to win without proving
that you are unworthy of winning.

—*Adlai Stevenson*, 1956

Although in the nature of American politics Stevenson's second
campaign for the Presidency had to be much like the first, it involved
some significant differences. This time he could not be charged with
"indecisiveness"—from the beginning he plainly wanted to run. He
had made up his mind to do so early in 1955, even before President
Eisenhower's heart attack made it uncertain whether he would run
again, and he formally announced his candidacy in November of that
year. The reasons he gave were conventional but honest: he believed it
important for the Democratic Party to take charge of the nation
again, he was assured his candidacy would be welcomed, and he
considered it his duty to contribute all he could to "the search for a
safer, saner world." Eisenhower had turned out to be a worse
President than he had expected; he now believed we were losing the
cold war. All polls indicated that Stevenson was far more popular
than any other Democratic candidate. If his motives naturally included personal ambition, he was unquestionably acting out of a
sense of duty too, for he could scarcely be confident of winning. All

polls indicated as well the exceptional popularity of President Eisenhower.

The immediate embarrassment for Stevenson was his ambiguous status as a "titular leader" of his party. Sam Rayburn and Lyndon Johnson, its leaders in Congress, neglected ostentatiously to consult him about matters of policy. In spite of a friendship dating from the early days of the New Deal, Johnson was too much a professional to approve of Stevenson's ways of doing politics, and he was already entertaining Presidential ambitions of his own. Ex-President Truman, not yet aware that he was nearing his political death, had changed his mind again. After the campaign of 1954, in which Stevenson helped the Democrats to win both houses of Congress by giving some eighty speeches in thirty-three states, Truman was so elated that he declared Stevenson was his choice for the Presidency in 1956; but now he was preparing to come out for Governor Averell Harriman of New York. (In his *Memoirs* he explained that he felt Stevenson was "still embarrassed by this farmer from Missouri.") Senator Estes Kefauver, the front-runner in 1952, was again running hard in the primaries; though an earnest liberal, he was known to voters chiefly for his handshaking and his folksiness. Stevenson had not planned to campaign in the primaries, but he changed his mind after Kefauver upset him in Minnesota, where he had been heavily favored to win because of support by the state organization.

He then went out to do battle in Florida, the scene of the next primary. In the course of a whistle-stop campaign—the prescribed ritual for primaries—Stevenson acquired a somewhat different "new look." Kefauver's victory in Minnesota persuaded him that Truman and the professionals might be right in their standard complaint that his speeches did not get over to the ordinary voter; so he went to the small towns smiling and glad-handing, even to the tune of cowboy music—putting on an "image" that might seem suited to his natural geniality. It did not really become him, however. Harry Ashmore, who accompanied him on his campaign through Florida, tells of how he could not help being himself. Once when Stevenson asked him how he had done in a small town they were leaving, Ashmore replied that it wasn't a bad show but he still had something to learn: "When you are shaking hands in a supermarket and a little girl in a starched dress steps out of the crowd and hands you a stuffed alligator, what you say is, 'Thanks very much, I've always wanted one of these for the mantelpiece at Libertyville.' What you don't say is what you did say: 'For Christ's sake, what's this?' " Ashmore adds that Stevenson was delighted by the lesson and told it on himself at the next stop, thereby probably losing another hundred votes to Kefauver, who was born knowing what to do with stuffed alligators.

Nevertheless Stevenson managed to win in Florida, and not by beating Kefauver at his own game; his sophistication and wit kept showing through the new image. (When informed about a citrus disease called "spreading decline," he said he thought it was attacking him.) He won again in the Oregon primary and then clinched his position as favorite by an overwhelming victory in California, where in speeches he was his old self. That he carried both the small towns and the big cities suggests again that the "average" American voter may not be quite so inert or uniform a creature as he appears in statistics.

In other respects, however, his primary campaigns did not augur well for the big campaign ahead. Since there was little difference between Stevenson and Kefauver on major issues, their contest in Florida degenerated into conventional politicking, with considerable unpleasantness. Stevenson neglected to disclaim the charges made by one of his supporters, on the same platform with him, that Kefauver was an "integrationist" and "sycophant of the Negro vote." Naturally angry, Kefauver retaliated with what Stevenson called distortions and abuse. Reporters noted other signs of stooping to low-level politics. Although at the national convention Stevenson could truly say that he had made no deals to win the nomination, he had sought support from some rather unsavory politicians, such as Herman Talmadge in Georgia. And at best his prolonged primary campaigns took a toll. He had to squander on them not only much energy but material he was preparing for the big campaign; he still disliked to repeat, and when he had to, the material seemed stale to him. He would not be in the best of fighting trim for another struggle against heavy odds.

The national convention he went to as a favorite was no better prepared to get him off to a rousing start. Since he had already been beaten once, the delegates were less spirited and united than those who had drafted him in 1952. Southerners caused trouble by a struggle over the plank on civil rights, in which his moderation offended both sides. Truman than killed himself politically by a last-ditch stand for Governor Harriman, having announced that Stevenson was "too defeatist to win." Stevenson was not worried by this, according to William Blair even feeling some relief, since he thought Truman had lost him votes in 1952 by giving General Eisenhower hell, perhaps cost him the election; and in any case he could take comfort in his nomination on the first ballot, followed by the ritual acclamation and move that it be made unanimous. But meanwhile the convention had agreed on a platform as uninspired as most. Although on the whole vaguely liberal, it wobbled on civil rights. While pledging continued efforts to eradicate all discrimination, the key plank added: "We reject all proposals for the use of force to interfere with orderly determination of these matters by the courts." By Stevenson's standards, the platform was least satisfactory in its declarations on foreign policy, his principal concern. Among other things, it not only pledged "determined opposition to the admission of Red China to the United Nations" but attacked the Republicans for "fraternizing with Communists," thus adopting the tactics of Richard Nixon.

After his nomination Stevenson introduced the only novelty in the routine proceedings, with ironic consequences. He defied all precedent by announcing his decision to throw open to the convention the nomination for the Vice-Presidency instead of choosing his running mate. Although this unique decision might seem to be a belated recognition of the importance of the Vice-Presidency in an age of perpetual crisis, it stupefied Sam Rayburn and Lyndon Johnson; they despaired of Stevenson when he held to it in spite of their pleas for political common sense. The convention responded by choosing Estes

Kefauver, no favorite of the professionals. (Truman had been referring to him privately as "cowfever.") He and Stevenson of course promptly made up their unnecessary differences in the primaries, but these had given the Republicans more campaign ammunition. The real winner would turn out to be Senator John F. Kennedy, whom Kefauver defeated for the nomination by a slim margin; Kennedy profited by his leap to prominence while being spared the handicap of association with Stevenson in defeat. Four years later he would round out the story neatly by reverting to precedent and choosing his own running mate—Lyndon Johnson.

Much less novel, however, was Stevenson's speech of acceptance this time. After the customary tributes to the principals in the proceedings, from Eleanor Roosevelt and Harry Truman to Kennedy ("that great young American statesman"), he swung into a conventional fighting speech. He offered his vision of a New America in generalities that might not enthrall a nonpartisan audience, and that were tarnished by his dutiful praise of the party platform. He grew more convincing in a lengthy attack on the Eisenhower administration, beginning with its failures to enlighten, elevate, and inspire the American people, but one who agreed with his charges might consider his tone too strident. When he bodied out his vision of the New America, detailing what the country could do under Democratic leadership, it was to the refrain "We can and we will!" His own voice came through now and then in quiet statements, for example, of his belief that there was a spiritual hunger in the world which could not be satisfied by material things alone, better cars or longer credit terms. But in general his speech was by no means so moving as his first speech of acceptance. With its accent on promise and decisiveness, it conveyed no such solemn sense of the difficulties and responsibilities of world leadership. I doubt that it will be read by future generations.

The campaign that followed was the usual ordeal of sixteen to twenty hours a day of ceaseless activity. It was the more grueling because with the long primary campaigns that preceded it, Stevenson was on the stump for almost nine months, and also because he felt more sense of urgency, with less hope of victory. Having begun formally in New Mexico as a "grass-roots campaign," it involved more whistle stops than usual. (One might wonder why reputedly shrewd politicians endorse all this exertion to impress the infinitesimal fraction of the electorate that shows up at railroad stations.) Stevenson often looked and acted more tired than did President Eisenhower, supposedly in uncertain health. Although the campaign gave him some genial memories, such as a very pregnant lady carrying a banner "Stevenson Is the Man," he was not rewarded in this second swing around the country by the excitement of seeing so much of it for the first time. In his Author's Note to a collection of his speeches published as *The New America,* he did not say that this campaign was an exhilarating experience.

For a student of American politics, the main question about it was raised by a particular difference from his first campaign. This one was managed by a professional, James Finnegan, who in Philadelphia had demonstrated his ability to get along with liberals and egghead amateurs. He and other of Stevenson's professional advisers did not see eye to eye with his staff of policy advisers and ghost writers, most of whom had worked for him in 1952. They asked him to give more attention to the party organization, the interests of partisan audiences, and the tactics of expediency. When he made some effort to comply, his intellectual advisers feared that he was losing some of his old appeal. The differences between the two groups were not sharp, being softened or blurred by mutual respect and common devotion to Stevenson, but they were serious enough to unsettle him. "Am I master in my own house?" he once asked wryly. As I see it, the outcome was an unhappy compromise. It is generally agreed that Stevenson campaigned on a lower level this time, and there is no question that his speeches were less witty and urbane, less often eloquent too. And to all appearances during the campaign, confirmed by its result, he was appealing no more effectively to the voters, if anything less so.

In Stevenson's defense it may be said that he was compelled to go on the attack, and so was bound to seem more partisan. Given

President Eisenhower's popularity as a folk hero, his only hope lay in the fact that registered Democrats still outnumbered Republicans. He had to win back many who had voted for Eisenhower, had to identify him with the Republican Party, since after all the President had said that he "favored the election of every Republican over every Democrat for every office any place." However partisan, moreover, he was never being merely expedient, but speaking out of genuine conviction. He attacked not merely the President's lapses but "his philosophical attitude toward the office and his consistent rejection of the positive responsibilities of leadership." The intellectual level of Stevenson's campaign was indeed in some respects higher than that of 1952. The editors of *The New America* (Seymour Harris, John Bartlow Martin, and Arthur Schlesinger) could maintain in their introduction that on almost every issue Stevenson's position was "more considered, informed and thoughtful" than it had been in his first effort. And on major speeches he remained a perfectionist, to the despair of both his campaign managers and the reporters who had to make deadlines. "Sometimes," James Finnegan later told Emmet Hughes, "we'd have to keep our campaign plane in the air—with important local politicians waiting on the ground—while we circled and circled in the sky, as Adlai edited on and on."

The speeches collected in *The New America* do not include, however, or at least adequately represent, the many Stevenson gave to partisan audiences. Newsmen reported that these accentuated a paradox of the campaign noted by James Reston—both candidates did better with their weak arguments than their strong ones. In hitting hard, Stevenson at times swung wildly. He blamed the Eisenhower administration, for example, for extending aid to the dictator of Argentina, Juan Perón—a policy inherited from the Truman administration. At times, too, his punches could be called low. Although in his speech of acceptance he said that he did not propose to make political capital out of the President's illness, on election eve he told the country, "I must say bluntly that every piece of scientific evidence we have, every lesson of history and experience, indicates that a Republican victory tomorrow would mean that

Richard M. Nixon would probably be President of this country within the next four years." He had some excuse in that this frightening possibility was real enough to justify a warning to the voters, short of dragging in all the lessons of history and medicine; but it recalls the sense of urgency that made the campaign more of an ordeal for Stevenson and exacted some cost in urbanity. *The New America* is on the whole distinctly less readable than the campaign speeches of 1952. Most of it is not clearly worth reading today, or quoting, except for its historical significance.

Yet this significance is considerable, great enough to warrant a review of Stevenson's far-ranging campaign. He stated most fully the challenges of abundance, stemming from the "breath-taking realization" that in America today "for the first time in history we have the material instruments for accomplishing virtually any goal we set ourselves." Much of the program that the voters rejected in 1956 would be endorsed by President Kennedy, put through Congress by President Johnson, and become as widely accepted as the basic reforms of the New Deal—all this within a decade. While catching up with Stevenson on some matters, the country outdistanced him on others. On both counts his campaign offers a perspective on the extraordinary pace of change in our time, the remarkable efforts to keep up with the history that man has been making, and the invariable lag, less surprising than ever before, but more dismaying because of the irresistible, ever accelerating drive of modern technology. Stevenson's faith remained that a country that had gone so far in so short a time would keep on going steadily. The question always remained whether it would move fast enough, and whether man could control the mighty movements that had got under way without conscious plan.

Because of his moderation Stevenson lagged most conspicuously on the movement for civil rights and equal opportunities for Negroes. There is no question of his sincere support of their cause, which he had consistently backed ever since in wartime Washington he persuaded the Navy to give Negroes more opportunity. As in 1952 he told Southern audiences that he stood squarely for civil rights, so in

1956 he went out of his way to repeat in Arkansas that he entirely agreed with the Supreme Court decision prohibiting segregation in the schools—a matter on which President Eisenhower refused to commit himself. (The President said characteristically, "I think it makes no difference whether or not I endorse it.") But Stevenson also said in Arkansas—and manfully repeated in Harlem—that he supported the Democratic plank opposing the use of force in these matters. Before the campaign started he was booed by a Negro audience in Los Angeles when he said he thought the use of troops to enforce the Supreme Court decision would be a great mistake: "That is exactly what brought on the Civil War. . . . We must proceed gradually, not upsetting habits or traditions that are older than the Republic." He disappointed many of his supporters by not facing up to the actual problem—that Southerners were stubbornly resolved to defy the Supreme Court, and had long been addicted to the use of force to keep Negroes in their lowly place.

One reason for his position was his belief that the states should take care of such matters. Another was the defect of his virtue of reasonableness; distressed by the increasing bitterness, he clung to his hopes of the many moderate Southerners, and so asked Negroes to be more patient than could reasonably be expected after all they had put up with for a century. Stevenson was consciously loyal as well to the spirit of Abraham Lincoln, though perhaps he forgot that his idol had wobbled on this issue in his debates with Stephen Douglas: Lincoln told voters frightened by his famous statement about a house divided, "I am not, nor ever have been, in favor of bringing about in any way the social and political equality of the white and black races." And like his idol, Stevenson apparently grew up with some feeling of the natural inferiority of Negroes that is deeply embedded in American tradition; as a patrician little boy he was accustomed to Negro servants.[1] Later, as Ambassador at the United Nations, he provoked some animus among Negro intellectuals by resisting efforts to add a Negro delegate to his lily-white staff, and then virtually ignoring one who was appointed. Stevenson might therefore be given

[1] One of his old friends remarked to me that he never really outgrew this feeling.

more credit for the pains he took to be especially cordial to the ambassadors of the new African nations, with whom he was most popular. At home he was nevertheless slow to realize how fierce the resentment of Negroes had grown, and how serious the danger of explosions unless much more was done for them soon.

On other of his proposals for a New America, bodied out in program papers prepared by his staff, Stevenson likewise did not go far enough to satisfy some of his supporters. While reminding the country of its uneven prosperity, he sounded no call for a war on poverty, nor a crash program to aid Negroes in particular. He was more disturbed by the failure of farmers to share in the prosperity because he still thought of the family farm as "the backbone of American agriculture," or the heart of the rural life he idealized, but again he had little to offer them beyond the traditional policy of supports incorporated in the Democratic platform. The program papers do not include one on labor, on which the platform called for outright repeal of the Taft-Hartley Act; to this Stevenson gave rather perfunctory assent, evidently believing that labor was mostly faring well enough. Yet for the most part he was farsighted, well in advance of both his party platform and the country at large, not to mention his opponent.

First he took up the inevitable question raised by all he wanted the government to do for public services: Where was the money coming from? He gave the obvious answer, which was not at all obvious to President Eisenhower and his team, and today still is not to the many conservatives who argue that we can afford to spend billions only on weapons. The answer was that the money would come from an expanding economy, with rising tax revenues. As for the standard complaints that taxpayers in the high-income brackets were suffering "severe hardships" and being deprived of "incentive," he gave as easy an answer that is better known to Congressmen but likewise still ignored: with all the deductions and loopholes carefully provided in the tax laws, very few of the wealthy paid anything like the pre-scribed rate. He could have added that on the record big businessmen were hardly suffering from loss of incentive. Stevenson's programs were in fact quite modest, calling for an expenditure of only a few billion in the first two or three years, rising steadily thereafter but remaining a small fraction of the estimated rise in the national income. Nothing of a radical in fiscal matters, he continued to talk of economy in government and the desirability of balanced budgets, a reduction in the national debt, and lower taxes. But at the time it was enough that he called for a rethinking of economic policy in terms of the technological revolution, proposed much more government action, pointed out that an ever smaller proportion of the national income was going into public services, and insisted that it was not economical to neglect the education, health, and welfare of American citizens.

On the "crisis in education" Stevenson amplified what he had been saying in recent years. His program paper and a campaign speech on the subject make unexciting reading because of their thoroughness, being loaded with facts, figures, and detailed recommendations. The main problems he identified as the shortages of buildings, teachers, talent, information, and policy. The Eisenhower administration had done nothing about these problems except arrange a White House conference, a favorite excuse for inaction, which took two years to convene; out of this came only an inadequate bill for limited aid to school construction, which a majority of the Republicans in Congress helped to kill. (The President had written one of them that we must indeed guard against "yet another vehicle by which the believers in paternalism, if not outright socialism, will gain still additional power for the Central Government.") Stevenson's proposals included federal aid to the states, grants for higher education, more exchange programs, and the expansion of vocational and adult education. In calling for a clear-cut national policy, he also emphasized again that the goal should be "the fullest possible development of each individual's capacities and talents." This ideal, difficult to realize in a system of mass education, would not guide the national effort when his main proposals were put into effect. One reason was a complication he neglected in his own fear of federal paternalism. He insisted that the control of education could and would stay in the local communities, particularly their school boards, since this was "the crowning feature of our democracy at work" and the "safeguard of our individual liberties." Unfortunately for those who cherish this democratic institution (as I do too), local control of the schools, especially in small-town America, is often the major obstacle to an improvement in the quality of education, and to provisions for highly individual, creative, or gifted students, except star athletes.

To support his program to better the nation's health—another cluster of problems that the Eisenhower administration had done almost nothing about in spite of the President's avowed liberalism in "human" affairs—Stevenson cited some shocking statistics, probably still unknown to most Americans. The Department of Agriculture was spending more money on research on plant and animal diseases than the Public Health Service was spending on research on cancer, arthritis, heart disease, and mental illness together. At a time when "economy" was the official password, it was grimly appropriate that Americans spent less on medical research than on tombstones. Stevenson's primary concerns, however, were the problems that the government would belatedly attack in the years to come: the inability of millions of Americans to afford decent medical care, the cost of which was rising steadily and steeply; the inadequacy of health insurance, which covered only about a quarter of the nation's medical bill; the overcrowded, often poorly equipped hospitals; and the shortage of doctors, now fewer in proportion to population than they were a century ago. Here again Stevenson's proposals were somewhat less than radical. He insisted repeatedly that he was against any form of socialized medicine, he would not lay down the law to doctors, he was all for voluntary health insurance so far as possible. Liberals could complain that he failed to attack the immediate enemy, the American Medical Association—the tightest union in the country, politically the most powerful, and by his standards among the most selfish and irresponsible. Yet his program called for more than the government has yet been willing to do. He held that the goal should and could be to make comprehensive health insurance available to all Americans. Although this would require federal aid, a country willing to subsidize agriculture, railroads, airlines, the merchant marine, and power plants ought to be willing and able to subsidize public health.

Most novel was Stevenson's program for older citizens. Far in advance of his party platform, or any platform in the past, it was the clearest response to the challenges of abundance—an abundance, he pointed out, to which the elderly had contributed most and from which they were benefiting least. There were proportionately more than twice as many people sixty-five years or older than there had been when he started to school. The great majority of them had pitifully small incomes, were poorly housed, lacked hospital insurance, and got inadequate treatment for their commonly poor health. The increasing number who were breaking down, suffering from mental illness, heightened Stevenson's concern over their deeper frustrations, the common emptiness of their lives. Most of them wanted to keep on working but could find no suitable work; industry had no room for them, their communities no need of them. He accordingly set up three goals for the New America: to enable the elderly to maintain their accustomed standards of living after their retirement, to provide the special facilities and services they needed, and to give purpose and significance to their lives. The objective was not merely social security but "the guarantee of human dignity." This was no matter of charity, he insisted—it was a matter of *right*, simple fairness, and good sense.

As it was, little was being done beyond the provision of Social Security benefits, which were not keeping up with the rising cost of living. Little new housing was being built to suit the needs of older people; social service agencies were inadequately staffed to assist them; the federal government was investing a penny a person for research on arthritis and rheumatic diseases, their common afflictions. Characteristically the administration had forty thousand employees working on the problems of business concerns, but just nine people in the Department of Health, Education and Welfare, with a budget of $65,000, working on the problems of fourteen million senior citizens. As characteristic was a recent announcement by President Eisenhower, with the usual fanfare, that he was setting up a Federal Council on Aging to review existing government programs and make recommendations. Stevenson remarked "how consistently the corporations have got action from this administration, while the people have got conferences, councils, commissions and confabs." These had the added attraction of costing nothing to speak of.

Stevenson's program of action included increased old-age benefits, provision of medical and hospital insurance, federal financing of special housing, training programs in kinds of work that can be done better by older people, and the establishment of an Office of Older Persons' Welfare. All this would be only a beginning, he said. Even so one might wonder whether a new office could do much to relieve his particular concern, the "terrible loneliness" of many old people, millions of them living away from any relative and feeling what an old lady told him—"We just want to be wanted." In a rapidly changing urban suburban society, in which ever fewer people live and die in the house where they were born, the old will necessarily be more liable to feelings of loneliness, and their wisdom count for less than it did in the days of the old family homestead. Still having such a homestead in Bloomington, Stevenson could state too brightly the good American belief: "We have never yet in this country met a problem we couldn't lick." But at least much more could be done to ease the problems of the old and enrich the independence that might compensate for the loss of the rooted life. As Governor of Illinois Stevenson had been able to do some pioneering work, among other things establishing the first or second Geriatrics Research Hospital in the country. Most important, as he said, is "that we *want* to do these things," set our goals high, and not be content with minimums.

The rest of his domestic program was more familiar, though at the time controversial enough. It included public housing, still denounced as socialistic; conservation of natural resources, which the administration inclined to turn over to private enterprise whenever possible; and attention to such growing problems as water supply and municipal pollution that were only beginning to stir alarm. As a whole his program was certainly liberal.

Before the campaign started, Stevenson gave a short talk in which he returned to the semantic issue, "What is a liberal?" A popular magazine that had posed this question got a rich variety of answers from self-styled liberals, which delighted the editors; they concluded that a modern liberal was a zombie who didn't know who or where he was. Stevenson commented that he thought variety of opinion was the hallmark of the American Way, not so funny or silly as they implied. Believing that liberalism was not a set of answers but an approach, he ventured his definition of the basic beliefs of a liberal today. One was "that *people* are all that is important, and that *all* people are equally important"; property and business are only means, not ends. Another was faith in the possibility of a better future. The liberal "has never seen from on high any slightest indication that Heaven itself wishes to return to the good old days—and so he walks ahead, in courage and steadfastness, with a minimum of backward glances, into the perpetually obscure, the perpetually dangerous, the perpetually unknown future. No wonder he cannot always tell where he is going." By contrast, "the reactionary can always tell you where he has been, so he has an air of authority." Without mentioning Edmund Burke, whom he admired and often cited, Stevenson suggested the basic objection to Burke's conservatism and reverence for tradition in a revolutionary age—the truism that we simply cannot stand on time-tested ways, since modern science and technology forever demand new thinking. As for America, blessed with abundance, the next frontier was "the quality, the moral, intellectual and aesthetic standards of the free way of life." Philosophical conservatives like Burke, one might add, would naturally believe in the importance of such standards, but American political conservatives have typically been indifferent to them because of their belief in the primacy of business. In this respect too President Eisenhower was scarcely liberal in human affairs.

As in the 1952 campaign, Stevenson gave one of his most genial, relaxed speeches at a Liberal Party convention. Again he noted the natural disagreements among liberals, whether with a large or small *l:* "No man can precisely define liberalism without getting into an argument with another liberal; that is the nature of our creed—and our breed." But feeling quite at home, and one suspects happy not to be tied down to one of his "program papers," he gave free rein to his wit in noting the remarkable changes in the political scenery since

1952. Whereas the Republicans had then rallied the country against the egghead menace, they now had organized "a committee devoted to the care and feeding of the egghead vote"; if the infiltration of intellectuals into their party might not change things much, it had to be recognized as "a minor triumph of mind over matter." The most striking change was the emergence of the "new" Nixon, in the image of Little Lord Fauntleroy. While awed by the lack of conviction that made possible so swift a transformation, Stevenson added, "I do wish that we might hear some word from him repudiating the irresponsible, vindictive and malicious words so often spoken by the impostor who has been using his name all these years." He commiserated with Harold Stassen, now campaigning faithfully after having been clobbered by the regulars for his effort to stop the renomination of Nixon. "In this new Republican Party liberal Republicans are like opera singers: when they are stabbed they don't die; they sing." He gave a pretty example of the workings of the President's staff system:

> When the Russians recently said they were going to reduce their army by 1.2 million men, the Secretary of Defense said it was a "step in the right direction"; the Secretary of State said it was a step in the wrong direction; Mr. Stassen said it was just what we wanted—and the President blessed everybody and appointed a committee to decide what we thought.

Stevenson again felt able to relax and forget his homework in a speech at Yale to an audience of fellow eggheads, all "hard-boiled now." Noting that Republican talent scouts were beating the darkest recesses of *Time* and the Ivy League in a search for intellectuals, he said seriously that he thought the prospects of intellectuals were improving and they were not so unpopular as they supposed. He approached his main theme, a plea for honest, responsible debate, by observing that the new Nixon was taking the high road by associating Democrats with socialism instead of communism. On his own "hard-hitting" campaign he quoted an old friend who had congratulated him a bit sourly: "I am glad at last to see the declarative sentence begin to triumph over the subjunctive." In entire seriousness he deplored again the common practice of debauching the language of politics, corrupting the basic terms of democracy, and now exploiting all the high-powered machinery of an age of mass manipulation. "The premise of such manipulations is contempt—contempt for people's intelligence, common sense and dignity." Stevenson would as always regret some ill-considered remarks he made in the heat of the campaign, but as always he carried through his earnest effort—this time if anything too painfully earnest—to prove himself worthy of winning. Here he dwelt on a particular difficulty of a second campaign against the same opponent:

> I am peculiarly exposed to the temptation of thinking that the issues are the same because the faces are the same. But I try to resist it because I know that to yield is to defy the overriding law of life, which is change. And the way I resist is by continually asking myself: What is this election really all about this year? What are the watchwords of the past which have no relevance for the present? What should we be thinking, planning, initiating, doing—now?

Such persistence led him to reject what appeared to be his best chance of winning.

At the beginning of his campaign Stevenson reluctantly accepted the advice of his staff to minimize foreign affairs. The polls showed that there was little public interest in them, and his advisers feared, rightly enough, that emphasis on them would only lend force to the shopworn Republican argument that theirs was always the party of peace, the Democrats were the party of war. Most of the voters knew little except that President Eisenhower had brought peace in Korea, avoided war in Indochina, and gone to Geneva to reach an understanding with the Soviet Union, while at the same time they believed he had the Commies on the run. But Stevenson, always convinced that foreign policy was the most important issue, therefore believed that the people ought to be shown we were not winning the cold war as the Republicans boasted. When early in the year both he and the President had addressed the American Society of Newspaper Editors, the editors had voted informally two to one in maintaining that we were losing the cold war. As the campaign wore on, he persisted more and more in his belief that the people *could* be made to see the truth. In the last weeks of the campaign he hammered away chiefly at foreign policy, without regard to political expediency.

In reviewing his basic objections to the policies of Secretary Dulles, Stevenson added a further charge, that too often he had deliberately misinformed the people, in keeping with the growing tendency of the administration to suppress or manage news for the sake of its own security rather than the security of the nation. It could not have been pure ignorance that inspired the Secretary to tell a House committee in 1955 that the Soviet Union was "on the point of collapsing," or later to announce that "we have the initiative, very distinctly," in both the Middle East and South Asia. Similarly after the loss of Indochina he wrote an article for *Life* magazine boasting about our victory there. As for our initiative in Asia, in less than four years we had had four different ambassadors in India—or would have when the administration got around to filling a vacancy that had existed for several months. Stevenson then had all too easy a time exposing the President's abdications in leadership. He cited a number of critical events—before his heart attack—that took place while he was off on a golf course or about to leave for another golfing vacation. When asked about a unanimous House resolution condemning colonialism, Eisenhower answered: "I did not know about that. Maybe I was fishing that day. I don't know." He had not read the Dulles article about our great victory in Indochina, he had not heard about an urgent message Prime Minister Eden sent him ten days before, and so on. But all such criticisms were drowned out in the hullabaloo over two specific proposals of Stevenson's, that we cut back the draft in order to build a professional army and that we end the testing of big hydrogen bombs.

In his proposal about the draft, Stevenson's main objective was not to lighten the burdens of defense, much less to weaken the armed forces. It was rather to strengthen the armed forces by enabling them to recruit and retain experienced men, keep up the kind of professional army required by modern technology, and reduce the waste of time, effort, and money caused by the constant turnover, since up to a million trained men had to be replaced every year. He cited military authorities on the damage done to military effectiveness by the incessant turnover and long training of raw recruits. General Nathan Twining, Air Force Chief of Staff, had told a Congressional committee: "If this trend continues, there would be more than a 100 percent turnover in the Air Force every five years. No industry could absorb this rate of personnel turnover. Nor can the Air Force." But whether feasible or no, Stevenson's proposal was given short shrift. He was at once charged with playing cheap politics, risking our vital defenses to win votes. His repeated efforts to explain his proposal only called out more abuse. Who was he anyway to advise General Eisenhower on how to run a military machine? It made no difference that the President's incompetent Secretary of Defense had weakened the Army in particular.

Much more disastrous was Stevenson's suggestion that we halt the testing of H-bombs. When he first made it, in his talk to the newspaper editors early in the year, there was no uproar; men everywhere were deploring the nuclear arms race for the obvious reasons. But he immediately got into trouble when he repeated it during the campaign. His professional advisers, who had pleaded with him to drop the idea, gave him up for lost when he refused out of a sense of moral obligation.[2] While President Eisenhower refused to debate the proposal, dismissing it as a theatrical gesture, other Republicans at once accused Stevenson of advocating unilateral disarmament, letting down our defenses without getting any guarantees from the Soviet Union, and so inviting catastrophe. The press joined in, and Truman too said he flatly disagreed. Instead of dropping the unpopular issue, Stevenson returned to it again and again, patiently explaining his position, stubbornly defending it.

Now, there was ample room for disagreement among informed men of good will. Both the Truman and Eisenhower administrations

---

[2] I have been told that one of his campaign managers went off on a two-week binge, and that another at this point wrote down a prediction of how the election would turn out, missing the final count by only three electoral votes.

had listened to arguments for a moratorium, but rejected them. Scientists differed on the danger of radioactive fallout from the H-bombs and on the safeguards required against the Soviet Union. It was never certain that we could trust the word of the Russians. But all the reasons for honorable disagreement accentuated the unreasonableness of the Republicans and their press in refusing to consider Stevenson's arguments, which in time most Americans would come around to accepting. He made clear that he was not proposing unilateral disarmament, only urging that the United States take the lead in suspending tests; if other nations refused to follow our lead, we could resume our tests. Meanwhile there was no need of the inspection the Russians refused to permit, for the President himself had stated that the testing of an H-bomb anywhere could be quickly detected. We would not be permitting other countries to get the jump on us either, for we had our stockpile and would of course go on with our research. These countries pointed rather to an obvious reason for trying to stop the tests before the "secret" of this appalling power spread all over the world, to leaders much less trustworthy than those of Britain, which was preparing to explode its H-bomb. To Stevenson it seemed as obvious that America needed to resume its leadership in the cause of peace, on which Republicans were claiming a monopoly. The wisdom of his proposal may still be debated, even though he would be vindicated by the event. There is no question of the integrity that led him to insist on it despite its political unwisdom at the time: "I say to you that leaders must lead; that where the issue is of such magnitude, I have no right to stand silent; I owe it to you to express my views, whatever the consequences."

In retrospect it seems clear that Stevenson never had a real chance in this campaign, as many if not most of his advisers felt all along. Possibly he did not lose as many votes by this stand as the professionals thought (estimates ran up to three million), since they also assumed that the voters were little interested in foreign policy. But he surely suffered to some extent from just such public indifference, which made the charges against him sound plausible. In particular he suffered more when, in the last week of the campaign, foreign policy was made the main issue by the most lurid demonstration of the ineptitude of the Eisenhower administration—the Middle East crisis, brought to a head when war broke out there. This piece of ancient history may now seem a little quaint, like a forgotten nightmare; but it was all too real to Stevenson.

During his six-month tour in 1953 he had learned at first hand the complexities out of which the crisis developed: the slowness of the British in making reasonable concessions, since Churchill and the Tories did not realize that the old incompetent, corrupt crowd that had been kicked out of office in Egypt were finished for good; the ferocious hostility of the Arabs to Israel and their refusal to admit publicly any possibility of compromise, which made it hard to sympathize with their understandable aspirations; and the stubbornness of Israel, rightly proud of its achievements, but inclined to be as uncompromising in its attitudes toward the Arabs. The situation changed when the Soviet Union initiated its aggression in the Middle East by sending in arms to the Arab countries. Stevenson protested against the Eisenhower administration's policy of maintaining our "neutrality" by refusing to send Israel arms, or to guarantee its integrity as it had that of other countries. Dulles at first wooed Colonel Nasser by pressuring the British to give in to his demand that they evacuate their military base along the Suez Canal, and by giving him expectations of aid in building the Aswan Dam; but when Nasser flaunted his friendship with the Soviets, the Secretary decided to teach him a lesson by suddenly withdrawing offers of aid. As might have been expected, Nasser retaliated by seizing the Suez Canal from the British. The President expressed concern because of the "tremendous importance" of the Canal, whose "continuous and effective operation is vital to the economics of our country," but a few days later his Secretary of State explained his own calm: "The United States is not dependent to any appreciable degree at all upon the Suez Canal." In mid-October, when Dulles knew that the Israeli were mobilizing and the British too were prepared to use force, the President happily told the nation that he had the "best announcement" he could possibly make: the United Nations was making fine progress in settling the Suez dispute, and "it looks like there's a very great problem behind us."

Two weeks later war broke out as Israel in desperation invaded Egypt; Britain and France followed suit by invading the Canal Zone. In a hastily improvised speech the President condemned their action on the high grounds that we must oppose any violation of international law, though acknowledging that they had been subjected to "grave and repeated provocations." By this time he perhaps could have done nothing else in good conscience about the rash invasions; but unfortunately it meant lining us up with the Soviet Union against our allies, just when the Russians were preparing to crush the Hungarian Revolution that Dulles and a Republican "truth squad" had hailed as "a clear-cut result of the new American foreign policy." Stevenson summed up the whole affair:

> Here we stand today. We have alienated our chief European allies. We have alienated Israel. We have alienated Egypt and the Arab countries. And in the UN our main associate in Middle Eastern matters now appears to be Communist Russia—in the very week when the Red Army has been shooting down the brave people of Hungary and Poland. We have lost every point in the game. I doubt if ever before in our diplomatic history has any policy been such an abysmal, such a complete and such a catastrophic failure.

Vice-President Nixon gave the nation a different version of the crisis: our bold break with our allies was "a declaration of independence that has had an electrifying effect throughout the world." This statement had been written for him by Secretary Dulles, but on his own he denounced the "partisan" criticism of the administration's policy, which smacked of disloyalty or worse. Possibly he appreciated more than the harried President how perfectly timed the diplomatic catastrophe was for campaign purposes. Given another week or so, the voters might have begun to realize the truth in what Stevenson said, but their immediate impulse was as usual to rally behind the President in an emergency. The catastrophe assured another stampede. This time Eisenhower polled 57.8 percent of the vote, against 55.4 in 1952, and swept all regions except the South, carrying forty states. Someone observed that it was impossible to defeat a President whose aces in the hole were peace, prosperity—and war.

So we are brought back to the mentality of American voters, in whose good sense Stevenson still trusted. Again they had not been simply stampeded into electing President Eisenhower. Voters sensed something of the high resolve in him that led Emmet Hughes to return to his service as a ghost writer. It was a sense of duty, not the goading of Republican politicians, that had made him decide to run again in spite of his age and his heart attack. If this was first of all duty to his party, which had no other strong candidate available, it was also duty to the country as he saw it; he told Hughes he was resolved to create a new image of the party, make it worthier of appeal to independents and liberals. He conducted his campaign on a distinctly higher level than the "great crusade" in 1952. He spoke gravely of the need for sacrifice, without trumpets calling upon the nation to meet its challenges and to strive for a peace that was "not a prize" but "a quest." Although his writers made him seem loftier by implying that Stevenson was cheapening his campaign by easy promises, they at least helped him to sound much like Stevenson:

> As your President, I cannot and will not tell you that our quest for peace is simple, or its rewards swift. This quest may, in fact, cost us much—in time, in effort, and in sacrifice. . . . We shall seek escape from no toil—or any sacrifice—that freedom demands of us. For we know that a people that values its privileges above its principles soon loses both.

Only the cynical or the rabidly partisan could doubt the earnestness of the simple pledge the President made to the people on election night: "With whatever talents the good God has given me, with whatever strength there is within me, I will continue . . . to do just one thing: to work for 168 million Americans here at home—and for peace in the world."

True, Eisenhower had a much easier time than Stevenson in the campaign. As President, he did not have to campaign all over the country and give countless speeches. He had little trouble maintaining a dignified manner because his proved popularity made it unnecessary for him either to attack or to defend vigorously. No perfectionist, he gave no trouble to the public-relations engineers who managed his campaign with unsurpassed slickness, nor to the production experts who made him up for his carefully staged appearances on television. Having no detailed programs to expound, he could accommodate himself more readily than Stevenson to the TV experts who believed that short speeches were better suited to a mass audience. And he owed something to Stevenson for the improved style of his speeches, which his ghost writers now took pains to give more literary quality.

Their content, however, gave little more to sink one's teeth into. In expressing his satisfaction with these speeches, Hughes neglected to consider a legitimate complaint of Stevenson—that again there was no real debate of the issues. If the President could hardly have been expected to acknowledge the failings of his leadership or of his party, he might at least have offered a positive program to support his habitual assertion that "modern Republicanism looks to the future." In fact, as Stevenson pointed out, he not only offered no new ideas but refused to discuss ideas when presented with them. Having briefly dismissed the proposal to suspend tests of H-bombs, he told a press conference he had spoken his "last word" on the subject—as if there were nothing more to say on so vital an issue. On the domestic issues raised by Stevenson's detailed program for a New America he had no more to say. Near the end of the campaign Stevenson drew up a list of questions for the voters. What did the President propose to do about the Taft-Hartley Act? About improving medical care? About the plight of older citizens? What about his housing program? His conservation program? His education program? His defense program? His program to combat inflation? The answer was that the voters did not know and could not know—he had said nothing. His party had offered them a blank check, saying, "Just trust Ike."

And always in the wings stalked the heir apparent, Vice-President Nixon. At times Eisenhower's public behavior suggested the misgivings about his choice that he privately confided to intimates, as when he permitted Harold Stassen—a member of his team—to battle

for a new Vice-President. He had something to do with the dressing
up of the "new" Nixon, who this time was supposed to campaign on
a loftier level too. But then he turned his deputy loose on the country,
without a tutor to keep an eye on Fauntleroy. While Nixon generally
contented himself with charges that the Democrats were socialists in
disguise, not dupes of communism, his style still justified Stevenson's
comment: "The Vice-President seems to sail downwind no matter
which way the wind blows." If the President's health failed, the
people would just have to trust Dick too. Meanwhile Nixon's new
public image might recall another factor in Eisenhower's victory.
Soon after his first inauguration C. D. Jackson, a high official re-
cruited from the mass media, had said: "We're going to merchandise
the living hell out of the Eisenhower administration."

In his speech of acceptance Stevenson had deplored "this idea that
you can merchandise candidates for high office like breakfast cereal"
as "the ultimate indignity to the democratic process," and toward the
end of the campaign he repeated that it would be a sorry day for
American democracy if "we replace responsible leaders with a personality cult," reduce a Presidential election to a kind of beauty
contest. Nevertheless for most voters the campaign came down to a
personality contest. The close studies of their attitudes indicate that
the appeal of Eisenhower had become overwhelmingly personal;
many fewer voters referred to his experience or skill as a leader than
had in 1952. What most impressed Americans was his sincerity, his
patriotism, his earnestness, or simply his likableness. Other popular
traits were his virtues as a family man and his growing religiosity.
(He came out for prayer, for example, suggesting that it was a
necessary condition of American democracy.) For similar reasons
voters expressed more disapproval of Stevenson's divorce than they
had at first, and generally were much less impressed by his personality. Fewer expressed a warm admiration for him as a person, many
more were critical of him. It was not so much that he was too highbrow or too satirical, since he restrained his sophistication and wit in
this campaign. The main reason he made a bad impression on so
many voters was evidently his aggressive attacks on good old Ike.

Hence the candidate's party counted for less when voters thought of the overriding issues of the campaign, peace and prosperity. ("Progress," which completed the alliteration in the Republican campaign slogan, would take care of itself.) A great majority thought Eisenhower would do better than Stevenson at maintaining peace, and a smaller but significant majority even at maintaining prosperity—once the Democrats' ace in the hole. Specific domestic issues had little effect on thought or feeling about the President. In view of his pride in his fiscal responsibility, he himself might have been dismayed by the extraordinary slight extent to which he was associated with the domestic record of his administration, except that he was not blamed for its failures. Having established himself as a benign man above politics, V. O. Key observed, he was by 1956 "the chieftain of a crusade that he could lead neither to the left nor to the right, even if he had been so disposed." Stevenson had more reason to be dismayed by popular thought on foreign affairs, with which the President was more closely associated. For most voters the issue was simply peace or war, with only a dim idea of the road to either, slight understanding of the specific issues that Stevenson tried so hard to educate them on; they knew only that Eisenhower was a strong man who could keep the peace. The public remained largely unaware of not only Stevenson's wide experience in foreign affairs but his positions.

This might have dismayed newspaper publishers, who had gone out of their way to denounce these positions. But the press, more overwhelmingly Republican than ever, had at least contributed to the public apathy by helping to merchandise the Eisenhower administration and cover up its failings. The editors who had voted two to one that Stevenson was right about our losing the cold war forgot this once the campaign had started. Almost all attacked his views on foreign policy, especially his proposal about the hydrogen bomb; most charged that he was simply desperate and irresponsible. On the whole the press gave his campaign fair enough news coverage, though with the usual conspicuous exceptions, and the networks were somewhat more scrupulous, but the whole climate of the mass media was charged with pro-Eisenhower sentiment. Given the further advantage that the Republicans had almost twice as much money to spend as the Democrats, beloved Ike got far more publicity.

Still, this again suggests some reservations about the foolish, ignorant electorate. Considering that the voters had been subjected to the most prolonged, massive, and expert merchandising campaign to date, one might wonder why more than 40 percent of them persisted in voting for Stevenson. At that, Eisenhower's victory was not due primarily to the skill of his public-relations engineers, for no merchandising could ever make Richard Nixon so popular. There remained the plainer reasons for his popularity, including the good reasons that won over many thoughtful people and made many others (like Hughes) hope for the best. If he was more beloved as a father symbol than any President since George Washington, the unreflective majority who voted for peace and prosperity were not simply taken in by this either, but were exhibiting at least a rudimentary good sense, of the kind suggested by Key. They were judging by their experience since the last election, and the fact was they had enjoyed peace, on the average they were better off. Hence the most considerable defection from Eisenhower was among farmers, who were worse off. Farmers also swelled another demonstration of independent judgment in voters. While President Eisenhower won a still greater personal victory, his party suffered a worse defeat in the Congressional elections. He himself could never realize, or at least admit, that he had been aided by the Republican defeat in the elections of 1954, which somewhat weakened the opposition of the reactionary, isolationist Old Guard that had given his party its public image. And the millions of split tickets pointed to further evidence that voters were doing some thinking on their own. The total shift to Eisenhower of 2.4 percent of the voters was rather slight, once more, in view of four years of high-powered merchandising, of a popular product to begin with; but analysis reveals a great deal of shifting that canceled out, because many voters switched to Stevenson too.

For Stevenson there remained the obvious consolation of his devoted following. Although their fervor hardly shows in the statistics, he had some intimation that it would count for much in the long run, and that he had made a deeper, more lasting impression than President Eisenhower would in victory. In his election eve speech he told how he had been "deeply moved and sustained" by the millions of Americans he had seen, of all conditions of life, and especially by the many who had come up to tell him that they had gone into politics in the last four years because of things they heard him say in his 1952 campaign. After conceding his defeat he told his hard-working followers that he too had been disappointed, of course, but they should not be downhearted. They had been defeated in a vigorous partisan contest that had proved again the vitality of democracy, since partisanship was its life blood:

> So I say to you, my dear and loyal friends, take heart—there are things more precious than political victory; there is the right to political contest. And who knows better how vigorous and alive it is than you who bear the fresh, painful wounds of battle?

Beneath the partisanship America was still united by love of freedom, of justice, and of peace. The aftermath would suggest that Stevenson was more depressed by this defeat than he had been in 1952, but it would also make plain that his conclusion was heartfelt:

> Be of good cheer. And remember, my dear friends, what a wise man said: "A merry heart doeth good like a medicine, but a broken spirit dryeth the bones."

9

❧❧❧

The Critic of an Affluent Society

The world is now too dangerous for anything but the
truth, too small for anything but brotherhood.

—*A. Powell Davies*

A month after the 1956 election Stevenson said, "I will not run again
for the Presidency." For some time it appeared that he might at last
retire from public life as he relaxed on his beloved farm at Libertyville. He said little to the country, taking up only a few of many
invitations to speak. In the spring of 1957 he accepted a congenial
position as chairman of the advisory board of Encyclopaedia Britannica Films, and shortly afterward a partnership in a distinguished law
firm. When he went abroad he said it was a business trip, which
would include a visit to his friend Albert Schweitzer in the Congo.

But all this got into the newspapers, as did every public appearance. Stevenson soon made it clear that he was not content to be
simply a private citizen again, or even an "elder statesman"—in
America a kind of ex-titular leader who keeps aloof from politics.
Among his early speeches after the election was one to a Democratic
Party conference, at which he sharply criticized the foreign policy of
the Eisenhower administration and called for a vigorous opposition.
The party should not operate on the "fallacy" that Eisenhower's
victory was a purely personal triumph, he said, and in particular it

should show the nation what a responsible, "creative" opposition really is. Already it was apparent that Stevenson would have to lead such an opposition, for other Democratic leaders were sure that Eisenhower's victory had been personal and were in no mood to buck his popularity. In Congress Sam Rayburn and Lyndon Johnson settled on their policy of polite collaboration. Johnson told insiders of his relief because at last the party was done with Stevenson and his kind of partisanship; his own ambitions drew him rather to Eisenhower's ideal of Consensus, with or without clear conviction. Stevenson was more "titular" than ever as he kept up a running criticism of the administration.

It was then Eisenhower himself who called him back to public service, in the late fall of 1957. Deciding at last to make use of Stevenson's prestige and popularity abroad, the President and Secretary Dulles invited him to serve as a consultant in shaping a nonpartisan "American" policy and program for a forthcoming NATO conference in Paris, called to meet the grave challenge of the Russian Sputniks. Stevenson agreed to help, but after some thought declined a further invitation to serve on the American delegation in Paris. The reason he gave was an embarrassment he would suffer from in his last years at the United Nations: he would be put in a position "without authority and necessarily identified with decisions I might not always agree with and could not publicly oppose." He also suspected that the administration was not really bent on reappraising its policy, but merely wanted to make a show of American unity and put his name on its old program. In the recommendations that he proceeded to draw up, Stevenson wrote: "I doubt very much if it will be possible to communicate much sense of urgency and determination to our allies in Paris if we have not made the measure of the emergency clear at home." He urged especially much more attention to economic assistance, saying that "the exclusively military emphasis" in NATO had not heightened respect for us in the cold war. "Beyond its frontiers, NATO must serve to extend to others the advantages of the modern industrial society which we enjoy." Finally, he suggested, the conference ought to conclude with "a brief and ringing statement summing up NATO policies in simple language—'Arms only for defense. Aid for the needy, underdeveloped nations. Cooperation with all states, including the Communist nations, to promote world peace and progress.' "

Thereupon the President and the Secretary publicly thanked Stevenson for his efforts. In the State Department he had his picture taken with Dulles and the Democratic chairman of the Senate Foreign Relations Committee. When the Secretary observed to the reporters, "You've got me surrounded by Democrats here," Stevenson explained: "This is what is called 'containment,' gentlemen." But his suspicions were soon confirmed by the outcome in Paris. Still uncontained, Secretary Dulles put through a program that reasserted America's might and remained exclusively military in emphasis. President Eisenhower expressed "interest" in the idea of economic development but as usual then dropped it, doing nothing about it for two years. He showed no more "sense of urgency" and conveyed none to the country. Thereafter he helped to keep Stevenson in public life chiefly by his continued failings in leadership, coupled with a continued popularity that deepened Stevenson's misgivings about the moral, spiritual state of the nation. We must again pause to recall a period that already seems strangely remote, at moments fantastically unreal, but that is still with us, very much alive in popular thought and feeling.

President Eisenhower's Second Inaugural Address, carefully worked over with Emmet Hughes, brought out all the nonpartisan best in him, in a style that impressed Democrats too:

> We live in a land of plenty, but rarely has this earth known such peril as today. . . .
>
> One truth must rule all we think and all we do. No people can live to itself alone. . . . No nation can longer be a fortress, lone and strong and safe. And any people seeking such shelter for themselves can now build only their own prison.
>
> We honor the aspirations of those nations which, now captive, long for freedom. . . . We honor, no less in this divided world than in a less tormented time, the people of Russia. We do not dread, rather do we welcome, their progress in education and industry. . . .

And so we voice our hope and our belief that we can help to heal this divided world. . . . May the turbulence of our age yield to a true time of peace, when men and nations shall share a life that honours the dignity of each, the brotherhood of all.

A few months later the President roused himself briefly to defend his foreign aid program, needed to make good his promises and his hopes, against the attacks of Senator Knowland and other Republican reactionaries, whom we had privately resolved to stand up against. But this was only a flicker. Immediately after the Inaugural his administration had relapsed into somnolent normalcy, committed chiefly to economy, which made a mockery of the self-righteous rhetoric and posturing of its foreign policy.

In his own account of his second administration, *Waging Peace: 1956–1961,* Eisenhower remembers a few incidental disappointments but mainly a series of triumphs, achieved by unflinching resolution in the face of ignorant or irresponsible opposition. Actually he did little "waging" until the end, after a series of setbacks. These began at once when his own Secretary Humphrey attacked the budget he submitted to back up the commitments of his Inaugural Address; upon his feeble defense of it, the budget was mutilated to the taste of the Knowlands. Then followed the disaster at Little Rock, when Governor Faubus defied the Supreme Court by calling in his National Guard to prevent a few Negro children from entering the schools. This time the President took firm action, sending in federal troops to uphold constitutional authority, but he had temporized long enough to give Faubus false hopes—and Communist propagandists a field day. He kept to himself his best excuse for shying away from the whole issue: insiders say he did not really approve of the Supreme Court decision he was obliged to uphold.[1] The rest of the world, made up chiefly of colored peoples, was quicker to see the ugliness of racism in a country supposedly defending the cause of freedom and brotherhood.

---

[1] The conservative journalist whom I sought out as a devil's advocate on behalf of Richard Nixon had been told by Eisenhower that what he most regretted in his administration was his appointment of Earl Warren as Chief Justice. Warren had proved not "moderate" enough.

On the heels of this came a more obvious blow to American prestige: in the fall of 1957 the Soviet Union launched its first Sputnik. The President at once assured the nation that we had never considered our space program a race and the satellite did not raise his apprehensions, "not one iota," while his assistant Sherman Adams dismissed the Russian triumph as a mere publicity stunt. This was too much even for the faithful Eisenhower press. The administration's publicity men had been trumpeting what we were going to do in outer space—a policy of fanfare in advance that would long continue to cause embarrassments. Again the rest of the world got the point: the once backward Russians were beating the boastful Americans at their own technological game. Asians and Africans were especially excited by their triumph as a demonstration of what they had been able to achieve in less than a lifetime, presumably by virtue of communism. And the blow was worse because the Eisenhower administration still had no real foreign policy, only a military policy of containing communism by superior power. It betrayed its futility by flaunting the pointless "Eisenhower Doctrine"—a pledge of American aid to any Middle Eastern country wanting help to resist Communist aggression. As General Nasser's scorn of it emphasized, the chief danger was not Russian aggression but the welcome of Russian aid and subversion by native Communists.

The President inaugurated 1958 by a striking exhibition of his failure to comprehend the challenges of a changing world. He presented Congress with the most traditionally Republican of his budgets, in which the unavoidably large appropriations for the defense and space programs were offset by reductions in domestic welfare programs and a surrender of such efforts as aid in building more schools. His conservatism was not rewarded on any front. In spite of his "sound" fiscal policies the country went into the deepest recession since the world war, suggesting to the impious the tabooed word "depression" as unemployment reached a new peak of well over five million; it accentuated the failure of the United States to keep pace with the rate of economic growth in the Soviet Union. Abroad the decline of American prestige was dramatized by the unprecedented humiliation of Vice-President Nixon during his tour of Latin America, where he and his wife were jeered, stoned, and spat upon. The White House followed custom by blaming this simply on Communist agitators. Although the President knew better, at least being disturbed by how much anti-American feeling these agitators had been able to whip up, he would be stuck with the old slogans when at the end of the year Fidel Castro drove the dictator Batista out of Cuba. He was quite unprepared to deal sensitively and flexibly with Castro because official policy had it that revolution must be the work of Communists alone.

Meanwhile 1958 had been climaxed by the Republican disaster in the Congressional elections, the worst in more than twenty years. This President Eisenhower had coming because he knew nothing better than to call critics of his administration "political radicals" or "socialists," at best "self-styled liberals" who wanted only to squander the voters' money. Vice-President Nixon dropped his new mask and took to the low road again, campaigning vigorously against Truman, Acheson, and all Democratic "appeasers." The President himself went out of his way to campaign hard for Senator Knowland, now running for Governor of California. In this company he forgot his dignity and himself reached a low in partisanship. "There will be no appeasing Communist aggression while I am President," he assured the voters. They redeemed Stevenson's faith in their good sense by burying Knowland under a million votes.

The kindest explanation of Eisenhower's behavior—and of the period that idolized him—was suggested in passing by Emmet Hughes: "intellectual and moral confusion." There is no question that the President sincerely wanted to give his party a "new image," quite different from Knowland's. Despite the almost incredible complacence of *Waging Peace,* his memoirs have a melancholy cast because of his awareness that he failed to do so, and his inability to understand why he failed. Thus he wrote that Kennedy's defeat of Nixon "showed again how much elections can be controlled by sentiment and emotion," for "I cannot ascribe any rational cause for the outcome." He had been as confused when it became known that his most trusted assistant, Sherman Adams, was tainted by the kind of corruption he had denounced in the Truman administration. At first he defended Adams, announcing that he personally liked him, admired his abilities, trusted his integrity, and "needed him"—as he surely did, especially since his three illnesses, Adams having taken the most pains to ease his duties and shield him from news that might upset him. But when the publicity grew embarrassing, as vengeful Democrats were joined by more implacable right-wing Republicans whooping after the scalp of this "liberal" in the White House, the President turned the problem over to professionals (including Nixon) and eventually accepted the resignation of Adams, which he had neither requested nor opposed. And confusion clouded a worse bereavement in the early months of 1959, the fatal illness of John Foster Dulles, who for two years had been afflicted with cancer. Dulles appears most courageous in his prolonged illness, on his deathbed constantly conferring with the President almost to the last; and *Waging Peace* is most touching in the passages recording Eisenhower's sorrow and sense of loss. Thereafter, however, he took foreign policy into his own hands and embarrassed the ghost of the Secretary of State by abruptly changing course, seemingly unaware that he was reversing the policy of the man he revered, or when reminded, angry at any such suggestion. In his view he was only pursuing the same high moral purposes.

At any rate, President Eisenhower began actually to "wage peace" in 1959. Having set a Presidential record for time spent on golf courses, he now set a record for personal diplomacy by the many thousands of miles he traveled. After flying visits to the capitals of Western Europe, he went to countries all around the world, including neutral India. Cheering crowds testified to his popularity as a peace-loving man, resources of admiration and affection that he had neglected to tap. He enhanced his popularity by initiating efforts to get along better with the Soviets. He sent Vice-President Nixon to Moscow, where his deputy held a much publicized informal "debate" with Khrushchev, and he extended the Premier a personal invitation to visit the United States, which was accepted and reciprocated.[2] When Truman expressed misgivings about these summit meetings, he explained to a press conference that he was only looking for "some little bridge, some little avenue yet unexplored" to better relations—what Stevenson had been urging for years. He also moved toward Stevenson's position on disarmament, offering to begin a "phased" suspension of testing that would not require inspections in the first stage. Likewise he at last began acting on Stevenson's recommendation of more emphasis on economic instead of military aid. In 1960, at the United Nations, the President committed the United States and the West to large-scale programs of economic development in Africa and Latin America.

Yet Eisenhower still showed little "sense of urgency" or clear comprehension of the state of the world. On the home front he dedicated himself more fervently than ever to the supreme challenge, the need of balancing the nation's budget. Abroad he dissipated some of the good will he built up in our European allies by paying a state call on Generalissimo Franco, whom they still distrusted as a Fascist dictator; the President saw only that "whatever the reasons for the Spanish revolution," Franco was "a strong and enduring leader." He did not fare so well on a swing through Latin America, where the police had to take pains to keep demonstrators out of his ken; the enthusiasm of Latin-American leaders was dampened by the thought that he had put them off to the last, after visits to such countries as Afghanistan. In his memoirs he reveals that the invitation to Khrushchev resulted from an error, his own failure—he admits humbly—to make clear to the State Department conditions he tried to specify. ("After all, here were some of the most capable men I knew in their field, and apparently all had failed to comprehend the idea in my mind.") And finally the President's earnest efforts were crowned by disaster, another fantastic exhibition of the ineptitude of his administration.

[2] In thus building up Nixon, the President incidentally betrayed his ambiguous attitude toward him. He neglected to consult the Vice-President about his invitation to Khrushchev, informing him just before he took off for Moscow, some days after it had been sent through the routine channels.

Two weeks before a big Summit Conference scheduled in Paris, the Russians shot down the U-2 plane flying across the Soviet Union on a spying mission. The State Department promptly lied, announcing that no American plane had ever been sent deliberately across the Soviet borders. When the Russians presented clear proof that the U-2 had been on a spying mission, the Department got around this by asserting that no such flight had been authorized by Washington. Khrushchev was still willing to accept its explanation, saying he "fully admitted" that the President did not know of the flight, but then the Department let Eisenhower assume full responsibility for the flights, which were defended as "a distasteful but vital necessity." Soon the word was that they were a sovereign right; so just before the President left for Paris his Press Secretary, James Haggerty, flatly denied reports that they had been suspended. Three days later in Paris Eisenhower as flatly repudiated this statement, earnestly assuring Khrushchev that the flights had been suspended and "are not to be resumed." But this surrender of a "vital necessity" was too late, even had it not been followed incongruously by an order of a world-wide alert of our combat forces. By now it was impossible to conciliate Khrushchev, who broke up the Summit Conference in a storm of invective.

The Soviet Premier weakened his case before the world by his outrageous rudeness to the humiliated President. At home Republicans could more easily attack "appeasers" who were critical of the administration's policy, and Americans more easily forget that they would feel outraged if Russians claimed the right to send planes over this country. In his memoirs Eisenhower managed to see a kind of diplomatic victory even in this appalling botch, intimating a carefully concealed shrewdness: had the Summit Conference been held, he wrote, it "would have proved to be a failure and thus would have brought the Free World only further disillusionment." But other peoples persisted in seeing what was in front of their nose. The free world could feel only sympathy for the President, not respect; to our allies the plain truth was what Stevenson said in one of his most powerful speeches: "We handed Khrushchev the crowbar and the sledge hammer to wreck this meeting." In Turkey riots broke out against the government, our staunchest supporter; in Korea students overthrew the regime of Syngman Rhee, next to Chiang our most pampered dictator. Everywhere Communist propagandists had an easier time making out that we were the great enemies of peace. And for Eisenhower there remained another humiliation such as no American President had ever experienced. In Japan, where we had bases for U-2 operations, anti-American demonstrations were so violent and continual that he was advised to give up a scheduled state visit there; and when his staff decided to go on with the plans, thinking that the perils would enable him to make a more impressive display of courage and dignity, he was forced to change his mind en route. A message from the Japanese Cabinet, met in an emergency session, requested him to postpone his trip for safety's sake.

Meanwhile Stevenson over these years held consistently to the basic policies he had urged. Repeatedly he called for more aid in economic development, on which we were spending only about a tenth of what we were spending on military aid, to doubtful effect. The population explosion was magnifying "the most important and fateful fact in the world today," widening the already immense gulf between the Western and the underdeveloped nations; the rich were getting richer and the poor poorer. "We are heading for a new crisis," he warned, "one no less dire than the crisis of 1947, and no less certain to lead to catastrophe unless we act in time." He warned as well that the Russians fully recognized the value of economic assistance for their political purposes, and for this reason too were doing better in the cold war. At the same time he urged more effort to negotiate with the Russians. While warning against high hopes of dealings with such tough and tricky bargainers, he met the persistent objections that it was impossible to negotiate with the Communists by pointing out that we would obviously have to talk and bargain with them for years to come. Similarly he deplored the administration's halfhearted, wavering efforts at a start on disarmament. As he said in 1960, "Our approach to disarmament had been 'Yes but.' It ought to be: 'Why not?' " Stevenson might have made more of another deep confusion in a businessman's administration, which wanted to keep its defense budget as low as possible, but feared that any large-scale disarmament would cause a depression.

His convictions about foreign affairs had again been deepened and sharpened by firsthand experience through travel. In 1957, when his future career was still uncertain, Stevenson was heartened by surprising ovations he received at staid Oxford University, both before and after he gave a speech upon receiving an honorary degree. (He began by remarking that since Oxford was known as the home of Lost Causes, its recognition of him was fitting—he was perhaps the world's greatest living exponent of the Lost Cause.) In 1958 he renewed his self-education by another long tour, climaxed by a summer in the Soviet. His impressions of the Russians he reported in articles for the *New York Times,* later collected in a book, *Friends and Enemies* (1959). A readable book, this has lost some topical interest because the Soviet has since then welcomed tourists and given them liberties that Stevenson enjoyed as a special privilege, but his report is still pertinent—not to mention that it would be a revelation to the depressingly large majority of Americans who remain ignorant or misinformed about the Russians. And for my purposes here it is especially pertinent because his experience stirred him to reconsider soberly, even somberly, the state of affluent America.[3]

First and last he emphasized the challenge of the Soviet Union in no ordinary sense. It was not only military but economic, intellectual, moral, and spiritual. The Soviet Union was of course very different from the backward peasant nation that Stevenson had seen as a young journalist in 1926. He visited the scenes of its most obviously impressive achievements, such as Central Asia, a region once almost wholly primitive, illiterate, and disease-ridden, and especially Siberia, once a wilderness—a land bigger than the United States, now sprouting industrial cities. Near Novosibirsk the Russians were building the "City of Science" to house 25,000 scholars and scientists, to work on the economic development of "the vast Siberian treasure house."

---

[3] I have learned that Stevenson was actually less eager and curious, and more harassed, than he appears in this largely ghost-written book. But in his speeches thereafter he adhered to the main ideas expressed in it. On the public record, the impressions he reports sank in.

Stevenson was most impressed by the intense purposefulness. Everywhere went up "the constant refrain of signs, songs, speeches": catch up with America, beat America. "The whole gigantic power apparatus—education, science, industry, agriculture and administration—is harnessed with ruthless, concentrated purpose on increased production, higher living standards, security, power and influence." Unexpectedly Stevenson was granted a long interview with Khrushchev. He found the person who would later become familiar to newspaper readers—hearty, vivid, shrewd, tough, sometimes amiable, always outspoken and sure of himself. Khrushchev confided that Communist leaders regularly toasted "their best friend," Secretary Dulles, but even without the help of "President Eisenhower's Sputnik" he was supremely confident that the Soviet would soon overtake America and the whole world would go Communist. As he had boasted, "We will bury you!"

Since then Khrushchev has himself been buried alive, not only disgraced but blotted out, denied even the recognition of being mentioned by name when his "subjectivism" is denounced. The Communist achievement looks less awesome since the economic growth has slowed down. Visitors to the Soviet Union today are less impressed too by the national purposefulness, reporting more complacence than ardor in the people.[4] Stevenson's report prepared one for such changes, however. He pointed out the inherent instability of a system that had no legalized opposition or clear provision for an orderly transfer of power. Aware that agriculture had been the Soviets' worst failure, he noted that the success of Khrushchev's bold experiments with marginal lands was still highly uncertain. He noticed too the decline of fanaticism in the young Russians, and expected that with continued economic improvement they would become more like Western peoples. Today one might add that university students in particular, assured a good safe berth in the bureaucracy, look much like all the prospective little organization men in American fraternities.

[4] In this section I am drawing as well on personal impressions, gathered from a month spent in the Soviet Union five years after Stevenson's tour. I met no dignitaries whatever and enjoyed no privileges, but as a simple tourist I got much the same impression as he did—except for the changes that had taken place.

Yet the challenge that directly concerned Stevenson is just as real and serious today. This was the advantage the Russians had in dealing with what seemed to him more than ever "the greatest threat of all," the economic difficulties of the many have-not nations that were getting relatively poorer. The Soviet Union was always more attractive to these nations as itself a once poor country that had made good. Now its leaders were saying that their primary weapon was economic power and were exerting it more effectively than Americans were their enormous power. The Russians were training many more specialists to work with non-Western peoples, and could always commandeer their services. They could buy, sell, or barter more flexibly, to suit both the needs of other peoples and their own political interests. They could easily plan long-range programs.

By contrast, it was almost impossible for American executive agencies "to plan and carry out a coherent, farsighted strategy of economic warfare, so long as imports, exports and overseas investments are subject to the whims and self-interest of every domestic pressure group." Every year the agencies had to go to Congress hat in hand, never sure what their appropriation would be or what strings might be attached to it; they could be sure only of an annual wrangle in which Congressmen would think first of their local interests or the special interests of businessmen. Our Foreign Service could not attract our ablest talents, for it had to compete against the far higher pay offered by advertising and other industries; and "no Congressman can hope to win a single vote by fighting to get better pay and representation allowances for the men who are now, literally, the first line of our defense." Stevenson summed up the basic issues:

> Can our American system prevail in competition with the central planning, control and direction of the Soviet system?
> Can we mobilize, organize and utilize our human and natural resources as effectively as they can?
> Can we do so without imposing controls that imperil the very freedom and values we in the United States are trying to preserve?
> Are our institutions adequate to conduct foreign policy in competition with the speed, secrecy, and certainty of the Kremlin?

Stevenson also dwelt on the abiding difficulties of getting along with the Communists. Their government remained a dictatorship, whose leaders were never subject to popular control or public criticism. The leaders were still bombarding the people with incessant propaganda, featuring the old devil of "capitalist imperialism," while never permitting them to hear the American side; one of the chief functions of their Ministry of Communications was "to prevent communication." Khrushchev heartily agreed with Stevenson on one basic principle, "No interference in the affairs of smaller countries," but he violently disagreed on what constituted interference. The United States was always interfering, the Soviet Union never, least of all when it crushed the Hungarian Revolution—it was only saving the Hungarian people. In effect Khrushchev was saying that "whatever goes on in the Communist world is a family affair and doesn't concern outsiders," while he said quite explicitly that what went on in the "capitalist" world was a proper concern of the Soviet Union. The Soviet Union could never admit that the people in the satellite countries had not chosen communism, and that "the new Russian Empire is a jail—you can't get out once you're in." Hence "peaceful coexistence" meant constant economic, political, and ideological warfare.

Nevertheless Stevenson came away more hopeful of the possibilities of getting along with the Soviets, for reasons that have since become more evident. One was the liberalizing tendencies introduced by Khrushchev, which were making the government more considerate of both public opinion and world opinion than the ruthless Stalin had been; Stevenson expected these to grow stronger as prosperity increased. He therefore welcomed the word he got from the leaders that they very much wanted to do more business with the "capitalist" countries, and especially to carry on more trade with the United States. "Why not trade with the Russians?" he asked. "Why not encourage the growth and material abundance and thereby make it harder to preserve the secrecy, ignorance and tight controls of the Soviet system? Why not help the Soviet leaders subvert their own system of fear with the confidence bred of plenty?" Above all, Stevenson now felt that the Russians really wanted peace, no more wanted war than Americans did. Only in peace could they go on with their mighty program of economic development, make good Khrushchev's promise of surpassing the American standard of living by 1970. His boast about the Communists burying us, Stevenson pointed out, did not mean that they would kill us first.[5] Hence Khrushchev seemed really afraid of the United States. We had encircled the Soviet with air bases, and what, he asked Stevenson, would Americans think if it set up bases in Mexico? Our official answer remains that our bases are purely defensive, we would never launch aggression from them; but Stevenson could see that the fears of the Russians were not wholly unreasonable, and that our peaceful intentions might not shine through our threats of massive retaliation.

Another reason for the uneasiness he detected beneath their confidence was anxiety about Red China. Although he did not foresee the open split between them, he devoted a prophetic chapter to China as the number one problem of the future for both the Soviet and the United States. To Americans this should have been obvious. China was at the time making striking progress, its 600 million people were multiplying so fast that before many years they should number a billion, and they were being brought up on a "hate-America" campaign of frightening intensity, which throve on our foreign policy. The Russians were more realistic and farsighted. Officials always looked troubled when Stevenson raised a question: What about the day when a powerful China, bursting with population, sees in her neighbor the "largest, emptiest land in the world"? More than once they raised their vodka glasses and replied, "Another reason for better Soviet-American relations." Having visited Poland too and observed how conspicuously different it was from the Soviet Union, Stevenson pointed out that the supposedly monolithic Communist world was full of contradictions and discords, and that Americans were making a great mistake in treating all Communist countries alike. But to this day the State Department would go on talking about

[5] Robert Tucker, who served as Stevenson's guide in the Soviet Union, has since added that as translated this boast sounded more aggressive and sinister than it was. In colloquial Russian Khrushchev's words meant: "We will be present at your funeral," i.e., "We will outlive you."

the "Sino-Soviet bloc," and Congressmen go on opposing freer trade with the satellites.

Stevenson also knew that ordinary Russians in particular wanted peace. Like many travelers since, he reported how friendly and courteous he found the people everywhere, and how pleased they seemed to meet Americans. (Even in Samarkand I was told that Americans were the favorite tourists.) Their pleasure was strange, inasmuch as for years they had been bombarded daily with ugly propaganda about American imperialism; they knew little about us, and that little was likely to be sadly distorted. Nonetheless they were curious and eager. Hence Stevenson wondered: Whence this contrast between the friendly people and the savage propaganda? He speculated that people must have some immunity to propaganda. In the spirit of Lincoln he might have reflected on the simple decency and warmheartedness to be found in common people all over the world, and a measure of simple wisdom, on which democracy has to count. If Americans got pretty much the kind of government they deserved, they too were in some ways more decent and honest than their representatives, friendlier than their official spokesmen.

At any rate, ordinary Russians had plain reasons for not wanting war, even apart from their more vivid realization of its horrors than Americans could have. They were rejoicing in a higher standard of living than they had ever known under Stalin, with prospects of further improvements now that their government was giving more attention to consumer goods. By the same token they knew that they were still a long way from the standards of America, which they admired as the most "advanced" country. Meanwhile they were aware of some compensations, such as free medical care, free hospitalization, and free higher education, while their Sputniks gave further assurance that the Americans were not superior in everything. Accordingly, they were neither the zealots nor the sullen, terrorized helots too often pictured in America. Like Americans, they were basically content with their system, proud of their nation. They made foolish any foreign policy based on the assumption that the Soviet Union was bound to disintegrate if contained long enough. Once more Stevenson concluded: "The Soviet challenge is formidable, and it will be with us for a long time to come."

In trying to promote a better understanding between the peoples, with an eye as well to his vision of a New America, he presented a balanced account of Russian life that would remain essentially valid despite the continued improvement in living conditions in the years ahead. To meet the desperate shortage in housing, for example, the government had begun the crash program that already had produced miles of poorly built, monotonous apartment houses, uniformly drab, lacking the least architectural distinction. Today, in their pride and their continued ignorance of the rest of the world, tourist guides show off first of all the latest miles of construction; and there is no more depressing sight in Russia.[6] Stevenson had similar feelings about the cities, now clean, with their spacious boulevards, parks, and squares, undefiled by billboards, but also their monotonous statues of Lenin and Stalin (the latter since torn down), the subways "famous and foolishly magnificent," and the overdecorated buildings, "in socialist imitation of prerevolutionary bourgeois grandeur." On the other hand, the government provided lavishly for recreation through not only sports and circuses but concerts, ballets, the opera, and the theater. Stevenson was impressed by how much more of its income it devoted to public services than did America. Health services were not only free but more adequate; the Soviet had more doctors per capita than we did.

Most of all Stevenson was interested in what the Soviet Union was doing for education, fundamental to any program for a better society. None of its achievements seemed to him more spectacular than the almost complete literacy of its people, uncounted millions of whom had been illiterate a generation ago. Now it was spending on education about twice the proportion of its national income that the United

[6] In Alma-Ata, which Stevenson visited, my guide was embarrassed by my interest in some charming old houses. He assured me that in five years they would all be gone—the whole city would be brand-new. Because of his love of markets, Stevenson might have brooded more over the probable fate of the old cities in Central Asia, such as Tashkent and Samarkand. Five years later in Tashkent, then a city of a million, little was left of the old Uzbek quarter he loved. Now I wonder what is left of Bukhara, where several years ago industrialization was under way.

States was. The poor boy working his way through college was unknown; all bright boys could be sure of an opportunity to go as far as their abilities could take them. But all this still fell far short of Stevenson's ideal. The objective of the mighty national effort was the immediate national interest, to prepare the youth to serve the state. It was not to develop the individual's capacities for his sake, much less to encourage him to think for himself. From kindergarten on, the youth were not only carefully indoctrinated but put through a rigid curriculum, given little choice and less opportunity to inquire and explore by themselves. The Minister of Education stated firmly to Stevenson the basic difference between the Soviet and American systems: "Here *we* decide what they are to learn." The Russian youth had to do much more solid intellectual work, but with no more idea of learning for its own sake, or just for fun.

The important point nevertheless remained that learning was more highly valued in the Soviet Union. Stevenson emphasized that professors and scholars, like writers, were among the most highly rewarded groups; the intellectually gifted would naturally go on with research instead of going off into business. And though science and technology were favored by the government for its practical purposes, it did not neglect the humanities. Russians had much more respect for their great writers than Americans had for their classics. Stevenson was struck by all the bookstores in Moscow, evidence that millions of Russians were avidly reading books, or going on with their self-education, while their American counterparts stared at TV. Although the Sputniks had jolted Americans out of their self-satisfaction, they were only beginning to take a hard look at what the Soviet Union was doing for education. Shortly before leaving on his tour Stevenson had told the United Parents Association that we might yet live to hail Khrushchev as an educational reformer, but he added that no merely external reforms would do:

> The softness which has crept into our educational system is a reflection of something much broader, of a national complacency, if you will, of a confusion of the priorities of the body, the mind and the spirit. . . . Respect for excellence—an idea which we can confidently draw

from our classical heritage of freedom—this respect we must learn for ourselves.

And so the ultimate challenge was intellectual and spiritual. That Americans were showing few signs of willingness to do what was necessary to win the long contest with Russia was due in part to lack of leadership, Stevenson wrote; their leaders were not telling them what had to be done, what sacrifices made. But in his introduction to *Friends and Enemies* he confessed that he was not sure whether any President could persuade them, at least without the stimulus of war:

> Maybe our kind of democracy has a fatal addiction to short views rather than long; to present comforts rather than future safety; to private satisfactions rather than public necessities. Else why do we spend more money on advertising than on college education—on tobacco than on textbooks—on entertainment than on urban renewal?
>
> The next ten years, I would guess, will *really* prove whether this nation or any nation so conceived and so dedicated can long endure— and right now the prognosis is not good. We are losing ground nearly everywhere; we are not taking measures necessary to stop the loss; and hardly anybody seems to care. . . .
>
> This time we might get licked, unless we are willing to change our habits, our political behavior and our complacent outlook on the world.

Stevenson ended the book on a typical note of "calm and final confidence." Our free economy had again confounded the Communists' prediction of an inevitable shattering capitalist depression; their parties in Europe were losing ground as the economic strength of the West had grown greater than ever before; Khrushchev himself wanted more than anything else to attain the standard of living that America had under capitalism; "and we still have the supreme advantage of living under the system most people want if they can get it and afford it." His confidence was strengthened when Khrushchev visited the United States and they spent a genial day together on an up-to-date corn farm. "I have seen how the slaves of capitalism live, and they live pretty well," said the Premier upon taking leave. "The slaves of Communism live pretty well too, so let's all live the way we want to live and be friends." Yet calm confidence was not the dominant note Stevenson sounded after his return home. The economic success of America and the West was no answer, after all, to the questions that troubled him—it only forced the questions. In his next little book, *Putting First Things First* (1960), he dwelt chiefly on what was wrong with affluent America and the way its people wanted to live. A collection of eight addresses and papers composed in 1959, all nonpolitical, this reached a smaller audience than his campaign speeches and popular articles, and it is apparently unknown to many of his admirers; but it contains his maturest thought about American society.

The title piece, an article that appeared in *Foreign Affairs,* was addressed to the question: "Why haven't we really led the postwar world since the Korean War?" Stevenson's answer inevitably involved some criticism of "the small aims and large fears of the Eisenhower-Dulles era," the failures of political leadership. In reviewing his main ideas about "the two most dangerous realities" confronting us, the multiplication of nuclear weapons and the growing disparity between the rich and the poor nations, he insisted once more on the need of a positive policy of our own, instead of the negative policy of merely containing communism: "Our goal is not just to win a cold *war* but to persuade a cold *world.*" But Stevenson began and ended with what seemed to him the root problem—the want of a sense of national purpose. Thus at the outset he coupled his immediate question with other questions:

> Why are many Americans fearful that we have lost our sense of national purpose? Why is there confusion about intellectual and moral values? Why is there a slackness about public problems and a wholesale retreat to the joys of private life? Why is balancing the budget a greater national concern than exertion, self-denial and hard work? Have we confused prosperity with security? Why is there a growing uneasiness over the contrast between a society like that of the Soviets which believes in its destiny and our own which seems to regard itself as fulfilled?

In returning to these questions at the end Stevenson again felt obliged to criticize the Eisenhower administration, whose purposes were confined by fear of deficits, despite the huge increase in the national income, but again he placed the blame on the American people, saying that nations could not demonstrate a sense of purpose abroad when they had lost it at home. Americans appeared to have little purpose except more affluence. "Freedom is not an ideal, it is not even a protection, if it means nothing more than freedom to stagnate, to live without dreams, to have no greater aim than a second car and another television set—and this in a world where half our fellow men have less than enough to eat." This time he concluded on a note of qualified confidence:

> I believe the United States is ready for a new awakening and the achievement of greater goals. Within it are the moral and material elements of new purpose and new policy. It is the task of leadership to marshal our will and point the way. We had better start soon, for time is wasting.

As he looked into the sources of this lassitude, Stevenson had some second thoughts about American business. In a campaign speech of 1956 he had mentioned the sayings that the New Deal had made America safe for capitalism, and made capitalism safe for America— "safe especially for the responsible businessman"; the main trouble had been an "irresponsible minority in the business community." Now he saw a more basic, pervasive, systematic irresponsibility. He chose a meeting of the Institute of Life Insurance to give a talk on "The Public Responsibility of Private Power." Remarking that he understood his audience represented the largest aggregation of investment capital in the world ("a most unusual environment for a Democrat!"), he dispensed with the usual compliments and directly introduced his thesis, that in the face of the most powerful, dangerous challenge of communism to free enterprise and democracy, he had seen little awareness of such public responsibility. We could no longer bank on our tradition of dispersing power and trusting to luck to make it responsible. Specifically he cited the crippling strikes, such as a steel strike that had just gone on for four months, which now resulted from the industry-wide bargaining conducted by big business and big labor. He therefore proposed a scheme of compulsory arbitration when they were unable to settle their differences, recalling that as long ago as 1952 he had told a Labor Day audience in Detroit that new methods had to be found for settling national disputes, the country could no longer tolerate shutdowns that threatened its safety. Even so it may be doubted that his present audience was much impressed. Both labor and management still cherish their right to promote their own interests at the expense of the public interest, as if their quarrels were purely private affairs.

Kindly political scientists, such as Andrew Hacker, observe that the big corporations cannot be held socially responsible for their decisions about how to conduct their business, since their primary aim always is and must be to make profits, and that social problems resulting from their decisions must be the province of government. If so, Stevenson's main point is more pertinent: "Businessmen will have to get over their neurosis about government," as if its power were always the chief danger to society. They were not cooperating in the effort "to give some reasonable direction to the greatest irresponsible power at large in the world, the power of technology." Like the Eisenhower administration, they were always warning the nation against "spending ourselves into bankruptcy." Forever doing their utmost to encourage extravagance in private spending on selfish wants, they condemned only spending in the public domain. Such irresponsibility had grown thoroughly respectable in America:

> Nobody cries "reckless spending" when perfectly good office build-
> ings on Park Avenue with years of life ahead of them are pulled down
> to make room for new ones carrying higher rents and higher profits.
> The charge of spending is hurled instead against attempts at the other
> end of the same avenue to pull down ghastly tenements and rehouse
> families with the elements of human decency.

At that Stevenson perhaps did not know that the new office buildings everywhere were not even well built—shoddy construction has become more profitable.

In speaking on the same theme to the National Business Conference at the Harvard Business School, he took his text from Alfred North Whitehead: "A great society is a society in which its men of

business think greatly of their function." To the question whether
American businessmen were thinking greatly, Stevenson answered
bluntly No. He sweetened the pill by reminding his audience how
very important businessmen were today, illustrating by the prayer of a
little English boy in the war: "God bless Mother and Daddy, my
brother and sister, and save the King! And, oh God, do take care of
yourself, because if anything happens to you we're all sunk!" But
then he reviewed the remarkably consistent record of shortsightedness
of businessmen since the beginning of the century: they had fought
bitterly almost every major social reform. Now they were not facing
up to the world challenges to America, but still parading their
stereotyped prejudices and myths about the American way of life, in
which government was simply a "bad thing." Stevenson expressed no
calm confidence that businessmen could be induced to think greatly
of their great responsibilities, or even think freshly about our economic system. He ventured only "to do a little hoping greatly." Was
it "too much to ask business to help us graduate from the nineteenth
century, to throw off the semantic shackles of the dear, dead past, and
get into position to meet the full scale of the real and rising attack on
our way of life?" In our kind of society they had to think beyond the
immediate interests of business. As it was, their shirking of their
social responsibilities was poor strategy, bad for business itself:

> The difficulty with the business community is that its concept of the
> public interest is so often limited to individual companies or at most
> to business as a whole. Consequently, the intellectuals and the politi-
> cians, not the businessmen, have taken the lead in shaping national
> thinking on public affairs. You have, in a sense, abandoned the field.
> Instead of putting the labor of thought into the job of articulating your
> views on the shape of American society, your time is spent with your
> lawyers and your lobbyists and your public relations officers on how
> to argue "your side" of the case. And you complained because "some-
> one else" was creating a bad public image of American business.

Stevenson took up another missed opportunity in a topic he was
assigned by a group concerned with urban renewal, "The American

City—A Cause for Statesmanship." In a rambling discussion he confessed at once that he was not expert at the problems of the city, not even living in it, being himself "a form of parasitical growth taking income and culture from the city, and in return only adding to the morning and evening traffic jams." He did know, however, that the population explosion was making this a world-wide problem, and that most affluent America was not "even arresting the spread of blight and decay in our cities." Although as usual he wanted local communities to assume the major responsibility, he knew too from experience the political difficulties, that in our urban society state legislatures are still dominated by rural lawmakers and most cities have to operate under archaic revenue authority, live on leftovers from federal and state taxes. Hence it was plain that again the federal government would have to help, and "those who oppose federal aid for urban renewal are actually against urban renewal." And as usual Stevenson called on Americans to set their sights high. Our proper concern was not only the slums and minority ghettos, the growing traffic congestion, the sprawling offensiveness—it was not even just urban renewal. "Rather it is the construction of an entirely new mode of living—the exciting, exhilarating adventure of constructing economic, financial, social and political tools to build—not a city—but a metropolis." Thus, he concluded, will we "renew and rekindle our faith in ourselves and the limitless creativeness of free men."

Architects and city-planners excited by such prospects might remark that Stevenson was pretty vague about the means of realizing them. Urban renewal alone would call for a mightier effort by government than he envisaged. He said nothing about a primary cause of the blight of the American city, the priority given the needs of the automobile. In his rosy vision of the possible cooperation between public and private enterprise he said simply: "Business, especially big business, has a great opportunity here to make a contribution—and to make a profit." Actually, builders and realtors were making enough profit out of new housing projects, but no notable contribution to municipal well-being; big business was by its bureaucratic nature unlikely to be enterprising, imaginative, and creative in public ventures.[7] As for financing the new metropolis, New York would soon show how hard it was to keep the old ones going. When the wealthiest city in the world somehow found itself on the verge of bankruptcy, big business (first of all the Stock Market) opposed new taxes that directly affected it. I mention these complications because at this stage Stevenson expressed most optimism about a problem he admittedly knew little about.

He was more at home when he addressed the National School Boards Association on the needs of education, again beginning with the challenge forced by the achievements of the Soviet Union. For both the Russian government and Russian students there was no problem of "motivation" (one of the favorite words of educationists), for they were alike bent on excelling, not merely getting by. On the prevailing attitudes in America Stevenson cited Robert Hutchins:

> History will have trouble with American education in the twentieth century. It will see a people who say they are dedicated to education and are unwilling to pay for it. It will see an educational system that delivers less education per dollar than almost any other, saying that all it needs is more money. The people and the educators are united only in this: they both want education without pain, either intellectual or financial. . . .
>
> We might as well make up our minds to it. If our hopes of democracy are to be realized, every citizen of this country is going to have to be educated to the limit of his capacity. And I don't mean trained, amused, exercised, accommodated or adjusted. I mean that his intellectual power must be developed.

In taking this view Stevenson no longer stressed the supreme democratic value of local control of the schools. Although he still thought legitimate the fears of centralized control, he dwelt more on education as a national problem, and the political fact that it was the only

---

[7] In Stevenson's own Chicago Bertrand Goldberg was providing an example by his difficulties in financing his highly original twin-towered Marina City, designed as a complete, self-contained community for real city-lovers. Bankers and insurance executives, the usual sources of capital, frowned on his project because of their typically conservative, ultraconventional tastes. Goldberg finally got the money he needed from the national janitors' union.

such problem not handled on a national basis. And the limitations of local control were most apparent in what he considered the most important problem of education—what he preferred to call "respect for excellence" instead of "motivation."

The school boards reflected the demands of the parents or the local community, which among other things assured overemphasis on athletics. The local taxpayers were typically unwilling to spend freely on education, as well as to give much thought to the selection of their school board. Perhaps out of politeness to his audience, Stevenson neglected to say that the school boards themselves were as typically more concerned about "life-adjustment" than training of the mind or intellectual excellence. But again he concluded that "we the people" were finally most to blame for the failures of our education. The primary need was to ask ourselves searching questions about our values, what kind of people we really are:

> If our freedom means ease alone, if it means shirking the hard disciplines of learning, if it means evading the rigors and rewards of creative activity, if it means more expenditure on advertising than education, if it means in the schools the steady cult of the trivial and the mediocre, if it means—worst of all—indifference or even contempt for all but athletic excellence, we may keep for a time the forms of free society, but its spirit will be dead.

He added that Americans would fail even in their pursuit of happiness, know only the boredom of the pursuit of distraction: "A nation glued to the television screen is not simply at a loss before the iron pioneers of the new collective society. It isn't even having a good time."

Stevenson took his hardest look at the basic failings of America in "Our Broken Mainspring," a lecture in memory of A. Powell Davies, for many years a Unitarian minister in the nation's capital. The most somber of his addresses, this is perhaps the most deeply considered. It contains no startling, original ideas; many observations are as familiar as the one he quoted from his friend Albert Schweitzer, that ours is the most dangerous period in history because man has learned to control elemental forces of nature before he learned to control himself. Nevertheless what he had to say, and said with his usual felicity, was most important—as important as what Lincoln said in his great addresses, which contained no more novel ideas. It was a bold address for a statesman. I think it worth quoting at length as an eloquent expression of the qualities of mind and character that placed Stevenson among the greater Americans of our time.

After a brief tribute to Davies as a Christian dedicated to the cause of social justice and liberty, he began:

> From the mountain of his vision, Dr. Davies constantly proclaimed the political relevance of moral principle and of religion as a "judgment of righteousness." From the dusty plain of politics I would like in my turn to reaffirm this relevance. I like to believe that there may be some value in echoing testimony from a layman who has spent his middle life in the press and confusion of great events—in government service, in diplomacy and in politics.
>
> There is a phrase of Dr. Davies that stays in my mind. I do not know when I have heard a more terse and pregnant summing up of our predicament. "The world," he said, "is now too dangerous for anything but the truth, too small for anything but brotherhood."

Once more Stevenson told of the "overwhelming impression of thrust and purpose" he had got during his summer in the Soviet Union. Although the revolutionary ardor of the early days had cooled, even its very pragmatic leaders seemed to believe profoundly in the truth of their cause and its destiny to sweep the whole world. Certainly the activities of the Russians were world-wide, no corner of the earth seeming too insignificant for their attention. "All this we know—or begin to know." But do we really?

> I wonder how often we try to grasp the scale of dedication that lies behind it. Why should they be so busy? Why so much work and thought? Why such diversion of precious resources? Why such patience through every setback, such forward thrusts through every point of Western weakness? Heaven knows, we only want to stay home. Why don't they? Why do we never meet an isolationist Communist? These are some of the questions that haunted me when I confronted at first hand this iron, forceful, formidable way of life.

And I do not think that there is any doubt about the answer. Part of it is simply need for foreign trade. Part is fear, the search for security through friends. And part is the historical centrifugal forces in Russia which have been pressing outward for two hundred years—to the Pacific, the Balkans, the Middle East, the Straits, and so on. But the important thing is that the Soviet Russians believe in their truth, as the men of the Western world once believed in theirs. They, not we, are firing the shots that are heard round the world—and also the satellites that orbit above it. The fact that their faith is in many ways an evil perversion of the great propositions that once made the blood course in Western veins does not alter the fact that their tempo is dynamic and rapid, ours sluggish—even, I think, to ourselves.

Stevenson then recalled that America was born "dedicated to a proposition," and that its greatest leaders—the Jeffersons, the Lincolns, the Wilsons—were great because they spoke for mankind, not merely for Americans. He reaffirmed his faith in the American dream and its "self-evident" truths. "The possession of liberty and the pursuit of happiness—rightly understood—these have not been overthrown as the highest goods of human society." Complaining again about our purely negative foreign policy, he inquired more closely into the reasons for it:

We have offered aid not to help others but to shield ourselves. We have reacted to countless Soviet initiatives; acted on our own initiative barely at all. We watch the skies for other people's Sputniks and listen to the telegraph wires for other people's moves. Yet we are the free men of this universe; we are the children of liberty, the beneficiaries of unequaled abundance, and heirs of the highest, proudest political tradition ever known to man!

Why this lack of initiative? Why this paralysis of will? What have we done to our truth, our brotherhood—the supreme truth of freedom, the Christian truth of brotherly love? Have they failed? Or have we?

There is no more urgent duty than to discover why we have failed, if we have, and I think we have, and to get back into the arena, aspiring, striving, fighting, if you please, once more for what we believe. An examination of what you might call our collective conscience is to my mind far more important than particular projects or programs. You can have a perfect assembly of pieces in your watch, but they are worthless if the mainspring is broken. I am not worried about our various pieces—our technology, our science, our machines, our resources. But I am concerned, desperately concerned, about our mainspring. That it has run down, we know. But is it broken; is it broken beyond repair? In the last analysis, no question is worth more consideration in America today.

His own consideration of it was deepened by a historical perspective, in which the "self-evident" truths no longer look like man's birthright:

> I believe—as I have said before—that we have confused the free with the free and easy. If freedom had been the happy, simple, relaxed state of ordinary humanity, man would have everywhere been free— whereas through most of time and space he has been in chains. Do not let us make any mistake about this. The natural government of man is servitude. Tyranny is the normal pattern of government. It is only by intense thought, by great effort, by burning idealism and unlimited sacrifice that freedom has prevailed as a system of government. And the efforts which were first necessary to create it are fully as necessary to sustain it in our own day.
>
> He who offers this thing that we call freedom as the soft option is a deceiver or himself deceived. He who sells it cheap or offers it as the by-product of this or that economic system is knave or fool. For freedom demands infinitely more care and devotion than any other political system. It puts consent and personal initiative in the place of command and obedience. By relying upon the devotion and initiative of ordinary citizens, it gives up the harsh but effective disciplines that underpin all the tyrannies which over the millennia have stunted the full stature of man. . . .
>
> I believe we have had enough of adjustment, of conformity, of easy options, and the least common denominator in our system. . . . The dreary failure in history of all classes committed to pleasure and profit alone, the vacuity and misery accompanying the sole pursuit of ease— the collapse of the French aristocracy, the corruption of Imperial Rome, the decline and fall of the resplendent Manchus—all these facts of history do not lose their point because the pleasures of today are mass pleasures and no longer the enjoyments of an elite. If we become a

nation of Bourbons, numbers will not save us. We shall go their way, too. Vacuity and indifference are not redeemed by the fact that everyone can share in them. They merely restrict the circle from which regeneration can come. . . .

How are we to defend freedom if, for the tyranny of external control we substitute the clattering, cluttering tyranny of internal aimlessness and fuss? This freedom of our souls, freedom at the profoundest level of our being, is not a gift to us by our contemporary way of life. On the contrary, much of this life is a direct conspiracy against it. . . . And between a chaotic, selfish, indifferent, commercial society and the iron discipline of the Communist world, I would not like to predict the outcome. Outer tyranny with purpose may well triumph over the inner, purposeless tyranny of a confused and aimless way of life.

Ultimately, the challenge to America was a moral challenge— perhaps, Stevenson said, the greatest any society had ever faced. Most of our major problems presented themselves in moral terms and were probably insoluble without some measure of generosity and moral vision, for example the plight of the Negroes, the poverty of millions of other Americans, and the worse poverty of the non-Western world. So he concluded by repeating his old-fashioned views about politics:

> You may argue that these qualities of dedication, of selflessness, are pretty remote from the realities of politics. They are all very well for private life, but what part can they play in the rough and tumble of partisanship, of primaries, conventions and election campaigns? Ambition, drive, material interests, political skills, the arts of maneuver— all these, you say, have their part, but do not let us pretend that the democratic process is primarily a school of virtue or an arena of moral combat.
>
> And yet, I wonder. It has been the view of great philosophers and great statesmen that our system of free government depends in the first instance upon the virtue of its citizens. Montesquieu made virtue the condition of republican government; Washington declared that it could not survive without it. We have had a hundred and seventy-five years of it and no one can deny that the system has survived a remarkable amount of skulduggery. In fact, it is probably a tougher system

than its founders imagined. Yet I believe they are right. For no democratic system can survive without at least a large and active leaven of citizens in whom dedication and selflessness are not confined to private life but are the fundamental principles of their activity in the public sphere. . . .

There has never been any disinterested reform without disinterested reformers. And here we come to the essential contribution made by dedication and selflessness to the public good. No one ever did any good in politics without readiness for endless hard work—for the grinding, boring, tedious work, as well as the glamorous, high-sounding, headline-hitting work. Each [reform] is carried to us on the bent and the weary backs of patient, dedicated men and women.

At the end Stevenson recalled the Lincoln-Douglas debates, listened to by the multitudes in the prairie towns. Did these citizens have fewer responsibilities than the citizens today to whom the great issues are conveyed in fifteen-second television flashes?

In a century in which so many of the mentors of the public mind— from the psychiatrists to the ad-men—speak to us in terms of "what we owe ourselves," may there not indeed have been a slackening of devotion compared with those days, not so long distant, when what man owes to God and his neighbor was a common theme of public discourse? If so, this is a dangerous hour of our politics and for government by consent of the governed.

Stevenson concluded with this *if*—a question instead of his usual affirmation of faith in the American people. To repeat, he expressed no really original ideas in this address, only some that might seem novel to sophisticates because they were old-fashioned and heartfelt. But how rare an address it was for an American of Stevenson's political stature may be appreciated by considering a simple question. Who else can one imagine delivering such a speech? Not Dwight Eisenhower or Richard Nixon, surely, but not Franklin Roosevelt, Harry Truman, or today Lyndon Johnson either. Conceivably John F. Kennedy might have come close to it—once he felt secure in the Presidency he had set his heart on, and felt freer to express his deepest beliefs and doubts. As it was, "Our Broken Mainspring" recalls both the reasons for Stevenson's defeats and the intimations of the new order he pioneered.

It was given favorable publicity by the press, which was now worrying over the fashionable theme of the slackness and moral decay in America. The Luce magazines in particular were playing up this theme, in keeping with their fondness for moral, spiritual crusades. Like the bulk of the Republican press, however, they did not associate this slackness and decay with the Eisenhower administration, which on election day they could be trusted to support. Like Eisenhower himself, they did not clearly specify the "spiritual" values to which they were devoted, except to call them Christian, and they neglected the apparent conflict with the business values of free private enterprise, which they more obviously cherished. While more sophisticated than the President, aware of the shallowness of popular religion in America, they in effect subscribed to the religiosity that had made him more beloved—a "sincere" belief in a vague God who blessed capitalism, tolerated the worship of mammon too, demanded no sacrifices to speak of, imposed no strict "judgment of righteousness," but simply made people feel better. The God who blessed America in the Eisenhower era was comfortably known as the "Man Upstairs."

The religious spirit reflected in Stevenson's Davies lecture was comparable in that it was not transcendental but this-worldly, humanistic, primarily ethical. Essentially it came down to the living religion of Albert Schweitzer, a "reverence for life." It expressed itself in a social gospel rather than a gospel of salvation; it addressed the spirit in man that may or may not be an immortal soul, but that in any case seeks truth, goodness, and beauty on earth. The difference was that Stevenson was deeply concerned with the values of this spirit. He was trying to awaken the conscience of America, lulled by complacence over its material prosperity. He was demanding good works of the constantly paraded good intentions. He was appealing to reason, not merely practical sense, or appealing to both head and heart. He was seeking to free the spirit from the narrow aims of private enterprise, from the conformity it encouraged, and from the fears of bold enterprise in thought.

Stevenson's kind of spirituality could scarcely be popular in affluent America. Still, he had reasons for clinging to his living belief that the mainspring was not broken beyond repair. Beneath the complacent surface Americans seemed troubled, however vaguely. A simple editorial, "What's wrong with us?" had been reprinted all over the land. In the election year ahead Congress itself would hold formal hearings on the National Purpose. Always a large following assured Stevenson that his was not a lost cause.

Toward the end of 1959 another spontaneous boom for him got under way. Like Lyndon Johnson, most of the professional politicians wanted no more of him as a Presidential candidate, but some veterans encouraged the many amateurs who very much wanted him. Volunteer groups began organizing to draft him again, old friends went to work enlisting support and raising funds, and a strategic center was set up in Washington to coordinate what Senator Mike Monroney has described as "the plot against Adlai." As in 1952, Stevenson steadfastly refused to encourage the enthusiasts, saying over and over that he would not seek the nomination. Again, however, he refused to say either that he would decline it. Deeply touched by the loyalty of his supporters, he gave more signs that he was not simply dismayed by the movement to draft him, but at heart would like another chance. While inviting nobody, he received a steady stream of important visitors at his home in Libertyville. When other candidates, especially John Kennedy and his old friend Hubert Humphrey, began throwing their hats into the ring, he was put under mounting pressures to declare his candidacy or else his preference among the others, but he still refused to do either. It was with mixed motives that early in 1960 he set off on a two-month tour of Latin America, on the excuse of legal business, in the company of ex-Senator William Benton, chairman and publisher of the Encyclopaedia Britannica. He would escape the pressures of the spring primaries, he would see for himself what was going on in a continent he had not yet visited, and as he told newsmen, he hoped to return a "much better citizen of the hemisphere," which might mean a better-prepared as well as refreshed candidate.

Immediately Stevenson learned again how popular he was over the rest of the world. Everywhere he was besieged by crowds of admirers, greeted by enthusiastic receptions even warmer than President Eisenhower met when he honored Latin America by his visit shortly before—not to mention the reception of Vice-President Nixon two years before on his "good-will" tour. As on his world tour in 1953, Stevenson earned and repaid the hospitality by arduous effort. William Benton has told of their fourteen-hour days, filled with official receptions, formal dinners, speeches, interviews with presidents and cabinet members, talks with intellectuals, labor leaders, and students, and greetings to crowds, after which Stevenson still found time to go off by himself and explore markets, chat with ordinary people. Again he made an ideal unofficial ambassador, always sympathetic, tactful, ready to listen, yet not simply polite, ready too to state firmly his beliefs and contend against distorted views of America. He had an advantage over President Eisenhower in that he was not only as obviously friendly but articulate, cultivated, and urbane—qualities more admired in Latin America than in his own country. More important, he had a far better understanding of its problems, realizing that it was in the throes of the same revolution as the non-Western world.

Thus the President had come back from a quick ten-day trip with an optimistic report, based on an acquaintance only with bowing officials and hand-waving crowds. He ignored (if he ever read) an open letter addressed to him by the Federation of Chilean Students, detailing the grievances of Latin America, which was widely discussed in its journals. Stevenson came back deeply concerned over the urgency of its problems. He had spent a whole morning with a delegation of these Chilean students, including some Communists with set speeches. He sympathized with their grievances, agreeing that the United States should do much more for its neighbors, which it had neglected ever since the war. As he reported later in an article in *Look,* the Eisenhower administration had been primarily concerned "with making Latin America safe for American business, not for democracy," and American businessmen were "interested only in the profits they can make, not in the country and its development." Most emphatically Stevenson agreed with the students' complaints about their own society—the wretchedly poor and illiterate many, the very wealthy and irresponsible few. But he therefore reminded them that the United States had put through its New Deal before the war. The main point was that Latin-American countries would have to do likewise, their destiny must depend finally on what they did for themselves, and there was no easy, quick way to solve all their problems. In *Look* he expressed more concern over both American ignorance of our neighbors and the dangers of increasing hostility to us. He warned that it was too easy for Latin Americans to blame us for all their frustrations and resentments, but foolish for us to attribute anti-Americanism just to Communist agitation.

Stevenson's tour was little publicized in the American press, for the reason he had just discovered—it gave little coverage to Latin America. At a press conference on his return he tried vainly to hold reporters to this subject. They were interested in only one question, his nomination, and pressed it harder because he seemed confident and relaxed, his old buoyant self. He repeated that he was not a candidate, but also said that he would not care to be a "draft evader." When asked whether he had observed any great change in Nixon, he said he would prefer not to go into that—"I believe in the redemption of souls." A few days later he elated his supporters by an address he gave at the University of Virginia, in which he illustrated the beliefs of Thomas Jefferson by a vigorous indictment of the Republican administration. He reviewed the basic shortcomings of America, the symptoms of moral flabbiness, the anti-intellectualism, the comfortable illusion that "history does not happen to us," but now he blamed the leaders who had failed to keep the people informed, tried to obscure the truth and hush up criticism. "The people have a right to know why" we were losing the cold war, falling behind in education, and so on through a dozen articles of his indictment. He then reaffirmed his Jeffersonian faith in "the capacity of the people to rise to greatness once they know, once they are told, once they are summoned." He concluded: "This is the Jeffersonian mission—the sacred obligation that confronts all Americans who honor his name today—the overwhelming challenge, the exciting opportunity to show the world that the American revolution still belongs to all mankind." Senator Monroney and other Stevensonians at once challenged him: Who else could summon the people and lead this mission?

Stevenson went on talking with verve, apparently enjoying the spotlight. He apologized to a Washington audience for being late, explaining that he had been held up at the airport by ceremonies welcoming President De Gaulle: "It's a curious thing how often some national hero seems to be in my way." But then came the sobering news of the U-2 plane shot down in the Soviet Union, followed by the crescendo of blunders of the administration; and once more a glaring demonstration of the truth of his charges against it did his cause no good. As the country rallied around the President, Stevenson commented temperately that while we of course had to gather intelligence for our security, he questioned the propriety of sending a plane over the Soviet Union on the very eve of the long awaited Summit Conference. At length, angered by the Republican effort to stifle criticism, he took upon himself the duty of heading a responsible opposition, giving his famous "crowbar and sledge hammer" speech at a meeting of Cook County Democrats. Even our incredible blunders could not justify the shocking behavior of Khrushchev at Paris, he said, but neither could they be condoned:

> We cannot sweep this whole sorry mess under the rug in the name of national unity. We cannot and must not. Too much is at stake. Rather we must try to help the American people understand the nature of the crisis, to see how we got into this predicament, how we can get out of it, and how we can get on with the business of improving relations and mutual confidence and building a safer, saner world in the nuclear age.

Most of the press at once denounced the speech as a blow to national unity. Nixon added piously that he was sure "right-thinking Democrats" would stand with the President. Lyndon Johnson thought Stevenson had gone too far. A flood of mail suggested that

Johnson was right, at least for political purposes: most of the letters were critical. If many Democrats admired Stevenson's courage in standing out against the invincibly popular President, it did not improve his standing with the professionals. When at the national convention he finally sought the support of the Illinois delegation, Mayor Richard Daley of Chicago informed him that he had none. Stevenson knew then that he would never be President.

10

The Triumph of Kennedy

The woods are lovely, dark and deep,
But I have promises to keep,
And miles to go before I sleep,
And miles to go before I sleep.
                              —*Robert Frost*

"I have read my epitaph so many times that I thought I was dead," Stevenson said on a television program a week before the Democratic National Convention, "and then, when I wake up in the morning and find I am alive, it is a matter of delight, I must confess." The next day he said that if he were drafted he would accept the nomination and do his utmost to win. As the convention assembled, it became clearer that he was not only very much alive but the most popular Democrat on the scene. Volunteers for Stevenson who had been streaming into Los Angeles by the thousands greeted his first appearance with the most tumultuous welcome in the memory of old political hands. For two days chains of marchers in and about the convention hall chanted and shouted "We want Stevenson!" One professional who was supporting Kennedy remarked that Adlai could have got the nomination then and there had he stepped up and asked for it. The managers of Kennedy's campaign were working desperately to get him nominated on the first ballot, knowing that his support was likely to crumble if there was a deadlock; and given the mood of the delegates, it seems probable that Stevenson would have won had he stepped up. As it was, he merely told the cheering delegates that after the trouble he had had pushing his way in and out of his hotel and the hall he knew whom they were going to nominate—"It will be the last survivor." He concluded a brief, noncommittal talk to another assembly of delegates by quoting from Robert Frost's poem on the traveler in the woods (a passage that was one of Kennedy's favorites too, often quoted during his campaign). Then he survived still another wild demonstration set off by the nominating speech of Senator Eugene McCarthy. But his last-minute decision to seek the nomination was too late. With no such enthusiasm, the convention proceeded on the first ballot to give a bare majority to young Senator John F. Kennedy.

This whole campaign of 1960 was the most ambiguous episode of Stevenson's career. To some of his supporters the convention was a heart-breaking demonstration of ingratitude to a devoted leader, to others the saddest demonstration of his own indecisiveness. He himself said that it had given him his "finest hour." In fact, it honored him by a deeper and more lasting recognition than he realized at the time, for his spirit would hover over the campaign that followed. Kennedy, whom at the 1956 convention he had perfunc-torily saluted as that "great young American statesman," would turn out to be a greater one than he then anticipated, and one more like himself. The new President would also disappoint him by not choosing him as Secretary of State. On this score, too, many of Stevenson's friends still deplore his indecisiveness, saying that he would surely have been made Secretary had he come out for the winner before the convention. And immediately Kennedy's triumph suggested some ambiguous lessons for the profession that Stevenson had for years been trying to make more respectable. He had a more complicated "new look" as an unacknowledged disciple, as the young-est Presidential nominee in history, and as a master of the latest techniques in the old art of politics—more proficient than Nixon, who prided himself on his political skills.

Most obviously Stevenson looked still more indecisive by contrast with an ambitious young man who ever since the election of 1956 had been working wholeheartedly and single-mindedly to win the nomination. He made his loyal supporters unhappy by his refusal to seek a nomination they felt he really wanted. His great and good friend Eleanor Roosevelt was among the many who urged him to become a candidate, once embarrassing him by publicly announcing in so many words that he was; he answered lamely something about a misunderstanding. Other friends agreed with the professionals that he should either have gone all the way into the campaign or have stayed all the way out. Some, like Arthur Schlesinger, went over to the Kennedy camp. By the time the convention met there was little doubt that Stevenson wanted to be drafted, but he still waited to the last, lost minute to make up his mind. He tacitly confessed his mistake when he took leave of the faithful who had worked for him to the end: "You have given me something far more precious than the nomination; you have taught me a lesson I should have learned long ago—to take counsel always of your courage and never of your fears."

Still, he had acted in character—and had not by any means hesitated out of simple weakness of mind or will. In the years following his last defeat, when he announced he would not run again, he had also said he believed the party needed new, younger leadership. When the candidates for 1960 began stirring, he promised to keep out so as to give them a clear field. What mattered most to him was that the party adhere to a liberal program, and all the leading candidates—Senators Humphrey, Kennedy, Johnson, and Symington—were talking like liberals. His once unpopular ideas about foreign policy, such as the need of halting bomb tests, negotiating with the Soviet, and reorganizing NATO, had become the commonplaces of Democrats. When the candidates announced themselves, he said in a television interview that he would try "to maintain an attitude of vertical neutrality." Always trusting to democratic processes, he never regarded himself as the indispensable man on horseback.

At the same time, he had sound reasons for keeping himself

vertical and available. Hubert Humphrey, the candidate closest to him both personally and politically, was eliminated early in the campaign; Stevenson feared anyway that he had antagonized too many conservative Democrats to keep the party united and strong. Although Kennedy was leading the field, he had obvious handicaps and was not a clear favorite to win; the odds favored a deadlock. None of the candidates was so experienced as Stevenson in foreign affairs, now more than ever his chief concern. None seemed so concerned either about the flabby complacence of the country. And always there remained the very real possibility, to him really alarming, of Richard Nixon's election as President.[1] In all modesty he could have agreed with his supporters, who believed that he had a better chance of defeating Nixon than did Kennedy, vulnerable to the charges of youth and inexperience. One may regret that American democracy was denied the test of a clear choice between Stevenson and Nixon, unclouded by the religious issue that counted for so much in the actual campaign.

His best reason for indecision was his attitude toward Kennedy, which would complicate his career in the years ahead. Friends of Stevenson who lament that he did not assure himself the appointment he wanted by backing the winner earlier forget that such expediency would have been quite out of character, for he did not at that time much admire the future President. When told that Kennedy was doing better than Humphrey in electioneering in the primaries, he observed, "I guess Hubert doesn't have enough charm and Jack has too much." He also expressed in private, too freely for his later good, his opinion that Jack was an "arrogant young man." Considering him at best too inexperienced in foreign affairs, Stevenson resented all the more the rude pressures on him by the Kennedy crowd. For on the record to date the Senator from Massachusetts was much more clearly an ambitious politician than a great young statesman. He had made some name for himself during his eight years in the Senate by a few

---

[1] The alarm was brought home to me early in 1960 by a prominent friend of Stevenson's, who said that Sam Rayburn had remarked to him that Nixon was the most "evil" man he had known in his many years in the House. Coming from a hard-boiled professional, "evil" was a startling word.

Yet the primaries were bringing out as well the best in the arrogant young man. Kennedy had shown courage in deciding, against the advice of most of his inner circle, to make a fight for Wisconsin, in the homeland of Humphrey. He showed more courage in risking his chances in West Virginia, 95 percent Protestant. Here he met the dangerous religious issue in Stevenson's manner, head on: again disregarding the advice of his staff, he brought up the issue himself in a dramatic broadcast, a forthright statement of his belief in the complete separation of church and state. In the mining districts of the state he was humbled by the discovery at first hand of a "new America" in fact, a lesson in the technological revolution that was throwing thousands of men out of their life's work by automation and the shift from coal to oil. Shocked by the poverty and hunger of these victims of industrial progress, he spoke out with more simple indignation than Stevenson generally had.

At the national convention Stevenson was still of two or more minds. While demonstrators were shouting "We want Adlai!" his own Illinois delegation was shouting back "We want Kennedy!"— but with less spontaneous enthusiasm; Joseph P. Kennedy, the father of the family, had worked long and hard on Boss Daley. Similarly with the New York delegation, in which Stevenson had the warm support of the stalwarts from the days of the New Deal, Eleanor Roosevelt, Herbert Lehman, and Thomas Finletter; Kennedy's father had worked on the city bosses to help line up the great majority of the delegates for his son. All along during the demonstrations for Stevenson Kennedy's lieutenants were going about their carefully organized job of holding the delegates pledged to him, pressuring others they needed to win on the first ballot, keeping a close tab on what mattered most at this stage—not fervor but votes. And Stevenson's feelings must have been mixed even as he listened to Senator McCarthy nominate him with an eloquence more oratorical than his, but rising out of what he had been telling the American people for eight years:

And I say to you that the time has come to raise again the cry of the ancient prophet, and what did he say? He said, "The prophets prophesy falsely. And the high priests," he said, "rule by their words. And my people love to have it so. But what will be the end thereof?"

I say to you the political prophets have prophesied falsely in these eight years. And the high priests of government have ruled by that false prophecy. And the people seem to have loved it so.

But there was one man—there was one man who did not prophesy falsely, let me remind you. There was one man who said: Let's talk sense to the American people. . . .

He said, this is a time for greatness for America. He did not say he possessed it. He did not even say he was destined for it. He did say that the heritage of America is one of greatness. . . .

And so I say to you Democrats here assembled: Do not turn away from this man. . . . Do not reject this man who made us all proud to be called Democrats. . . . Do not leave this prophet without honor in his own party. Do not reject this man.

In the tumultuous demonstration that then gave him his finest half-hour, spectators joined delegates on the floor in chanting "We want Stevenson!" But several hours before this Mayor Daley had informed him that he had no support in the Illinois delegation. He was not surprised when on the roll call only 79½ of these roaring delegates voted for him.

Like most of the delegates, however, he was startled by the first decision Kennedy made after his triumph, one that would prove more fateful than either of them could know—the selection of Lyndon Johnson as his running mate. Many were shocked by what they considered Kennedy's cynical betrayal of his avowed cause. Johnson's famous skills in handling the Senate had made liberals regard him as primarily a smart operator, not too principled. In campaigning as a dark horse he had not endeared himself to Kennedy either by focusing on him, harping on the charge that the young man was too inexperienced; one proof was the bad mistake he made in agreeing with Stevenson on the U-2 plane affair. (Johnson said that any apology over this affair was only "appeasement.") When Kennedy consulted his advisers about his proposed selection, labor leaders protested because the Senator from Texas had at first boasted of his support of the Taft-Hartley bill, but also because they feared he would lose the Negro vote in the North. There was considerable surprise in all quarters when Johnson swallowed his pride and accepted the offer. One may still read conflicting accounts of why he did so, and whether Kennedy expected or really wanted him to.

Nevertheless Stevenson was not simply shocked by Kennedy's decision. It made good political sense as a means of holding the South, healing the wounds within the party, and securing the full weight of Johnson's influence in Congress behind the President's legislative program, but he respected Johnson for more than his political skills. Although the Texan's record was spotty, he had supported most of the New Deal legislation and taken a far more advanced stand on civil rights than other Southern Senators. This also brought up the reasons why Stevenson could feel that he himself was far from being a rejected prophet. The convention approved the most liberal platform ever adopted by the Democratic Party, including a civil rights plank stronger than either party had dared to approve. The operators of the efficient Kennedy steam roller were not hard-bitten pros but mostly bright young men, the type Stevenson had inspired. Like Senator McCarthy other speakers suggested his inspiration by the tone of their political oratory. And none spoke his language more unmistakably than Kennedy himself in his speech of acceptance:

> I think the American people expect more from us than cries of indignation and attack. The times are too grave, the challenges too urgent, the stakes too high to permit the customary passions of political debate. We are not here to curse the darkness, but to light the candle that can guide us through that darkness to a safe and sane future. As Winston Churchill said on taking office some twenty years ago: "If we open a quarrel between the present and the past, we shall be in danger of losing the future. . . ." Today our concern must be with that future. For the world is changing. The old era is ending. The old ways will not do. . . .
>
> Woodrow Wilson's New Freedom promised our nation a new political and economic framework. Franklin Roosevelt's New Deal promised security and succor to those in need. But the New Frontier of which I speak is not a set of promises—it is a set of challenges. It sums up, not

what I intend to offer the American people, but what I intend to ask of them. It appeals to their pride, not their pocketbook—it holds out the promise of more sacrifice instead of more security. . . .

Can a nation organized and governed such as ours endure? That is the real question. Have we the nerve and the will? Can we carry through in an age where we will witness not only new breakthroughs in weapons of destruction—but also a race for mastery of the sky and the rain, the ocean and the tides, the far side of space and the inside of men's minds. . . .

Listening to such passages, Stevenson would not feel that Kennedy was merely arrogant when he appealed to his own younger generation:

It is time, in short, for a new generation of leadership—new men to cope with new problems and new opportunities. All over the world, particularly in the newer nations, young men are coming to power, men who are not bound by the traditions of the past, men who are not blinded by the old fears and hates and rivalries, young men who can cast off the old slogans and delusions and suspicions.

More surprising, there were already signs that Stevenson would be partially vindicated even by the Republicans, have some indirect influence on Nixon himself. In the proceedings that led to the virtually inevitable nomination of Vice-President Nixon, the only excitement was provided by Governor Nelson Rockefeller. Something of a maverick ever since he came through the Democratic landslide of 1958 with an impressive victory in New York, by a campaign in which he was careful not to associate himself with the Eisenhower administration, Rockefeller had given New York an efficient liberal administration that the President might otherwise have recognized as a model of "progressive conservatism." His public behavior intimated what he said privately, that he hated the thought of Dick Nixon's being President. In the fall of 1959 he had started a preliminary campaign for the nomination, working hard for two months, only to discover the truth in what Stevenson and other Democrats always said, that the Republicans were distinctly the party of business: the organization and the big money were lined up solidly behind Nixon, against the progressive Governor. He accordingly announced that he would not be a candidate for the nomination, explaining that the great majority of those who would control the Republican Convention were opposed to any contest. But he again bestirred himself when the U-2 plane affair ended in the collapse of the Summit Conference.

Rockefeller agreed with Stevenson that this sorry affair should be openly and thoroughly debated, and said as much in a public announcement. He then said that in view of the national crisis he would accept a draft. Like Stevenson, he was much disturbed by Eisenhower's subordination of the defense program and foreign policy to the needs of economy, and he also agreed that the government should do much more about civil rights, education, medicine, and other domestic problems. About six weeks before the Republican Convention he issued a remarkably impolitic statement. He was "deeply concerned that those now assuming control of the Republican Party have failed to make clear where this party is heading and where it proposes to lead the nation"; he bluntly condemned Nixon's refusal to make known his program and policies until after the nomination; and he then offered a specific nine-point program, which amounted to a complete repudiation of the policies of President Eisenhower. In the spirit of Stevenson he concluded: "The people want one thing above all others—leadership of clear purpose, candidly proclaimed." This manifesto of course killed any lingering chance of his nomination, but in many Republicans it stirred an enthusiasm like that of Stevenson's volunteers. "Citizens for Rockefeller" went to work as the convention approached, so effectively that the delegates were swamped by more than a million letters and telegrams on their arrival in Chicago. From New York Rockefeller prepared to do battle over the ordinarily meaningless platform, force the convention to face up to basic issues for a change. He rejected a tame compromise draft that satisfied Nixon. The Vice-President, knowing that he could never hope to win the election without the support of Rockefeller's large following, thereupon made a secret trip to New York to come to terms. The outcome was the once famous Fourteen Point Compact of Fifth Avenue, agreeing upon a new platform.

Although this too was naturally a compromise, Nixon made most of the concessions. The Compact was liberal enough to infuriate the party regulars, implicitly critical enough of the administration's defense policies to infuriate Eisenhower too. In the ensuing battle to get most of it into the platform, Nixon was aided by the confidence of the regulars that he was never a man to be feared, but even so he had to work hard to appease both them and the President. He fought most successfully for a stronger civil rights plank. Stevenson was probably most pleased by a plank that called for suspension of nuclear testing—what in 1956 Nixon had described as "catastrophic nonsense." Altogether, the new platform at least seemed forward-looking by contrast with the keynote address of Congressman Walter Judd, who roused the party rabble by beating all the straw out of Truman and Acheson again. ("Was it a Republican administration that divided Korea and gave North Korea to the Communists?") The unanimous nomination of Nixon was held up only momentarily by ten prophetic votes the Louisiana delegation gave to Barry Goldwater, who had called the Compact the "Munich of the Republican Party." Nixon then chose as running mate Henry Cabot Lodge, one of the more enlightened Republicans on foreign affairs, who was acceptable to both Eisenhower and Rockefeller.

Stevenson might also have rejoiced in the speech of acceptance with which Nixon closed the Republican Convention. In the same Stockyards Amphitheater where General Eisenhower had accepted his nomination in 1952, he sounded some familiar notes about the deadly danger of propaganda and subversion, but a new note that made it the most dignified of his campaign speeches. "I serve notice here and now," he said, "that whatever the political consequences, we are not going to try to outpromise our opponents in this campaign." His task would be difficult because "at times our next President must tell the people not what they want to hear but what they need to hear"—for example, that it might be "just as essential to build a dam in India as in California." He ended on a religious note, dear to Eisenhower, but more suggestive of Stevenson's kind of religion:

A hundred years ago, Abraham Lincoln was asked during the dark days of the tragic war between the states whether he thought God was on his side. His answer was, "My concern is not whether God is on our side but whether we are on God's side."

My fellow Americans, may that ever be our prayer for our country, and in that spirit, with faith in America, with faith in her ideals and in her people, I accept your nomination for President of the United States.

It sounded like an auspicious start for a crucial campaign, one that Stevenson believed might be a major turning point in the history of American democracy, and that certainly made a considerable difference, to both him and the country.

In some respects it necessarily resembled the campaigns he had gone through, beginning with the preposterously exorbitant effort demanded in America to sway the smallish minority of voters who had not already made up their minds by habit or hearsay. Always a hard campaigner, Nixon pledged himself to visit all fifty states; he felt impelled to do his utmost to fulfill his new role as leader of the party and to stamp in his new image as a statesman. Kennedy was simply obliged to work hard because of his handicaps. Polls taken after the Republican Convention showed what might have been expected, that he was the underdog; he was always kept aware that the country had never elected a Catholic President or a forty-three-year-old; and always he faced the same difficulty Stevenson had in 1956. Although Americans were troubled by one thing or another, most felt no sense of crisis or urgent need for a New Frontier. How could the nation be in a bad way after eight years of leadership by most popular Ike?

To meet these problems, Kennedy drew on the assistance of men who had worked for Stevenson. The indefatigable James Rowe was on hand again to help manage his campaign. His ghost writers included John Bartlow Martin, William Attwood, and in particular Richard Goodwin, who as a college senior had been inspired by Stevenson; Goodwin and Theodore Sorensen were his principal writers. Among the men who supplied him with ideas and made him increasingly popular with intellectuals were Kenneth Galbraith and Arthur Schlesinger. Stevenson himself worked hard for Kennedy. He had agreed to give ten campaign speeches, but once he got started he gave more than eighty, as usual refusing simply to repeat a set speech. The one that perhaps gave him most pleasure, if with some misgivings, was a major effort in Nixon's home state of California, for which his assistants scoured the record for choice examples of the old Nixon's style. His feeling that perhaps he had been too rough was confirmed when a reporter asked him, "Governor, since when have you become Jack Kennedy's hatchet man?" But at least he had no compunctions about attacking Nixon's record in world affairs, and repeating what he had said about the Republican "truth squads" that were following him around: "Those truth squads bear the same relation to the truth that the fire department does to the fire—they'll put it out if they can."

Kennedy's own performance was making it easier for Stevenson to go all out for him. The themes of his basic set speech were reminiscent of 1956: America's prestige in the world was falling; this was a time of burdens and sacrifice; we must start moving again. As the campaign went on, he developed these themes with more style, and with growing assurance more freely indulged his humor. He took over from Stevenson the theme of the two-headed elephant, ridiculing the Eisenhower-Rockefeller-Nixon circus parade. He sounded more like Stevenson too when in exhorting Americans to start moving again he appealed to their past. Whether or not he was consciously imitating the older man, or trying to prove that he was no callow youth, he constantly quoted from Franklin, Jefferson, Emerson, Lincoln, and Roosevelt. In general, the misgivings of Eleanor Roosevelt and others about Kennedy were allayed by his unmistakable growth during the campaign. On election eve he could sound convincing when he told a crowd of home folks: "The kind of society we build, the kind of power we generate, the kind of enthusiasm we incite, all this will tell whether, in the long run, darkness or light overtakes the world."

Indirectly Kennedy owed something to Stevenson for the clearest advantage he won over Nixon—their celebrated debates on television. In an article published in a popular magazine before the conventions, Stevenson urged that a series of televised debates be held between the two major candidates. He pointed out from his own experience how the grotesque demands of American Presidential campaigns made it impossible for a candidate to reach most voters with a thoughtful, coherent presentation of his program:

> I do not mean to criticize these candidates for succumbing to the inevitable. I have been in similar predicaments. I've worn silly hats and eaten indigestible food; I've bitterly denounced the Japanese beetle and fearlessly attacked the Mediterranean fruit fly.

Hence he proposed that "a great debate conducted in full view of all the people" be substituted for the present circus:

> It would end the tendency to reduce everything to assertions and slogans. It would diminish the temptation of politicians to entertain, to please and to evade the unpleasant realities. It might even help to restore what we seem to have lost—our sense of national purpose.

Stevenson repeated his arguments shortly afterward before a Senate committee that was considering legislation to make such debates possible. "In the long run," he prophesied, "it may turn out that the direction we give to political television is one of the great decisions of the decisive decade of the 1960's." Immediately he was helped by one of the symptoms of the moral decay he had been deploring: the networks were eager to cooperate in order to brighten their public image, which had been badly stained by the scandals of "payola" and rigged quiz shows.

For Kennedy the debates were a godsend, the best possible opportunity to prove that he was not immature and inexperienced. Nixon consented to them out of a self-confidence bolstered by the memory of his triumphant Checkers speech in 1952; although at first he held out for a single debate, he agreed to four. The debates turned out to be an immense popular success, beyond the dreams of the networks' publicity men. Each broadcast attracted an audience of 65 to 70 million, and all told more than 100 million Americans listened to one or more of them—by far the largest political audience in history. Elmo Roper's survey indicated that most voters thought they had been influenced by the debates. And there is no question that Kennedy was right when he said after the election, "It was TV more than anything else that turned the tide." Although the various professional surveys as usual gave different estimates, all agreed that most listeners thought he had won the contest.

By Stevenson's standards, however, the debates were no such success. They did little to clarify the issues as he had tried to do in his campaigns. Both Kennedy and Nixon confined themselves to generalities, neither offered a specific program. As Nixon said at the outset, they did not disagree about goals, only about means; but they were vague about means too. They were like high school debaters, too busy trying to score points ever to thresh out their differences. Kennedy gave the clearest example of missed opportunity when he at first spoke out sharply on the dangerous issue of the Quemoy and Matsu islands, then hedged under pressure from Nixon, and ended in a stand indistinguishable from Nixon's. Since both chiefly repeated themselves, their last session was the dreariest. Essentially the Great Debates came down to what campaign oratory in America usually is, an exchange of "assertions and slogans," appealing primarily to sentiment and emotion rather than reason. Of this appeal Nixon gave the clearest example in the third debate—the one in which according to the surveys he gave his most effective performance—when the issue of Truman's profanity came up. Some may remember the ineffably sanctimonious manner in which he expressed his disapproval of bad language, and added that President Eisenhower would never use such language. As I recall, the great audience did not see Kennedy at this point trying hard not to burst out laughing; and if so, it was no doubt better for his chances.

Now, one may doubt that political debate before a mass audience can ever come up to Stevenson's standards. The Lincoln-Douglas debates that he held up as a model did not actually maintain a high level; Lincoln and Douglas alike mostly repeated their stock arguments, tempered them to suit local interests or prejudices, scored points by rhetorical art or sophistry, and abused each other's good faith. Kennedy and Nixon had more excuse for their performance in the limited time allotted them by the networks—only eight minutes for their opening statements, two and a half minutes for their answers to questions, and this in the knowledge that more than a few seconds of silence is considered deathly in a medium that flourishes on ceaseless chatter and jingle. In so short a time they could not hope to give a comprehensive, specific statement of their program, or a decently considered response to questions about it. Political television is unlikely to help much in illuminating the "great decisions" of our decisive decade so long as the networks are controlled by men convinced that a mass audience must be given only small doses of food for thought instead of pap. And in the last ten days of the campaign the Republicans exploited the more obvious possibilities of the medium. Since Nixon had fallen behind Kennedy in the polls, they spent some two million dollars to stage a television blitz that came down to high-powered merchandising.

Still, this was further evidence that the more dignified debates had influenced people. Possibly they did restore some sense of national purpose, inasmuch as so many millions of Americans had been willing to give up their pap at a popular hour. At least something important came through with a rough idea of the attitudes and purposes of the candidates—an impression of them as persons, and of their style under pressure; voters might size up somewhat better the men who would have to make the decisions on many issues that ordinary people could not be expected to comprehend fully. At any rate, the impression Kennedy made was almost all to the good. Even those not charmed or persuaded by him could see that he was no boy, but as mature as Nixon. Many evidently were charmed by him. After the first debate he was greeted by much larger crowds on his campaign tour, often crowds frenzied in their enthusiasm.

They brought out qualities in him that distinguished his campaign from Stevenson's. Whereas the latter was usually uneasy in large crowds, Kennedy was stimulated by them; Eleanor Roosevelt remarked that he was much like her husband, who drew strength and vitality from the crowds and was likely to end a campaign in better shape than he started. Kennedy was also a shrewder campaigner than Stevenson, more inclined to tell his audiences what they wanted to hear. A key member of his staff from the outset was Louis Harris, the political analyst and pollster, who kept him informed about the interests and attitudes of voters. He was accordingly sensitive to the significant changes in the fifties, such as the movement of millions of people to the suburbs, by far the fastest-growing regions in the country. In campaigning he concentrated more than Stevenson had on the suburbs, which were inclined to vote Republican, and he was rewarded by doing much better in them on election day. A less agreeable name for Kennedy's shrewdness was lack of candor. Thus his whole campaign was premised on the failures of the Eisenhower administration, but knowing how popular the President himself still was, he did not dare to attack him directly as Stevenson had.

Another difference from the campaign of 1956 was the behavior of the press. In a talk to editors, at which Stevenson good-naturedly passed over their "ill-concealed zeal at certain sacrificial festivals of recent years," he reminded them again of the importance of giving the opposition an adequate hearing; but Kennedy had little reason to complain. Although editorially the press was still about 80 percent Republican, some eminent newspapers that had supported Eisenhower did not support Nixon, and others were at most lukewarm. Nixon could never arouse such enthusiasm as Eisenhower had or Kennedy could. And it was he that complained of the press this time, even though he had most of the publishers behind him. Convinced that newspapermen were inveterately hostile to him and never gave him a fair break, he pointedly kept them at a distance. Refusing to meet them privately or talk with them freely, as Kennedy did, Nixon made it harder for them to report the campaign objectively, or to add the intimate touches that might have given him more "personality." Even so a neutral observer might be impressed by how fairly they reported his campaign, managing to conceal their private opinions about the schmaltz he was addicted to, such as all the stories about his poverty in his youth and his honest, hard-working parents.[2] In any

---

[2] Among the newsmen he persistently refused to see was Theodore White, who in *The Making of the President 1960* made an especially conscientious effort to be fair to him. White even wrote that the "meanest" epithet, "Tricky Dick," that had always plagued him was unmerited, and that if in his first major campaign, against Helen Gahagan Douglas, he had won as a Red-baiter, "it was because that was the ethos of the time and place where he campaigned." I would remark that Mrs. Douglas managed to rise above that ethos, as did Stevenson, of whom Nixon has expressed only contempt. But in what follows I am drawing on White's

case it was Nixon, ironically, who did most to make this campaign different from that of 1956.

The main themes of the set speech he gave from beginning to end were expectable. Kennedy was much too inexperienced a leader for these grave times; the promises of his New Frontier would raise by 25 percent the cost of everything the housewife bought; and in asserting that American prestige in the world had declined he was "running America down and giving us an inferiority complex"—a charge that enabled Nixon to end on a "spiritual" note. He made much of how he had talked back to Khrushchev in Moscow, an episode that had boosted his standing in the polls even though Khrushchev gave no signs of having been put in his place. He made more of his own promise to keep America moving ahead, by means unclear. But he at least conducted himself with enough dignity to look like a "new" Nixon. Although he lapsed occasionally toward the end (for instance when he called Kennedy a "barefaced liar" for saying that the Republicans had opposed Social Security), he in general campaigned more responsibly than he ever had in the past. He refrained from the nasty innuendoes with which he had smeared Truman, Acheson, and Stevenson. He refused to exploit the religious issue in spite of pressures from Republican politicians. In the TV debates he performed too much like a statesman to suit these politicians, who sent in angry complaints from all over the land, demanding more of the old Nixon.

Otherwise, however, the change did not suggest a clear growth. In Congress Nixon had voted with the Old Guard, and under President Eisenhower he had taken a more liberal course, reversing his stand on some issues; but in either case his stand appeared to be dictated by political expediency rather than conviction. On his record no one could yet say with assurance just what his convictions were, beyond a devotion to the Republican Party in which he had made his career. He offered no visions of the future comparable to the visions of Steven-

book, an admirable piece of journalism that is indispensable for all students of the campaign of 1960. While recognizing Nixon's limitations as a statesman, he stirs sympathy for a solitary, pathetic man, more sensitive than he appears on the campaign platform, and lonelier than Stevenson ever was, for reasons quite different.

son and Kennedy, if only because he had neither historical sense nor a clear political philosophy. At most he had the homespun philosophy of small-town America, simple notions about a land of the free where poor boys could make good by hard work as he had. And though such limitations were by no means fatal handicaps, as the popularity of Eisenhower showed, they were hazardous because he was still first and last a politician in the ordinary sense of the word, never able to create the illusion that he was above politics. As a smart politician, he could make fatal errors.

The plainest example in the campaign was his stand—or failure to take a stand—on the issue of civil rights. Having fought hard for a strong plank in his party's platform, which might win the Negro vote in the North, he proceeded to talk out of the other side of his mouth in the South, hoping to win its vote too. Here he made use of Barry Goldwater, waving the Confederate banner of states' rights. His staff was therefore furious when Henry Cabot Lodge blithely made in Harlem a pledge that Nixon would appoint a Negro to his Cabinet. But the critical test came in the last days of the campaign when a Georgia judge sentenced the Rev. Martin Luther King to four months at hard labor. Kennedy, who had spoken out unequivocally on both the social and the economic injustice being done to Negroes, at once called up Mrs. King on long-distance, to console her and assure her that he would do what he could to secure her husband's release, even though Southern governors had warned him that any support he gave King would cost him the South; and as her friends spread the word, Negroes in the North were thrilled. Nixon remained silent, as did President Eisenhower, though a Republican Deputy Attorney General had sent them both an application he had prepared for King's release. In *Six Crises* Nixon explained that as a lawyer he properly did not wish to interfere with judicial proceedings—as if he had given no thought to political considerations. In his shocked inability to understand why his protégé lost to Kennedy, Eisenhower might have thought a bit about the obvious reasons why he lost both the South and the Negro vote in the North.

By his own evidence, Nixon was even more devious on another

portentous issue, which was to give Stevenson some of his worst moments, the handling of Castro in Cuba. In *Six Crises* he writes that the one and only time during the campaign when he got mad at his opponent personally was when Kennedy accused the Eisenhower administration of doing nothing about Castro, and called for intervention. What angered Nixon was the knowledge that Kennedy had been briefed by Allen Dulles about the Cuban refugees who were being armed and trained for an invasion. To protect security, the righteous Nixon then used their last TV debate to attack him for advocating intervention—an attack that would have been fair enough (as it seemed to me at the time) were it not that he himself was actually for intervention, being one of the authors of the invasion plan. According to his moral logic, in other words, the way to meet a falsehood is by opposing it with a more downright falsehood. One who values Stevenson's effort to make politics honest might add that both were properly punished—Nixon by defeat, Kennedy by humiliation at the Bay of Pigs fiasco. Only the poetic justice was flawed: Stevenson would be as humiliated by Kennedy's falsehood at that time too.

With Nixon there remains the crowning irony. He entered the campaign with by far the best cards, inherited from the most popular President. Despite some worries over unemployment, the people were still rejoicing in peace and prosperity, two out of three in polls approved of the performance of Eisenhower, most believed that the Republicans would do better at keeping the peace, and almost none reported worries over the declining prestige of America. Yet the shrewd Nixon managed to lose. Praised by Theodore White and others for his "enormous" skills in politics, he lost because he played his cards badly. He ignored a brilliant staff of Madison Avenue television men who were eager to improve on the expert merchandising job they had done for Eisenhower. Republican politicians believed he made a bad mistake anyway in agreeing to the debates with Kennedy, but he got off to a dismal start in the first one by coming in tired and unbriefed, having neglected to consult with his advisers, and poorly made up as well, with a stubble showing on his heavy jowls. Above all, until near the end he refused to call on Eisenhower to campaign for him, though the President was eager to do so. In the last ten days Ike and the TV men showed how much they could do, as they were most plainly responsible for the surge that almost carried Nixon to victory; but he had lost too much ground by his own efforts. So he ran about 8 percent behind Eisenhower's record in 1956—a considerably greater shift in the vote than in Stevenson's campaigns, in fact the largest since Franklin Roosevelt's election in 1932.

His blunders may be attributed to pride, an excessive confidence in his own abilities. In his prolonged failure to make use of Eisenhower, pride was intensified by a deep resentment that one may sense in *Six Crises* even though it is never openly expressed; he was the more determined to prove himself because for years he had been treated as "my boy," denied intimacy, denied complete trust. Hence the pathetic aspect of Richard Nixon. An extremely ambitious man who had had to work hard all the way up, he seemed eager to be liked and esteemed, but remained lonely because always self-conscious, wary, unable himself to trust others wholeheartedly, unable either to win or to lose graciously. Similarly he was the more determined to make good as the "new" Nixon because of the thin skin on the heavy jowls.[3] But the most significant reasons for his failure, I should say—the reasons why I have treated his campaign at such length—may be summed up in the statement that he was almost the complete antithesis of Adlai Stevenson.

Nixon was always more likely to go astray in his judgment because on the record he had no clear faith, no deep commitment, no real passion for any cause beyond his political advancement. When he sounded off on "the Spiritual Values of America," one had only to ask: What were his own spiritual values? Incapable of eloquence, he could seldom speak movingly about anything except perhaps his experience as a poor boy. By the same token he had little capacity for detachment, no ironic reserve, no humor—qualities that do not

[3] Theodore White reports that he was especially sensitive about the cartoons of Herblock, mercilessly satirizing the old Nixon. One of his friends said, "If he lives to be a hundred, he'll never forget that Herblock cartoon of the welcoming committee, and him climbing out of the sewer to greet it, all covered with that stubby beard of his."

guarantee political wisdom, but can help. Lacking them, he was further handicapped in his very self-conscious resolve to create a new public image by being "sincere," being "himself." *Six Crises* only deepens the mystery of what his "real" self is. Whittaker Chambers wrote him in a last letter that from the beginning of their acquaintance a dozen years before, "I sensed in you some quality, deep-going, difficult to identify in the world's glib way, but good, and meaningful for you and multitudes of others." Those who are unable to recognize this quality in Nixon, but find it easy to identify the admirable qualities of Stevenson, might ask: Could he himself identify it?

They then have to ask some questions about an election that he lost by a very small margin in the popular vote—a little more than 100,000 in a record turnout of almost 69 million voters (64.5 percent of the electorate). In view of the odds at the outset, Kennedy's victory may be considered a personal triumph. He did most to inspire so large a turnout; he won millions of voters by not only his personal charm but his earnestness, conveying a sense of driving purpose even though he never specified the sacrifices he intended to ask of the people. Yet it was a severely limited triumph. Kennedy was a minority President, getting only 49.7 percent of the vote to Nixon's 49.6. Barely winning against an uninspired candidate, he most likely would not have won had popular Ike entered the campaign earlier. He certainly won no clear victory for his New Frontier program; the Republicans captured a number of additional seats in both the Senate and the House, and the Democratic winners included the usual large number of conservative Southerners. At that Kennedy ran substantially behind his party ticket, outside the South too.

Once more we must pause to consider the mentality of the American voter whom Stevenson trusted to the end. Analyses of the election brought out some unsurprising results. Although Kennedy entered the national convention as the least popular of the Democratic candidates among Negroes, he won about 70 percent of the Negro vote, somewhat more than Stevenson got in 1956; this heavy majority, which swung a number of key states, he clearly merited by his forthrightness and political courage. As understandably, the shift of

Eisenhower voters to Kennedy was most marked in the lower-status groups; they voted sensibly on the basis of their experience since they had been the chief victims of unemployment, insecurity, rising costs of medical care, and Eisenhower's notions about fiscal responsibility. Voters who expressed any particular interest in domestic problems were in general strongly for Kennedy, for as good reasons. Other findings, however, made less apparent sense. Kennedy won more of the new voters than Stevenson had, but not so many as might have been expected in view of his direct appeal to youth; they split pretty evenly between Nixon and him. Some millions of Stevenson voters switched to Nixon, for various reasons that might be illuminating but remain unclear, naturally difficult for admirers of Stevenson to appreciate. More depressing, though I suppose not surprising, was the number of college graduates among these deserters—they supplied the highest proportion. Altogether, the total picture was at last report (Key's book) somewhat more confusing than usual.

The most obvious reason for the confusion was the religious issue, which cut across all others. Thoughtful, tolerant Protestants could reasonably feel uneasy about the election of a Catholic President, since the Church was obtruding its views on birth control, education, and other vital issues, but an assembly of churchmen that met in Washington to discuss such objections was headed by Norman Vincent Peale, whose great popular appeal was hardly to the thoughtful or enlightened. Kennedy then again met the issue directly by accepting an invitation to discuss it with a Protestant assembly in Houston, Texas—near the heartland of the old-time religion. In a short speech he stated views that should have allayed reasonable misgivings:

> I believe in an America where the separation of Church and State is absolute—where no Catholic prelate would tell the President (should he be a Catholic) how to act, and no Protestant minister would tell his parishioners for whom to vote—where no church or church school is granted any public funds or political preference—and where no man is denied public office merely because his religion differs from that of the President who might appoint him or the people who might elect him. . . .

I believe in a President whose views on religion are his own private affairs, neither imposed upon him by the nation nor imposed upon him as a condition to holding that office.

In answering questions from the floor, Kennedy said as plainly that although he was confident that his Church would attempt no interference, he denied the right of any ecclesiastical official to tell him what to do in the sphere of his public responsibility.

Nevertheless bigotry unquestionably influenced the outcome, if to an extent impossible to measure. A large majority of Catholics voted for Kennedy, millions of them just because he was a Catholic; they included many Irish who had voted for Eisenhower. A smaller majority of Protestants voted against him, millions for the same reason. They help to explain why the farm states went strongly for Nixon, as they never had for Stevenson even when farmers were faring poorly. The record is confused because Nixon also appealed more to small-town America by his stories about his poor boyhood, and many of those who voted primarily for religious reasons would not say so to pollsters; but on the face of it there was enough simple prejudice to recall the saying of Dean Swift: "We have just enough religion to make us hate, but not enough to make us love one another." For the long run, however, I assume the most important point is simply that Kennedy won in a preponderantly Protestant country. He then removed the religious issue from politics by not taking a Catholic stand on any public issue, leaning over backwards to avoid the least impression of favoritism to his Church. Unlike President Eisenhower, for example, he did not piously oppose government assistance to birth control programs in poor countries contending against the population explosion. (Out of office, Eisenhower changed his mind.) It now seems unlikely that a Catholic candidate will ever again stir up such controversy as Kennedy did, and before him the unhappy Al Smith.[4]

[4] Lest I sound too cheerful, let me add that no avowed agnostic could hope to be President of the United States. Stevenson perhaps remembered a passage from his grandfather's chapter on "The Lost Art of Oratory." Among the eloquent speakers cited was Robert Ingersoll, who was defeated for the governorship of Illinois by his agnosticism, or what he called "a slight difference between himself and some of the brethren upon the highly exciting question of total depravity." Today no politician would dare proclaim himself an agnostic.

And so, finally, with Kennedy's record as President. It was an ambiguous record apart from Stevenson's troubled role in his administration. On the domestic front Kennedy did not provide the bold, decisive leadership that many thought the "rejected" prophet was incapable of; the positive achievements of the first President born in the twentieth century, a herald of the "new generation of leadership," were on the whole disappointing. The reasons for his limited success may again illuminate speculation about how great a President Stevenson would have made. He did inaugurate, however, a new order that was mostly congenial to the old leader. If we cannot speak of a "Kennedy era," since he lived only three more years, we must speak of some important differences from the Eisenhower era. The gist of them is that Stevenson was vindicated, not rejected.

To begin with, President Kennedy staffed his administration with many men who had worked with or for Stevenson—George Ball, William Blair, Willard Wirtz, Newton Minow, David Bell, J. Edward Day, Kenneth Galbraith, Arthur Schlesinger, Richard Goodwin, and John Bartlow Martin, to name a few. As Chairman of the Federal Communications Commission, Newton Minow symbolized one important difference by telling the television networks that their standard programs had created a "wilderness"; President Eisenhower had made his harangues about creeping socialism seem more foolish by following the traditional Republican policy of appointing to the federal commissions men who favored the business interests they were supposed to regulate in the public interest. Among the newcomers brought on the political scene by Kennedy was Robert McNamara, a young business executive with a new outlook, who would prove the most capable and longest-lived of the series of Secretaries of Defense.[5] But most important was simply the change

---

[5] According to Arthur Schlesinger, whose book on Kennedy I am trusting for inside information, McNamara himself remarked upon the common limitations of businessmen as statesmen that had been so conspicuous in the Eisenhower administration. When Vice-President Johnson gave birth to "Operation Tycoon" by suggesting that the fifty largest corporations be asked to provide their best vice-presidents for a year of service in the foreign aid program, he commented that 10 percent of the vice-presidents might be good men but the rest would do no

in the political atmosphere, the end of the intellectual torpor of the Eisenhower years. Eager young men were bringing ideas to Washington again, and much more sense of purposefulness. Idealism was put to work instead of being paraded in talk about spiritual values. Criticism and satirical humor became respectable. The Kennedys themselves were mimicked in a popular record—a tribute the humorless Eisenhowers and Nixons would not have appreciated, any more than they appreciated the humor of Stevenson.

Liberals, disappointed by how little definite progress the Kennedy administration made toward the New Frontier, blamed the President's conciliatory treatment of a conservative Congress. Kennedy's excuse was that his very close victory had given him no clear mandate, he wanted first to win over public opinion, and he saw no point in battling Congress when he was certain to lose. Judging by his record as Governor, Stevenson would surely have fought harder for his program. Whether he would have had more success must remain forever uncertain. It is unlikely that he would have managed better with a balky Congress, unless he had been elected by an impressive majority; one reason why Kennedy refused to appoint him Secretary of State was a legitimate doubt of his ability to get along with Congress, where he was typically regarded as too visionary. In general Kennedy's problems illustrated both the validity of Stevenson's charges against the Eisenhower administration over the years and the much greater difficulties of a President than he had faced as Governor of Illinois.

"The only thing that really surprised us when we got into office," the President told a Democratic Party dinner, "was that things were just as bad as we had been saying they were." They were nowhere worse than in the Army, which for reasons of economy had not been fully equipped with modern weapons and was wholly unprepared to fight a limited war. But on almost all fronts the Eisenhower administration had failed to keep abreast of the changes coming over

---

good at all. The Operation was not in fact a great success, for most of the big executives were devoted to businesslike methods unsuited to the delicate problems of foreign aid.

America and the world. With an economy just recovering from the latest recession, Kennedy faced the needs for more housing, education, medical care, public services of all sorts. It appeared that everything had to be done. And then it had to be done through the bureaucracy, the "permanent government" that all Presidents have to reckon with. Always denounced by conservatives as a token of creeping socialism, the bureaucracy is actually the most conservative branch of the federal government, the most resistant to change in protecting its vested interests, and more closely allied with Congress than with the executive branch.

Most pertinent in this study was the problem of the Department of State. In a foreign policy report drawn up for Kennedy before he took office, Stevenson warned that the "tremendous institutional force" of the Department threatened to "overwhelm and dictate to the new regime," just as the Pentagon had "systematically absorbed a series of Secretaries of Defense." Kennedy soon discovered for himself that the *esprit de corps* that made the Foreign Service devoted also earned the Department its name of Foggy Bottom. According to Schlesinger, he liked to dream of "establishing a secret office of thirty people or so to run foreign policy while maintaining the State Department as a façade in which people might contentedly carry papers from bureau to bureau." The Department had grown even more conservative than usual under Dulles and had never recovered from the demoralization caused by his failure to resist McCarthy. Always disposed to support conservative governments, it was more hostile to mildly leftish ones than to dictatorial regimes whose only virtue might be that they were anti-Communist. It was oblivious to the irony remarked to Kennedy by the Italian Premier Fanfani, "that the Communists, who believe in dictatorship, are always addressing the masses; while the West, which believes in democracy, is always addressing the leaders." As for its U.S. Information Agency, this was preaching to the world the American gospel according to Herbert Hoover and George Humphrey. Kennedy never got the Department under control. Dean Rusk, the Secretary of State he chose in preference to Stevenson, lent no vigor for such purposes. Stevenson himself could hardly have overhauled a department in which so many top officers had earned their posts by long, faithful, unimaginative service.

The most successful of Kennedy's innovations was the Peace Corps. Described by Eisenhower as a "juvenile experiment" and by Nixon as a haven for draft dodgers, this tapped the resources of idealism in American youth that Stevenson too had appealed to. A related program after Stevenson's heart was Food for Peace. Otherwise the President often sounded like him when telling the people that there was no American solution to every world problem, we could not impose our will on all the rest of mankind, we always had to make clear our willingness to talk whenever talk would help, and so on. On the home front Kennedy devoted a speech to another congenial theme, the need for more critical thought:

> For the very enemy of truth is very often not the lie—deliberate, contrived and dishonest—but the myth, persistent, persuasive and unrealistic. Too often we hold fast to the clichés of our forebears. We subject all facts to a prefabricated set of interpretations. We enjoy the comfort of opinion without the discomfort of thought.

One obsessive myth his administration began to dispel was the fetish of the balanced budget. With the aid of what shocked Eisenhower as a "vast, reckless" plan for a "massive deficit," the economy achieved a faster rate of growth (5.6 percent) than it ever had since the Republicans had taken charge of the government, and began approaching the "miraculous" growth in Western Europe, where no country had worried over unbalanced budgets. Thereupon the President began planning a war on poverty that he did not live to carry out.

Kennedy's active interest in culture produced another innovation welcomed by Stevenson. The guests at President Eisenhower's bachelor dinners at the White House had been mostly businessmen and politicians, with now and then a scientist, since the value of basic research had at last been recognized; the President took no interest in the producers of American culture except a few big names in the mass media, other "successful" men. In 1957 William Faulkner expressed a common feeling: "The artist has no more actual place in the American culture of today than he has in the American economy of today, no place at all in the warp and woof, the thews and sinews, the mosaic of the American Dream." The Kennedys, themselves culti- vated people, invited in more of their own kind, including artists, writers, and intellectuals. Lewis Mumford hailed Kennedy as "the first American President to give art, literature and music a place of dignity and honor in our national life." At Amherst the President paid particular tribute to writers: "The men who create power make an indispensable contribution to the nation's greatness, but the men who question power make a contribution just as indispensable . . . for they determine whether we use power or power uses us." In honoring Robert Frost he went on to exalt one of Stevenson's loves: "When power leads man toward arrogance, poetry reminds him of his limitations. When power narrows the area of man's concern, poetry reminds him of the richness and diversity of existence. When power corrupts, poetry cleanses." The style of the Kennedys, perhaps most appreciated in Europe, made more impression at home than was realized until the shock of his assassination. For many young Ameri- cans the shock was intensified by a sudden awareness of how much it had meant to them to have such civilized people in the White House.

All in all, Kennedy's qualities of greatness were much like the qualities of Stevenson. He had not only a keen intelligence but sensitivity, an interest in new ideas, an open mind. His mind was freer because he too had the saving grace of philosophical humor, ironic detachment, and ability to laugh at himself. (When Eisen- hower's memoirs appeared he remarked dryly to Schlesinger that apparently Ike had never done anything wrong, and added, "When we come to writing the memoirs of this administration, we'll do it differently.") He was displaying a similar capacity for growth, perhaps more marked than Stevenson's; he was potentially more adventurous because of his self-confidence and love of power. Kennedy seldom displayed, however, the forceful qualities that he too thought Stevenson lacked. He was very cautious in not only his dealings with Congress but his regard for public opinion; he was more afraid than Stevenson of getting far ahead of public opinion. Although he could scarcely back up all his eloquent words with vigorous action, the discrepancy between his promise and his performance could be glaring. He never tried so hard as Stevenson either to educate public opinion, even though he was developing considerable gifts as an educator and could speak more easily to his generation. The question why he did not try harder brings up the most common doubts about Kennedy. Was he capable of passionate, wholehearted commitment to a cause? Did he have enough heart? I would not venture an answer; but I would say that there was no question about Stevenson on this score.

Hence Kennedy possibly achieved most by his shocking death. In a sense it was a tribute to him that no national leader since Franklin Roosevelt had inspired such hatred in the extreme Right as he had. Just before his assassination Stevenson went to Dallas, a leading center of the hatred and hysteria, to address a meeting on United Nations Day.[6] The local patriots arranged to take the curse off this performance by staging the day before it a "United States Day" (unfortunately blessed by Governor Connally with an official proclamation); they circulated handbills with photographs of President Kennedy and the legend "WANTED FOR TREASON." Many were on hand to hoot Stevenson when he spoke and to scream at him as he left the hall; before the police rescued him from the mob, a woman hit him over the head with a sign and a man spat in his face. Such patriotism produced the Dallas schoolchildren who cheered when informed of Kennedy's assassination. Shame deepened grief as the nation went into mourning. A chastened people had a more poignant sense of the best in their young President. Now one may observe that in idealizing what he stood for they paid unwitting tribute as well to the example Stevenson had set him. Thus Kennedy was honored as

[6] On his world tour in 1953 he had got news of Dallas. Its Minute Women had removed from the public library a volume of the *Encyclopaedia Britannica* that contained an article favorable to public housing, and had also got banned a travel book because it described the Alps as the most beautiful mountains in the world.

"the first Western politician to make politics a respectable profession for thirty years—to make it once again the highest of professions, and not just a fabric of fraud and sham." Stevenson was surely more deserving of this tribute.

11

Ambassador to the United Nations

Three Presidents of the United States sent Adlai Stevenson
to the United Nations. They sent you our best.
—*Dean Rusk,* at the United Nations memorial ceremony

Stevenson's last years as Ambassador at the United Nations brought
him to the peak of his popularity and world fame, and might seem to
be the most successful period in his career since his governorship; yet
it is by all odds the most troublesome, controversial period. The
paradox began with the overwhelming approval of his appointment
by the public—almost 90 percent in a Gallup poll. His appointment
was as popular in the rest of the world. He was superbly qualified,
without question the best man in the country for the position. There
is no question either that he performed with great distinction,
remaining the most popular, esteemed ambassador in the United
Nations. Even political enemies paid him sincere tributes after his
death, applauding—as Nixon did—his performance as defender of
the nation. But this role was precisely the root of the trouble. What
Stevenson defended was not necessarily the national interest—it was
the policies of the administration. He was often unhappy in the role,
sometimes deeply so, and as often talked of resigning. Although his
friends disagree on just how unhappy he was and how serious his
intention of resigning, his experience was certainly an ordeal; at least

one of his old associates regrets having urged him to accept the ambassadorship. Many of his old supporters were disappointed by his defense of policies they thought unworthy of him, some even questioning his integrity. There is much controversy over several stands he took, above all his defense of the war in Vietnam—an issue that grew much more critical after his death. This will be the most somber chapter of my study.

Since I could not in any case pretend to a wholly impartial survey of such burning issues, I should say at once that up to a point I agree with Stevenson's critics. I regret in particular his support of President Johnson's policy in Vietnam. I do not question, however, his integrity. The choices he faced seem to me, as they did to him, much more difficult than they seemed to writers who publicly expressed their disappointment in him. Friend or foe, no thoughtful man can be certain that Stevenson was right or wrong in his judgments. He himself suffered for just this reason. But this chapter will reflect my judgment that in spite of his sufferings his last years in the United Nations were on the whole a fitting, not a regrettable, conclusion to his public career.

When Kennedy was campaigning for the nomination, he said he "assumed" that any Democratic President would appoint Stevenson Secretary of State. His reasons for not doing so have already been suggested, but it was probably enough that he felt he could never be on easy, comfortable terms with him; in the U.N. he could keep him at a further distance while taking full advantage of his international prestige. The tension between them was not relaxed when Stevenson publicly deferred his acceptance of the post, waiting until he heard who was to be Secretary of State, the position everybody knew he wanted. Once more he went through a spell of anguished indecision, but this time for reasons easier to understand. Since 1948 he had been accustomed to giving, not taking, orders, and he had hoped as Secretary to have an important say in determining foreign policy. As Ambassador his job would be chiefly to explain or defend it. In remarking to Harry Ashmore that Kennedy would properly make his own foreign policy, he added, "And there simply isn't enough in his record to indicate how much of it I could agree with." He then stated the reason for the torments to come: "And yet if I accept this appointment, I am committed to support him this side of treason or madness. There is no way for a man as prominent as I am to quietly step down." Also he would have to work closely with the State Department. While this should as properly have the final say about American policy at the United Nations, and be consulted about all the gradations between "requesting" and "demanding," "regretting" and "denouncing," in the Ambassador's speeches, it meant that Stevenson would have to deal constantly with underlings whose judgment he might not respect. He accepted the appointment after Kennedy selected Dean Rusk as Secretary, gave the U.N. post Cabinet rank, and promised him "a key role in the formulation of foreign policy"; but when a reporter congratulated him he said, "You must be kidding."

One reason why he accepted was that he still did not really yearn for the relaxation of private life that he so often talked wistfully about. He needed to remain in public life, which he loved more because he felt lonely; or as Mary McGrory wrote, he "needed to be needed." An old friend now points out that Stevenson could have kept busy and influential as a syndicated newspaper columnist, a role in which he would surely have had a large audience, but at the time his many friends were urging him to accept the ambassadorship for the obvious reason, his ideal qualifications. Having visited most of the 110 nations now in the U.N., met their leaders, and received warm welcomes, he could not kid himself about his qualifications. Above all, he was dedicated to the cause of the United Nations, which he still considered the best hope for a "safer and saner world." As he wrote after two years of the ordeal, "Surely the most rewarding task of civilized man today is that of reconciling different points of view, of accommodating national positions, of producing a consensus from a workable design for a meeting of the minds—for looking not at each other but in the same direction." To the Senate Foreign Relations Committee that unanimously approved his appointment he observed that at best the U.N. "is not a formula for 'stability' but a framework for change." There was plenty of change that Stevenson hoped to work for. And since he habitually talked of "challenges," he was drawn by an immediate one in the low ebb of American prestige in the U.N. Eisenhower's Ambassador, Henry Cabot Lodge, had at best not been very effective or popular, but he had long been handicapped by having to defend policy made by Secretary Dulles.

Having committed himself, Stevenson settled down with his usual conscientiousness to the most grueling job in his career. From January 23, 1961, to his death in London on July 14, 1965, he put in fourteen-hour days on what his deputy Francis Plimpton described as "that always exacting, often exasperating, sometimes exciting, inevitably exhausting and occasionally exhilarating post on behalf of the United States." An outsider might call it an impossible job. Stevenson had to confer with 110 other ambassadors, attend many of the hundreds of meetings of the various councils and committees, and keep up with the hundred items on the annual agenda. While doing his best to negotiate tactfully with the representatives of all these diverse peoples, he had to keep in constant touch with the State Department and digest its latest advices. After a full day's work at the U.N. he also had to attend one or more of the many cocktail parties and dinners that defined diplomatic life, in his words, as "protocol, alcohol, and Geritol." In addition Stevenson prepared many speeches, with his usual pains: the formal speeches he had to give in the U.N., which cost him more pains because their wording had to be approved by the State Department, addicted to pompous rhetoric or jargon; and talks to public audiences, responses to some of the thousands of invitations he received. The latter he agreed to give because he believed that his duties included service as Ambassador to the American people, to inform them about the U.N. and explain American policy. In the introduction to a collection of the speeches he gave in this period, *Looking Outward* (1963), he summed up his life as Ambassador:

The crises are incessant; so is the travel back and forth between New York and Washington; the cables and reports from every quarter of the globe come in daily torrents; so does the mail; the conferences and meetings and politicking are unending; so are the speeches that have to be written, the visitors that have to be seen, and the luncheons, receptions and dinners that have to be attended. And they say I have diplomatic immunity! Add to all this the everlasting combat with the Russians and you may understand why there are times when I yearn for the peace and quiet of a political campaign. . . .

He then answered the question whether all this was worthwhile: "Of course it is—if peace is worthwhile." For the sake of peace Stevenson endured other trials too. The countless meetings of councils and committees lasted longer because of the endless flood of oratory. "Why," he asked parenthetically, "do so many people feel that to be immortal a speech must be eternal?" Most trying were the orations of the Russians, made monotonous by not only the stock invective but the incessant repetition of stock arguments, no matter how often or patiently they had been answered in detail. At this time the Russian delegates seldom bothered to carry on a dialogue, but appeared to be talking exclusively to the Communist world or its propagandists in the non-Western world, rehearsing crude or patently false charges that one would think could impress only the completely ignorant or systematically misinformed.[1] But most trying for Stevenson were the difficulties he anticipated at home. The State Department exasperated him by keeping a suspicious eye on his style, underlings sometimes treating him as a bright but erratic errand boy; in the middle of a televised debate with the Russians he would be slipped notes instructing him how to conclude his argument. In the White House he soon got intimations that he would not play a "key role" in determining foreign policy. After a year he seriously considered a request from Mayor Daley that he run for the seat of Senator Dirksen.

[1] As I write, the Chinese government press has come out with a glowing account of how Comrade Mao swam miles down a river, at a speed many times greater than all world records. The story is so utterly ridiculous that one must wonder: Do the rulers of China really believe that their people are so stupid and childish as to believe this? Can it be that they are preparing the people for some political demonstration of Mao's miraculous powers? Or are they merely trying to impress other superstitious Asians? In any case, how can diplomats deal with rulers who couple such utter nonsense with barbarous hate propaganda?

What chiefly kept him on as Ambassador, I assume, was the satisfaction he was nevertheless getting from his work, and the awareness that he was helping to keep the peace. Apart from his specific accomplishments, he enjoyed his immense popularity at the U.N., which was obvious from the day he began his duties there, among people almost all of whom knew him or his works and had hoped for his election. (He often said, "It was a damn shame I ran for President of the wrong country.") He enjoyed as well recognition of the patience, tact, and courtesy that made his job more arduous than people in Washington realized, but also his performance more masterful, earning him a sobriquet that greatly pleased him—"Housemother of the U.N." Possibly he got too much pleasure playing housemother, for some associates say that Kennedy's failure to consult him regularly was partly his own fault; he could have made a point of spending a day in Washington every week, as his successor Arthur Goldberg would.[2] And he managed despite the stuffy officials in Washington to carry on in his distinctive style. He soared above the flood of oratory, sometimes in eloquent passages, more often in graceful ones, but most consistently by maintaining a calm, lucid, reasonable manner and seeking understanding or solution of problems instead of victory in debates. As President Kennedy wrote in a preface to *Looking Outward,* Stevenson "raised the level of the international dialogue" just as he had the level of the national dialogue.

At home he raised it in his role of Ambassador of the U.N. to the American people. Although a large majority of Americans now approved of our membership, a great many thought of it as a kind of sacrifice, always entailing some menace to the national interest. Especially when talking to House or Senate committees, Stevenson felt obliged to answer a crude question: "What's in it for us?" He pointed out that our membership was quite cheap: we were spending

[2] While agreeing that he was pleasant to work for, his associates also report that he tended to be thoughtless or selfish in his demands on them. At this time Stevenson tried to dissuade an old friend from accepting an attractive ambassadorship, saying that he should work for him at the U.N., or if he insisted on being an ambassador, he should go to a country like Cambodia where he could do real good. His friend asked pointedly where was he? He was in his suite at the Waldorf-Astoria. Why didn't he get off his fat rear and go to Cambodia?

only about a dollar per capita on the U.N. Since Americans typically read its record in terms of "victories" and "defeats" for the United States, he could assure them that a large majority of its votes had supported the American position. But then he added: "I prefer to avoid the specious habit of treating the course of human affairs, even the massive conflicts in world affairs, like some sporting event which ends when the timekeeper blows his whistle." The U.N. was not and should never be an arm of the U.S.; it was a truly international organization, which could be truly effective only if it was not dominated by us. And just because it was an open forum, we had a clear advantage over the Communist nations. Operating more or less closed societies at home, they had to step out into the open society of the United Nations. Stevenson concluded:

> There is contention in all this; there is frustration and the stuff of headlines; there is danger that the fearful and the insecure will want to withdraw from the free interplay of conflicting ideas and concepts and terminology, especially if, now and again, things do not go exactly the way we would like them to.
>
> Yes it is we who do best in the open forum, for this is our natural habitat. And if we have the nerve to go ahead, if we have the stomach for the test of the open society, if we have the courage to build even that which is not perfect from our point of view, I can foresee nothing but a more meaningful dialogue coming out of it, a gradual erosion of tension, and finally the dominance of a set of ideas which are better, and better able also to stand the test, than the Marxist ideas as revealed to his successors.

In this faith Stevenson often repeated his usual warnings against self-righteousness: "We judge ourselves by our motives, others by their actions."

But the main subject here is perforce the incessant crises he had to deal with. It can be wearisome to review these crises—all the muddy water that has gone over the dam, leaving as much more piling up behind it. The Ambassador's speeches, Kennedy wrote, present "thought generated on the spot, not hindsight called up in tranquillity"; and the spot may already seem remote, the thought antiquated, the more so because we have our own crises. Nevertheless these were the conditions under which Stevenson had to work, the sources of his sufferings and his satisfactions, and they are of course not actually remote or at all foreign to our condition. He helped to contain the crises, as we hope to contain ours. In so doing he dealt with the same basic problems that confront us. He makes clearer some things we have learned, others we still have to learn.

When Stevenson began work at the U.N., he had at once to deal with a lurid illustration of why it would not be a "formula for stability." It was in the thick of the Congo crisis, which had erupted as soon as Belgium granted the Congo its independence in 1960. A preposterous nation, hopelessly unprepared to govern itself, it began to disintegrate the day its new government was set up with Patrice Lumumba as Premier and Joseph Kasavubu as President. Katanga, its rich mining province, broke away under the leadership of Moïse Tshombé, and some of its troops revolted, in their sprees attacking white women. When the Belgians sent in paratroopers to protect their civilians, Lumumba appealed for aid against both them and Tshombé, and the U.N. responded by sending in troops provided by neutrals. On the instructions of Secretary General Dag Hammarskjöld, how-ever, these troops merely tried to maintain order, refusing to help Lumumba against the Belgians, Tshombé, or any other rival or rebel; so he appealed for aid to the Soviet Union, which was all too willing to oblige. The pretense of native government grew more farcical as Kasavubu and Lumumba dismissed one another, then both were dismissed by Colonel Mobutu, who set up a new caretaker govern-ment. Insisting that Lumumba was the legitimate ruler, the Russians violently attacked both Hammarskjöld and the United States, which was supporting Mobutu. Stevenson came in just before Lumumba was murdered. Thereupon the Soviet Union grew still fiercer, de-manded the withdrawal of the U.N. troops, and gave more aid to Lumumba's successor, Gizenga.

The point of reviewing this messy affair is not merely the chaos that was called the Congo nation, but the colonialism that had produced it. Belgium, which had drawn immense wealth from the

Congo, had done nothing to prepare it for self-government. In a population of fifteen million there were only fifteen college graduates (they made up Mobutu's government); the few hundred natives in the civil service had all been petty officials, not one helping to make policy; and the Belgian-trained army had not one native officer. Now Tshombé got his power from Belgian mining interests. He was backed as well by Britain and France, which likewise had economic interests in rich Katanga. Nor was the United States free from taint in its diplomacy. The last official act of the Eisenhower delegation at the U.N. was to abstain from voting on a declaration against colonialism that was endorsed by almost all the nations except our European allies. In supporting Colonel Mobutu, who had no claim to legitimacy as ruler, we were adhering to our policy of preferring any ruler to a leftist; African and other neutral nations supported the Soviet demand that Lumumba be recognized as the legitimate ruler. As for the U.N. troops, Hammarskjöld had obvious reason for keeping them out of the internal fights of the Congolese, but Lumumba also had reason for his complaints. After his death he was vindicated by a reversal of U.N. policy: the troops helped a new Premier, Adoula, to put down Katanga—against the opposition of Belgium, Britain, and France. No premier could maintain order or begin to unite the Congo without foreign aid.

Out of this whole affair came another headache for the United Nations, as not only the Soviet Union but France refused to pay their share of the costs of operations they strongly disapproved of. As I see it, not even hindsight can tell the ideal way to have handled the embattled leaders of an impossible nation.[3] But at least the worst dangers of the crisis were overcome, with some credit to both the

[3] For a frankly biased but intimate history of the affair, see *To Katanga and Back* by Conor Cruise O'Brien, formerly commander of the U.N. troops. He is most convincing in his account of the skulduggery of Britain and France as well as Belgium, whose civilians spread reports of the "atrocities" committed by these troops in struggles with Tshombé's gendarmes and European mercenaries; most Western newspapers played up these sensational reports, in part because their wealthy publishers naturally favored the Belgian mining interests. O'Brien also believes that Hammarskjöld—the most devoted servant of the U.N.—issued false or misleading statements under pressure. He believes that the mercenaries were responsible for the airplane crash in which Hammarskjöld was killed.

United Nations and the United States—the only major power to support its operations. Stevenson made out a strong case for both.

In a reply to the welcome he received on his first official appearance at the U.N., he had lined up the United States against colonialism, declaring that as "the oldest anticolonial power" we believed in freedom and self-determination for all peoples, and did not wish to impose our system or our philosophy upon any of them. In his many debates with the Soviet Ambassador Zorin he focused attention on the main concern—the welfare of the Congolese people, which the Russians were subordinating to their own interests; their insistence on the immediate withdrawal of the U.N. troops could only mean civil war and worse chaos. With more feeling Stevenson defended Dag Hammarskjöld against their demands for his resignation and their vicious abuse of him, even to accusing him of "organizing the murder" of Lumumba—one of the worst examples of their contempt for the opinions of mankind outside their bloc. With the support of African and Asian nations, Stevenson put through the resolution giving Hammarskjöld more power in the Congo. Similarly he led the successful opposition to the Soviets' "troika" proposal for the General Assembly, which would have given it an effective veto over the Secretary General. And whether or not it was wise for the U.N. troops to aid Premier Adoula in subduing Katanga, American support of this change in policy indicated another change that accorded with Stevenson's assertion of the rights of neutrals: Adoula was neither pro-American nor pro-Russian, but wanted to remain neutral. In a later article reviewing the Congo crisis the Ambassador admitted that mistakes had been made, but expressed satisfaction in its outcome as "a victory for the rule of law and of peace."

Throughout this prolonged crisis his patience was often tried by African delegates too, some of them representing pro-Russian nations, almost all of them hypersensitive about their new independence and suspicious of moves by the Western democracies. When primitive rebels against still another Premier (the unlikely Tshombé) were threatening to kill hundreds of hostages they held in Stanleyville, mostly Europeans, and American planes dropped Belgian paratroopers to save the lives of these civilians, the Africans burst out with wild charges about this latest proof of Western imperialism and prejudice about "white supremacy." After listening to their harangues for some hours, Stevenson spoke to them bluntly: "Never before have I heard such irrational, irresponsible, insulting and repugnant language in these chambers—and language used, if you please, contemptuously to impugn and slander a gallant and success-ful effort to save human lives of many nationalities and colors."

The Congo was only an extreme example of the terrific problems besetting the African nations: all of them jealous of an independence they were ill-prepared to maintain because of their poverty, primitive technology, largely illiterate population, and lack of experience in self-government. Stevenson had mixed feelings about these nations, which in turn were extreme examples of the problems besetting the whole non-Western world. In his travels through Africa he had again perhaps hobnobbed with too many British and French colonials to fully realize the bitter resentment of the Africans and their need of self-assertion to bolster their self-respect. He betrayed some doubts of their capacity to live up to their new opportunities. On the other hand, he was favorably impressed by Nkrumah of Ghana, who entertained him in the days before this ruler exhibited delusions of grandeur. Another host was his good friend Barbara Ward, who was not only sympathetic to the Africans but inclined to be too optimistic about their potentialities in her pleas for much more aid to them. (She has pointed out that all Africa has a total national income less than a twentieth of that of the United States, less even than the annual increase in our income—and this to support more than 300 million people.) In any case, Stevenson's official position was clear. With the support of President Kennedy, he continued unequivocally to oppose colonialism, including *apartheid,* as a violation of human rights, and to appeal for more economic and educational aid to the new nations. On his own he went out of his way to be courteous to their ambassadors. In *Looking Outward* he warned against the fright-ening talk about stemming "the tide of black nationalism," but also warned that "this avalanche of nationhood" would bring graver responsibilities: "The next decade in Africa will be much more turbulent and much more dangerous than the last." Soon after his death his prophecy was borne out by the uprisings that finished Nkrumah and others he had known.

Stevenson's book makes no mention, however, of another affair that engrossed him in the early months of his ambassadorship, the Bay of Pigs invasion. A disaster too complete and indefensible perhaps to deserve the name of "crisis," this gave Stevenson the most humiliating experience of his whole public career. It also had deeper implications that unfortunately still need to be pondered.

Inasmuch as Castro exploited anti-Americanism to popularize his dictatorship, which denied the Cuban people the democratic elections and constitutional liberties he had promised them, it is well to recall that there was considerable justification for this feeling. Americans had controlled the great bulk of Cuba's utilities, mines, oil wells, and cattle ranches, and 40 percent of its sugar. The Eisenhower administration supported to the end the brutal dictatorship of Batista, who had been publicly embraced by the American Ambassador. Castro was popular as well because he began introducing social reforms on behalf of the peasants and workers, reforms to which American business interests were typically hostile or at best indifferent. By the time Kennedy took office, at any rate, Cuba was in the Soviet camp. The United States had stopped buying its sugar, and in January 1961 it broke off diplomatic relations. The Central Intelligence Agency and the Pentagon went on with their plans for an invasion, training and equipping Cuban refugees; according to their "intelligence," all Cuba was ready to rise up against its hated dictator. Kennedy had serious misgivings about the venture, but could not make up his mind either to drop it or to promote it. A few days before the invasion he told a press conference: "There will not be, under any conditions, an intervention in Cuba by the United States Armed Forces." He consented to a compromise that made the worst of the situation—preserving the fiction that we were not intervening by refusing to allow our planes to cover the invasion. So our armed forces merely ferried over to the Bay of Pigs a force of fifteen hundred refugees they had trained, to meet certain disaster. The United States was disgraced all over the world, while Khrushchev could again pose as a defender of small nations against American imperialism by threatening to come to the aid of Cuba.

The immediate question is how Kennedy could have made so incredibly stupid a blunder. The most significant reason was that he respected the advice of the CIA and the military, who since the war had had more influence on foreign policy than ever before. Robert McNamara also accepted their advice, while Dean Rusk voiced no opposition to the plan. All seemed blind to the plain truth stated by Senator William Fulbright, one of the few Kennedy consulted who did oppose it: "To give this activity even covert support is of a piece with the hypocrisy and cynicism for which the United States is constantly denouncing the Soviet Union in the United Nations and elsewhere." Adding that the rest of the world would not miss this point, Fulbright concluded: "The Castro regime is a thorn in the flesh; but it is not a dagger in the heart." Stevenson would surely have opposed the adventure, as he did when he caught wind of it too late, but he was neither consulted nor informed. He might have saved the young President from this humiliation had he been Secretary of State.

As Ambassador he suffered as much as Kennedy for no fault of his own. Within a few weeks after he took his seat in the U.N., the Cuban delegate began charging that the United States was planning "direct intervention," and Stevenson as regularly and angrily denounced the charge. When Cuban air bases were bombed two days before the invasions, he denied any American responsibility for the aggression; the CIA had given him faked photographs to bolster his case. Upon the invasion he again denied in good faith the Cuban charges. But shortly after this speech friends found Stevenson in a shocked daze: he had at last been told the truth, learned that unwittingly he had told the U.N. a clumsy lie. Feeling that he could never hand in his resignation at so critical a moment as this, he felt worse when gossip had it that Kennedy had referred to him as "my official liar." At the U.N. he was pained most of all by the conclusion a foreign delegate expressed to Norman Thomas: "What American

can we ever believe?" This feeling, however, Stevenson soon overcame. He was heartened to stay on by private apologies from Kennedy and assurances that he would never be kept in the dark again, but perhaps most heartened by the trust of the U.N. delegates. Knowing the devious ways of heads of states, they realized that the fault was not his, and his reputation remained about as high as ever.

At home the aftermath of the Bay of Pigs was on the surface heartening, but had disturbing implications. Kennedy at last acted decisively, in a public statement declaring that he bore the sole responsibility for the affair. (Privately he mentioned an old saying that "victory has a hundred fathers and defeat is an orphan.") As usual the people rallied unthinkingly behind the President in an emergency; a Gallup poll had 82 percent approving the administration, a new high in its popularity. Kennedy commented that it was just like Eisenhower—"The worse I do, the more popular I get." But judging by the record he apparently brooded no more than most Americans did over one lesson of the Bay of Pigs, that the people could not trust the official announcements of their government. The Kennedy administration remained vulnerable to the charge Stevenson had leveled against the Eisenhower administration, that it did not keep the people fully enough informed, and sometimes deliberately misinformed them. Newsmen complained that the White House now worked harder than ever at "managing" the news. The people's "right to know"—a right more important just because it was more difficult to define and enforce, given all the secrecy and security regulations required by modern defense programs—would be respected no more when the war in Vietnam was built up.

President Kennedy himself, lastly, was both humbled and toughened by the fiasco in Cuba. In the conduct of foreign affairs he was handicapped by the blow to his personal as well as the national prestige. Khrushchev treated him arrogantly when they first met in Vienna in the summer of 1961, rejecting his overtures to better relations, and the East Germans set about building their wall in Berlin. About this he did nothing but visit West Berlin and endear himself to its people by assuring them that he was wholeheartedly with and for them, committing the United States still more firmly to the questionable policy of making the reunification of Germany the primary condition of peace in Europe—for the Soviet Union an impossible condition. At the same time, he was resolved to prove himself to Khrushchev and the world by a demonstration of toughness. His chance came the next year with the missile crisis in Cuba, by far the most dramatic and dangerous crisis of his administration. This time Stevenson was consulted and listened to, if only because Kennedy had learned to mistrust the advice of the military. In the showdown at the United Nations he gave his most celebrated performance. But in the aftermath he was again humiliated, for reasons that throw light on Kennedy's life-or-death gamble, the basic issues of power, and—in my opinion—the riper wisdom of Stevenson.

Presumably Khrushchev was emboldened by Kennedy's apparent weakness to try his dangerous gamble of sending missiles secretly to Cuba, where they would be in easy range of Washington, New York, and the Panama Canal. When air surveillance brought in clear proof of an extensive, speedy build-up of offensive missile bases, Kennedy was determined upon a showdown. Most of his advisers approved the "quarantine," a naval blockade to keep out the Soviet freighters carrying missiles and back up his demand that the Russians dismantle the bases. He rejected the advice of the military, who wanted an immediate air strike, which might well have brought on a large-scale war.[4] He rejected as well Stevenson's proposals of political negotiations to go with the naval operation, including an offer to give up our own missile bases in Turkey. But Stevenson approved of the quarantine. It at least gave Khrushchev time to reconsider; Kennedy was resolved not to humiliate or exasperate him by too belligerent an attitude. The President also pleased Stevenson by agreeing on the need of consulting immediately with the Organization of American States to get its approval of his demands, which it soon gave almost unanimously. The United States could go before the world more

---

[4] The Air Force supported its argument by photographs of Cuban airfields with planes lined up in neat rows, sitting ducks for bombs. Now warier of the military mind, the President asked that photographs be taken of our own airfields. These of course showed our planes lined up just as neatly.

becomingly as the spokesman and defender of the Western Hemisphere.

The day after Kennedy went on the air to inform the people gravely about his decision, Stevenson explained and defended the American action before the United Nations in what listeners remembered as his most impressive speech to date. Read today, it may seem too long, and one basic inconsistency too apparent. The vision of the United Nations Charter, he said, assumes a pluralistic world, "quite large enough to shelter a great variety of economic systems, political creeds, philosophical beliefs and religious convictions"; whereas only a few days before he had said that Cuba could rejoin the American family by renouncing communism, our actual position was (and still is) that our hemisphere is not large enough to accommodate nations that might prefer communism. But delivered to a tense audience, aware that the fate of civilization was literally at stake, Stevenson's grim, patient, comprehensive review of the whole problem was most effective, especially because on the whole it was restrained and just. He exposed the myth about American imperialism that the Soviet began proclaiming in 1945, at a time when we were starting to dismantle our great military machine and it was starting its aggressions in Eastern Europe. He asked a fair question: "Has the Soviet Union ever really joined the United Nations? Or does its philosophy of history and its conception of the future run counter to the pluralistic concept of the Charter?" He pointed out that Khrushchev's innovations had not altered "the basic drive to abolish the world of the Charter." Similarly he reviewed the case against Castro, his suppression of other political parties at home and his aggressions on other Latin-American countries. Most important, Stevenson ended with neither a ringing denunciation of the Soviet nor a paean to the American cause, but a characteristic plea for sanity:

> The hopes of mankind are concentrated in this room. The action we take may determine the future of civilization. I know that this Council will approach the issue with a full sense of our responsibility and a solemn understanding of the import of our deliberations. . . .
> This is a solemn and significant day for the life of the United Na-

tions and the hope of world community. Let it be remembered, not as the day when the world came to the edge of nuclear war, but as the day when men resolved to let nothing thereafter stop them in their quest for peace.

In subsequent speeches Stevenson defended the quarantine more specifically in a rather different tone. Since the Soviet Union was arguing in effect that not it but the United States had created the crisis by the hullabaloo over the alleged missile bases it had discovered, he observed: "This is the first time I have ever heard it said that the crime is not the burglary, but the discovery of the burglar." Finally, in the most dramatic of his speeches, he showed that he could be as tough a debater as any. Gromyko had at first blandly denied that the Soviets had sent any missiles to Cuba, Ambassador Zorin had then said they were only defensive weapons, and in his latest "flood of rhetorical scorn" he had seemed to say either that the missiles did not exist or that the United States had not proved their existence. Stevenson began by saying that he had incontrovertible proof and then pinned Zorin down:

> All right, sir, let me ask you one simple question: Do you, Ambassador Zorin, deny that the U.S.S.R. has placed and is placing medium and intermediate-range missiles and sites in Cuba? Yes or no? Don't wait for the translation. Yes or no?

When Zorin refused to answer, saying he was "not in an American courtroom," Stevenson pressed him harder:

> You are in the courtroom of world opinion. You have denied they exist, and I want to know if I understood you correctly. I am prepared to wait for my answer until hell freezes over. . . .

When Zorin again refused to answer, Stevenson produced his incontrovertible proof—aerial photographs that this time he had taken precautions to be sure were not faked. But again he concluded his speech on a characteristic note:

> And now I hope that we can get down to business, that we can stop this sparring. We know the facts and so do you, sir, and we are ready

to talk about them. Our job here is not to score debating points. Our job, Mr. Zorin, is to save the peace. And if you are ready to try, we are.

In "the courtroom of world opinion" Stevenson unquestionably won his case, hands down. As unquestionably President Kennedy won in his "eyeball-to-eyeball" confrontation with Khrushchev. When he announced the quarantine, Khrushchev quickly gave signs of uncertainty: Cuba-bound Soviet freighters stopped on the high seas or changed their course. Later it became known that the Premier was very much afraid of war, almost frantic. The crisis ended abruptly with his agreement to remove the missiles. As the world breathed more easily again, there was much applause in the West over a triumph of wise diplomacy. Kennedy had prevented any further Russian miscalculation by taking a firm stand and making it absolutely clear that the United States was prepared to use force to defend this stand. At the same time, he had made it easier for Khrushchev to back down without losing all face. In a brief broadcast to the nation he was careful to refrain from boasting over the American victory, instead praising Khrushchev's "statesmanlike decision" and remarking what Stevenson had long emphasized, the "compelling necessity for ending the arms race and reducing world tensions."

Yet the success of this bold essay in brinkmanship obscured some important, disagreeable questions. I. F. Stone has observed that the many articles and books dealing with the missiles crisis have rarely asked: What if Khrushchev had not backed down? Kennedy and his staff were by no means confident that he would. This raises another question: Were the Russian missiles in Cuba actually so grave a threat to our security as to demand so serious a risk of nuclear catastrophe? The Soviet Union already had more than enough missiles at home capable of destroying the cities of Eastern America, or all America for that matter. Elie Abel quotes Robert McNamara as saying at the time that a missile is a missile, and "it makes no great difference whether you are killed by a missile fired from the Soviet Union or from Cuba." As the White House debates continued, McNamara conceded that the Cuban ones would have a considerable political effect on Latin America and the rest of the world; or as Sorensen wrote in his *Kennedy,* they would have had a slight effect on the "strategic balance *in fact"* but a substantial one on this balance *"in appearance."* In other words, what was at stake was American prestige, not national security. And though prestige or appearance is vitally important, it raises other troublesome questions. One reason for the gamble was the President's felt need of restoring his personal prestige. Another was domestic politics: the Congressional elections were only a few weeks off, and the Republicans would surely stage a profitable uproar if Kennedy failed to get the missiles out of Cuba.

Abroad our NATO allies were naturally relieved by Kennedy's success, but not altogether happy about his diplomacy. Prime Minister Macmillan of Britain was disturbed because Europeans—like the Russians—had lived so long within easy range of missiles that they found it hard to regard the missiles in Cuba as a dagger in the heart of the United States. They also knew that if a nuclear war broke out they would probably be the first victims. President De Gaulle put the matter bluntly when Dean Acheson was sent to him as a special envoy during the crisis: Was he being consulted or informed? The answer had to be that he was merely being informed. The United States always felt free—as it still does today—to make crucial decisions and take risks of world war without consulting its allies, only requesting their approval and feeling aggrieved if denied it. Exulting over Kennedy's victory, Americans would feel outraged when De Gaulle later declared his independence of NATO.

Our allies were accordingly disposed to welcome the proposals of Stevenson for negotiation that Kennedy turned down. On the offer to give up our missile bases in Turkey, for example, the Ambassador pointed out that it would be hard to make the United Nations understand why it was right for us to have bases in Turkey but wrong for the Russians to have bases in Cuba. During the crisis Khrushchev himself offered to remove the missiles from Cuba and give Turkey a nonaggression pledge if we would do likewise with our missiles in Turkey and give Cuba a similar pledge. Neither Sorensen nor Schlesinger makes clear just why Kennedy refused to consider this apparently reasonable compromise, which Walter Lippmann and others had been urging. His refusal seems stranger because early in 1961 the Joint Congressional Committee on Atomic Energy had recommended the removal of our missiles from both Italy and Turkey, on the grounds that they were unreliable and obsolete, and later that year the President himself had ordered their removal. (During the crisis he was shocked to learn that the Air Force had neglected to carry out his order.) One may suspect that personal pride and political considerations had considerable to do with his decision to make concessions whatever to the Soviet, but gamble on its surrender.

Such considerations may likewise have influenced his rejection of Stevenson's suggestion of a package plan to neutralize Cuba, including an offer to give up our naval base at Guantánamo and guarantee its territorial integrity. This might remind us that Cuba too had a real case. After the Bay of Pigs affair it had obvious reason to mistrust the United States and build up its defenses, especially since exile groups were still being encouraged in their plans to stage a counterrevolution. Two weeks before the crisis its President Dorticos had made a speech in the United Nations in which he declared that Cuba was ready to demilitarize if we pledged ourselves to commit no acts of aggression against it. This offer may have been a cover for the missiles already being installed, but in any case it was given no consideration at all. Stevenson delivered on the same day the habitual answer of the State Department: "The maintenance of Communism in the Americas is not negotiable." The frightening missile crisis made Stevenson reconsider, but not Kennedy.

Once the President had won his dangerous gamble he did reconsider. While he had more self-confidence thereafter, Schlesinger writes that his feelings underwent another change:

> A world in which nations threatened each other with nuclear weapons now seemed to him not just an irrational but an intolerable and impossible world. Cuba thus made vivid the sense that all humanity had a common interest in the prevention of nuclear war—an interest far above those national and ideological interests which had once seemed ultimate.

This is precisely what Stevenson had been feeling and saying for years. He was therefore the more deeply hurt when Kennedy turned down his proposals of negotiation and soon made it plainer that he considered him too soft: the President took up his brother Robert's suggestion that John McCloy be appointed Stevenson's assistant during the negotiations at the U.N., to assure that he would be tough enough in dealing with the Russians. (McCloy was among those who believed that it is foolish to worry about world opinion—the balance of power is what matters.) And this was the prelude to another humiliation. Charles Bartlett and Stewart Alsop published an article in the *Saturday Evening Post* about the meetings of the National Security Council during the two weeks of the missile crisis. After telling of the debates between the doves and the hawks, and the consensus that was reached on the naval blockade, they reported that only Stevenson had dissented, adding that one top official said he wanted another Munich. "There seems to be no doubt," they concluded, "that he preferred political negotiation to the alternative of military action." The article set off a furor because Bartlett was known to be one of the reporters whom the President favored with his confidences. The New York *Daily News* featured it with a headline: "Adlai on Skids over Pacifist Stand in Cuba."

Schlesinger denies what some of Stevenson's intimates say they heard on good authority, that Kennedy had prompted the article. At least the White House promptly repudiated the story, announcing that Ambassador Stevenson had strongly supported the quarantine. Several days later Kennedy made public a letter he wrote to him expressing regret over the "unfortunate stir" and admiration of his performance at the U.N., which was of "inestimable value." At their first public meeting, a dinner for scientists, Stevenson as master of ceremonies introduced the President as the "author, producer and star of Mr. Krushchev's new play, 'A Funny Thing Happened to Me on the Way to Cuba' "; and he added, "I'm proud to have been a member of the cast." Nevertheless he had been profoundly depressed by the "unfortunate stir." The article made more headlines than his immediate denial that he had opposed the blockade. Commentators noted that in his letter to the Ambassador Kennedy had expressed no opinion about the truth or falsity of his good friend's article, and Schlesinger also writes that there had been worry in the White House over Stevenson's persistence in urging negotiation. It was left to the Ambassador to voice indignation over the article:

> This must be some kind of record for irresponsible journalism. I hope the time hasn't come in the United States when it is considered better to advocate war to settle issues than peaceful means, because if that time should come the world is doomed. I think it's time to stop this childish talk about hard and soft lines among the advisers of the President. . . .

The last sentence, however, was not strictly accurate. There was in fact a sharp division in the President's advisers, as in Washington and the country at large. A "hard" line was recommended by not only the Chiefs of Staff but such civilians as Dean Acheson. Acheson simply despised Stevenson; to him the important thing was not negotiation but the organization of power. (He had been hardened, too, by the brutally unfair and prolonged attack on him by Republicans.) What Stevenson more properly resented was the word "soft" for his position. "Dove" was not a precise word either for such men as George Kennan, Averell Harriman, Chester Bowles, Thomas Finletter, Kenneth Galbraith, and Senator Fulbright, who like Stevenson argued only for less emphasis on military power alone, a flexible policy adapted to the important changes since the Truman administration, and more initiative in negotiations to reduce tensions. Kennedy on the whole sided with the latter camp, but with some reservations that always troubled Stevenson. The differences between the two camps bring us back to the fundamental issue of power.

Now, military men have by no means been unanimous in exerting their great influence simply on behalf of military power. "Hawk" is no more a precise word for General Marshall or General Eisenhower. Army men in particular were inclined to resist the policy of massive retaliation that Dulles and Wilson imposed on the Eisenhower administration, with the enthusiastic endorsement of the Air Force; Generals Matthew Ridgway, Maxwell Taylor, and James Gavin all resigned in order to fight publicly for the idea of limited war. General Gavin was also a sharp critic of the "military-industrial complex" that had acquired such great power in Washington, pointing out how costly the gospel of profits was to both the military and the taxpayers; through its lobbies industry was forcing on the services many obsolete weapons. Because of his awe of big business Eisenhower showed no concern over this complex during his Presidency, but he did accept a passage that Malcolm Moos composed for his Farewell Address, expressing worry over its threat to the freedom of the people.

Yet the Chiefs of Staff have usually distrusted mere diplomacy. Typically they see no hope of security except in military supremacy, preferably overwhelming, and as in the missiles crisis they are wont to invite a military showdown. The Air Force remains inclined to recommend all-out bombing as the one sure solution of all problems. General Curtis LeMay, Air Force Chief under Kennedy, tells in his memoirs how he kept urging that the way to end the war in Vietnam was to let them know that "we're going to bomb them back into the Stone Age."[5] Stevenson might have been more frightened than he seemed by the thought that a man so callous and ignorant outside his specialty should have a voice in the highest councils in Washington. The General embraced him in his contempt for the "Whiz Kid liberals," and "the intellectuals, the inveterate pacifists, the dreamers and idealists. . . ."

It is always possible that Stevenson was too idealistic in his hopes

[5] *Mission with LeMay,* fancied up for him by MacKinlay Kantor, is not a disarming revelation of his own Stone Age mentality. In writing that he "sought to slaughter as few civilians as possible," he adds a note of scorn: "I've tried to stay away from hospitals, prison camps, orphan asylums, nunneries and dog kennels." More heartily he boasts of the big fire raids on Japan, how "we burned up nearly sixteen square miles of Tokyo." He quotes another general on how one raid alone produced "more casualties than in any other military action in the history of the world," more even than those of Hiroshima and Nagasaki together; though he neglects to point out that the casualties were civilian men, women, and children. President Johnson kept LeMay on just long enough to prevent him from campaigning for Barry Goldwater, since he embarrassed the administration by his feud with McNamara to preserve manned bombers against the simpler, swifter missiles; but at least his exhortations for more bombing in Vietnam finally bore fruit.

of reasonableness and patient negotiation, just as he tended to bank too much on the good will he built up by his personal charm. He was not at all blind, however, to the realities of power. In his first speech on the missiles crisis he said: "Reluctantly and repeatedly, we have to face the sad fact that the only way to reinforce those on the other side who are for moderation and peaceful competition is to make it absolutely clear that aggression will be met with resistance, and force with force." Having known from the beginning that we could never bank on the good will of the Russians, he was the more grateful for the immense power of America. He had criticized the Eisenhower administration precisely because it was weakening America by economizing on defense, adopting the unrealistic policy of massive retaliation, and failing to deploy our economic power. The main point, once more, was that he always sought to use our power reasonably and responsibly, humanely and generously, in the interests of peace before victory or after victory. He kept more steadily in mind than most leaders the obvious danger of the power at our command, the obvious need of restraint. In a speech to the United Nations on disarmament, he again answered the invariable criticism that he was soft, visionary, wishful, escapist:

> Escapism, no—escape, yes. For a man *must* escape—not in wishful dreams, but in hard reality. We *must* escape from this spiral of fear, from the outmoded illusion that lasting security for people can be found by balancing out the wildly destructive power in the hands of their governments.

Early in the administration Stevenson had started pressing on Kennedy the idea of making disarmament the first business of the nation, at last demonstrating to the United Nations unequivocally that we wanted it. Schlesinger records an earnest discussion in which he said: "Your first decision, Mr. President, must be to make sure that you yourself are genuinely for general and complete disarmament." He was then dismayed by Kennedy's apparent skepticism, his political objections that disarmament was not a popular issue in either Congress or the country, and his eventual welcome of the idea of seizing the initiative from the Russians first as a smart move in the propaganda war. Wise or no, Kennedy was at this time certainly not passionately committed to the cause of disarmament. About all he did was to induce Congress to adopt a proposal made by Stevenson years before establishing a small Arms Control and Disarmament Agency, and to give a speech at the United Nations challenging the Soviet to a peace instead of an arms race. And by then Khrushchev had made it harder for Stevenson. Riding the crest of his self-confidence, he broke the moratorium on bomb-testing in the atmosphere that the Soviet Union itself had proposed, now announcing that stopping only one kind of test "would be a disservice to the cause of peace." The Russians proceeded to poison the atmosphere with more radioactive fallout than had Americans and British together by trying out a series of at least thirty big bombs, climaxed by a 50-megaton monster—one that Khrushchev boasted was 2,500 times bigger than the bomb dropped on Hiroshima. He did not inform his people of this service to the cause of peace until the end of the series.

Stevenson was deeply shocked. In a speech at the U.N. he prefaced a review of the double-dealing of the Soviet Union, which had been condemning nuclear tests at Geneva while preparing this atrocious series, with a statement of feeling that might have ended as despair:

> I confess a feeling of futility when I consider the immensity of the problems which confront us and the feebleness of our efforts to deal properly with them. We have lived for sixteen years in the Atomic Age. During these years we have ingeniously and steadily improved man's capacity to blow up the planet. But we have done little to improve man's control over the means of his own destruction. Instead, we have worried and wrangled and talked and trifled while time trickles away, and the hands of the clock creep toward midnight.

Nevertheless he declared that the United States was still ready to negotiate a test-ban treaty. Now more strongly convinced than ever that the nuclear arms race was the crisis of crises, he spoke with more feeling a month later:

> In past wars, there have been winners as well as losers, the victors and the vanquished, the decorated and the dead. In the end, valuable real estate and other riches have changed hands. Thrones have been won,

regimes transferred, rule extended, religions and ideologies imposed, empires gained and lost, aggressions halted or advanced. . . .

But war in the future would differ fundamentally from war in the past, not in degree but in kind. It is this which seems so difficult to grasp. Thermonuclear war cannot serve anyone's national interest—no matter how moral or immoral that interest may be, no matter how just or unjust, no matter how noble or ignoble, regardless of the nation's ideology, faith or social system.

In this speech Stevenson outlined a treaty that would at least make a start toward sanity by a limited ban on all but underground testing. At first rejected by the Soviet Union, this proposal became the basis of the treaty, signed in 1963, which finally vindicated the "theatrical gesture" that had cost Stevenson so heavily in his 1956 campaign against Eisenhower.[6]

In the national debate on the treaty the hard-liners ran true to form. The Chiefs of Staff, past and present, opposed any comprehensive ban; Senator Everett Dirksen deplored it as another exercise "in giveaway"; the hawk-scientist Edward Teller told Senators that if they ratified the treaty they would be giving away "the future safety of this country"; Admiral Lewis Strauss testified, "I am not sure that the reduction of tensions is necessarily a good thing"; and so on. But Kennedy had by now come closer to Stevenson, if still short of wholehearted commitment to the cause of disarmament; he spoke out for the treaty. Having done more to lead instead of heed public opinion, he was rewarded by a pronounced swing in favor of the treaty, which on polls reached 80 percent or more. This made it easier for the Senate to ratify it, only nineteen die-hards voting against it. The President went on to plead in the U.N. for more peaceful cooperation in space, another proposal that Stevenson had ventured there a year or so before. "Surely," said Kennedy, "we should explore whether the scientists and astronauts of our two countries—indeed of

[6] He was not invited to accompany Dean Rusk and the Senators in the American delegation that went to Moscow to sign the treaty. Sorensen writes that Kennedy regretfully left him out "to prevent reminders of a partisan nature." How Stevenson felt about this political delicacy I do not know.

all the world—cannot work together in the conquest of space, sending some day in this decade to the moon not the representatives of a single nation but the representatives of all our countries."

For the rest, other differences between Stevenson and him were not serious, and were offset by matters on which they saw more nearly eye to eye, such as economic aid to the needy nations. Kenneth Galbraith, one of Kennedy's advisers, stressed in particular the need of social and political as well as economic development, through education, social justice, and national planning; Galbraith was Ambassador to India, a country at last getting the attention Stevenson had pleaded for years back.[7] Similarly Stevenson was gratified by the Alliance for Progress that Kennedy set up for Latin America, long neglected by the Eisenhower administration; in pledging billions in aid over the next years, the President too emphasized the need of social reforms. But the differences between them were still characteristic because of the Ambassador's consistent tendency to take a longer, broader view of issues, with less fear of public opinion at home and more attention to world opinion.

One such difference was over policy regarding Red China and its admission to the U.N. Stevenson early raised the question he had for years, whether we should not deal with it more realistically and try to find a solution of the problem of the two Chinas. Kennedy agreed that it made no sense to pretend that Taiwan represented China, but said that for political reasons Red China must be kept out, at least for a year; its admission in the first year of his administration would be fatal. He had a further excuse in that Eisenhower had told him he hoped to support the administration on foreign policy, but would return to public life if it ever considered admitting Red China. Stevenson dutifully defended Taiwan and the short view in the

---

[7] Stevenson did not idealize India, whose representative in the U.N. was Krishna Menon, the surliest and most arrogant critic of America. When India made a mockery of Nehru's sanctimonious attitude by attacking Portuguese Goa, with troops commanded by Menon, he enjoyed giving a speech at the U.N. that began with a picture of the Indian Ambassador, "so well known in these halls for his advice on peace and his tireless enjoinders to everyone else to seek the way of compromise."

United Nations. The Chinese would make it easier for him by warring on India.

About the crisis of Berlin and the wall he was less concerned than the President. On a visit to Europe he learned that as usual Europeans were much less jittery than Americans over the possibility of a shooting war; they were rightly convinced that Khrushchev did not want war, any more than they did. Looking ahead again, Stevenson saw a more serious danger. "It would be extremely dangerous for us," he wrote Kennedy, "to allow our attention to be so absorbed by Berlin that we overlook attitudes in Asia, Africa, and Latin America, or take decisions on public positions based on the exigencies of our NATO allies rather than the exigencies of those areas." The President agreed on theory, but in practice gave more thought to the West Germans. Most fateful—for Stevenson too—would prove his relative neglect of Southeast Asia. Here the gap between promise and performance in his administration was most conspicuous.

Kennedy did give much thought to the mess in Laos that he inherited from the Eisenhower administration. By the time he took office, our effort to prop up a right-wing military government was a fiasco plain to all except our military and the intelligence service. The Laotian army on which we had squandered so many millions had almost as many generals as troops, who alike had no stomach for fighting tough Communists; they were losing ground steadily. Kennedy accordingly reversed the policy of trying to keep Laos pro-American, declaring that all we wanted was that it be truly independent and neutral. He rejected the proposal to send in American troops, recommended by the same advisers who had sold him the Bay of Pigs adventure; General Douglas MacArthur helped out by warning him never to commit American troops to fighting in mainland Asia. In his second State of the Union message the President pointed out to the nation an elementary truth, long taught by Stevenson, that it had yet to learn, "that no one nation has the power or the wisdom to solve all the problems of the world or manage its revolutionary tides; that extending our commitments does not always increase our security. . . ." Although he adhered to the old policy of threatening to intervene

if the Communists went on fighting to take over Laos, and like
Dulles had his bluff called, he managed by a show of force in
Thailand to get a face-saving agreement on a coalition government.
This at least left the country no more unsettled than he found it.

Yet Kennedy did not take sufficiently to heart one lesson of Laos—
that its people were not at all eager to fight for their independence or
against communism. In dealing with the more momentous problem
of Vietnam, he did not apply either the lessons he had learned when
he visited Indochina in 1951. Then he wrote that we had "allied
ourselves to the desperate effort of a French regime to hang on to the
remnants of an empire," and that the drive of communism could
never be checked by force of arms alone; the real task was "to build
strong native non-Communist sentiment." Now as President he failed
to concentrate on this task. The war in South Vietnam was going
badly, the Vietcong having won control of much of the country even
though their forces were outnumbered ten to one by the government
forces. Although he was startled to realize that Eisenhower had never
briefed him on Vietnam, he knew that the corrupt, dictatorial government of Ngo Dinh Diem had lost popular support by refusing to put
through social and political reforms, instead merely suppressing
opposition. But while he again rejected the advice of the Chiefs of
Staff and the CIA to send in American troops, he committed the
United States to checking the Communist drive by force of arms,
steadily building up the military assistance mission from some hundreds to fifteen thousand men. He had misgivings because he remembered the optimistic statements made about the prospects of
French victory that in the last years of their doomed war had been
issued by hard-line realists, such as Dean Acheson, Secretary of
Defense Wilson, and Admiral Radford. Ten years later the American
military were hewing to the same fatuous line. Robert McNamara
was taken in by it when he paid his first visit to Vietnam, announcing: "Every quantitative measurement we have shows we're winning
this war." Kennedy knew the reasons for distrusting such "quantitative" evidence.

Now, he had some good reasons for nevertheless deciding to

defend South Vietnam—reasons that would induce Stevenson to support our basic policy there until the end of his life. Unlike Laos, it had at least been fighting for some years, showing some resolution. Since the late fifties the Vietcong had been getting extensive aid from North Vietnam, and behind it China. While winning support from many peasants, they had cowed many others by their terrorism, and if they won the war they would surely liquidate the South Vietnamese whom we had encouraged to defend their country. Kennedy felt that somewhere a line had to be held against the unmistakable aggression of the Communists, especially the Chinese, and since 1954 the United States had pledged itself to defend that line in South Vietnam. It was not only the Chiefs of Staff who subscribed to the "dominoes" theory: most of the President's advisers agreed that if Vietnam fell, all Southeast Asia would most likely fall or move into the Communist camp. And under McNamara the Army had at last been prepared to fight a limited war. It was training American soldiers, and then the Vietnamese, for guerrilla instead of conventional warfare.

Still, Kennedy did not face up to the real problem that he himself had defined—the failure of the autocratic Diem government to build popular support and "non-Communist sentiment." When he decided to step up military assistance, he wrote President Diem urging him to begin introducing social and political reforms, but he demanded no commitment to match our own; Diem ignored the requests, doing nothing but spread some anti-American stories in his controlled press. Similarly Kennedy emphasized that it was up to the South Vietnamese, not to us, to win the war, but he neglected to set any limits to American aid or ever to say positively that we would not send in combat troops; if only to prove that he was not "soft," he ordered the departments to be ready to send them if necessary. Kennedy's indecisiveness was the more deplorable because the Pentagon was naturally indifferent to calls for social reforms. He paid little attention either to American newspapermen, who in spite of harassment by Diem's censors were managing to tell something of the truth that our generals were either blind to or bent on suppressing. So the war went on from bad to worse as American aid increased; the Diem government was busier repressing popular discontent. Repeated requests that it get down to its proper business called out a public complaint from Diem's brother Nhu, the effective ruler of the country, that there were too many Americans in South Vietnam. Madame Nhu came to the United States to regale Young Republicans with vicious attacks on Kennedy's interference with her country. Diem's troops carried out more brutal assaults on Buddhist monks who were protesting against his dictatorship. When his regime was finally overthrown, shortly before Kennedy's assassination, it was too late.

"No doubt," concluded Arthur Schlesinger in his book on Kennedy, "he realized that Vietnam was his great failure in foreign policy, and that he had never really given it his full attention." If the public record gives some reason to doubt that he realized this, unquestionably he failed to give Vietnam sufficient attention. With the legacy of American support to still another Asiatic dictator, he passed on the fiction that the war was not a civil war, only another Communist aggression against a legitimate government. Since we were defending the "freedom" of South Vietnam, "liberating" its gallant people, we ruled out any possibility of negotiation or compromise with the Vietcong, no matter how much popular support they obviously had. We would continue in fact to defend a shambles of successive military governments, none of them elected by the people, while it became ever plainer to all but American policy-makers that most of the South Vietnamese had little heart for this war of liberation. Finally President Johnson would give an ironic twist to Stevenson's fears about the Berlin crisis. Washington's attention became so absorbed by Vietnam that all the rest of the world was neglected, and we overlooked the disagreeable truth that most of the world disapproved of the war we were fighting. As usual we informed our allies about our decisions instead of consulting them.

With Lyndon Johnson, Stevenson at first had distinctly easier relations. It was reported that he phoned and saw more of the new President in three weeks than he had of Kennedy in three years. He had the obvious reasons for respecting Johnson: the extraordinary political skill and energy employed to push a comprehensive liberal program through Congress—a legislative record that neither he nor Kennedy could have matched, and that was approached by no other President except Roosevelt in the early days of the New Deal. In an introduction to a collection of Johnson's speeches, *A Time for Action,* Stevenson was lavish in praise of "his vitality, his courage, his intelligence," all in the service of "a master in the art of the possible in politics" who was unafraid to lead. He recognized the simple Populist in a character it is now fashionable to regard as incredibly complex. He wrote that although his style would of course be different from Kennedy's, "the drive, the convictions, the principles and programs that were a part of the New Frontier will never be lost so long as Lyndon Johnson is President." He could see that the President was really committed to the cause of the "Great Society." Because of his own experience with professionals in Illinois, and presumably some idea of the gruesome politics of Texas, he could condone some lapses from scruple.

Yet his relations with the President unmistakably worsened, contributing to the nagging if not deepening unhappiness of his last years. There were again obvious reasons why Stevenson could never feel wholly at ease with Johnson, or as he said privately, why he would hate ever to have to spend a weekend at the Ranch. The antithesis of the Texan in most respects, he would naturally be irked by the manners of the man he referred to dryly as "my lord and master," as well as by his callous treatment of his "buddy" Hubert Humphrey. Born and bred to the cultivated life, he perhaps found it too hard to condone or fully understand the hypersensitivity of one who had actually been a "country boy," poor and uncouth, and who was painfully aware that he was looked down on by intellectuals and sophisticates, the worldly people who had so much admired Kennedy, as they did Stevenson. But the important reason for Stevenson's troubles is spread all over the public record—the President's conduct of foreign affairs.

It is fair to say that Johnson's exceptional skills are confined to Congressional politics; he has hardly distinguished himself as a national politician, much less as a statesman. Stevenson knew he had a limited understanding of foreign affairs, and before long he realized what has since grown more apparent. As Philip Geyelin puts it, Johnson's foreign policy comes down to "foreign politics," played with an eye primarily to domestic politics. It is not played skillfully because the "treatment" that worked with Congressional politicians does not work with foreign statesmen; as Johnson himself lamented, foreigners are difficult because "they're not like folks you were reared with." They have been less impressed by his "rodeo diplomacy" because he has displayed no clear philosophy, no firm principle, no deep commitment. Sincere in his desire for peace, on the international scene he still looks more like a politician seeking votes than a statesman seeking the means to peace. His passion for "consensus" provoked Stevenson to observe that he "has not yet learned that you cannot always have a consensus on foreign affairs, that you sometimes have to do the bold, unpopular thing in order to lead." Having lost his consensus, he keeps a more feverish eye on public opinion polls— not on world opinion.

Given these limitations, Johnson was disposed to listen to Stevenson respectfully as a long-experienced authority on world affairs, aware too of the political value of his great prestige both at home and abroad; but he was also disposed to discount his advice, and with it his concern over America's standing in the United Nations. As Ambassador, Stevenson suffered from Johnson's notorious vanity too. Thus he wrote a major speech for the President to give at the twentieth anniversary of the U.N., with policy proposals including a compromise on the refusal of France, the Soviet Union, and other countries to pay their dues; but when James Reston published an article anticipating these proposals, Johnson was angry as usual over a "leak" of his intentions, and also fearful that the compromise would be unpopular at home. He had the speech rewritten, with all the meat cut out, and made a point of not showing it to Stevenson before he delivered it. His political judgment incidentally went awry this time, for when the compromise was put through later by Arthur Goldberg there was little fuss. But for the most part he was no doubt right in

judging that Stevenson's views were unlikely to be the most popular.
On his record, at any rate, he subscribed to the common opinion that
the Ambassador was too soft. He went his own way in dealing with
problems that were beyond his grasp or the reach of his passion for
getting things done.

On the specific issues that gave Stevenson trouble, one of some
consequence was Johnson's impulsive action in sending U.S. Marines
to the Dominican Republic when a revolution broke out against a
military-dominated government that had overthrown the democratic
regime of President Juan Bosch. At a White House conference (later
reported by Stevenson to Eric Sevareid) the President stressed only
the need of rescuing imperiled Americans, but when he went on the
air to defend his action he surprised Stevenson by stressing chiefly the
argument that Communists were about to take over the revolution,
and the United States would not permit another Cuba. As he saw the
whole affair, it was "just like the Alamo"; and it pretty much set the
course he would follow thereafter, the addiction to what has been
called "political overkill." On the rest of the world, including our
allies, his action made a bad impression. From past experience, Latin-
American countries were not inclined to welcome U.S. Marines on
their shores; we were violating the United Nations Charter and international law; we were in effect again aiding right-wing generals,
who were opposing the return of President Bosch; and it was
commonly supposed that the danger of a Communist takeover
was greatly exaggerated by our intelligence service, since the evidence
presented was pretty flimsy. (The State Department presently admitted that most of the evidence was assembled after the Marines
landed.) Stevenson, always troubled by resort to military action
before efforts at negotiation, was more upset by our failure to consult
first with the Organization of American States, of which the President had a low opinion. Our intervention was clearly unpopular in
Latin America, more grist for Castro's mill.

Nevertheless Stevenson dutifully defended it in the United
Nations. He evidently agreed there was real danger of the Communists' setting up another Castro regime; among those who had warned

the government was one of his former speech-writers, John Bartlow Martin, who under Kennedy had served as Ambassador to the Dominican Republic.[8] Stevenson's speeches at the U.N. strike me as halfhearted, however, not worth quoting. He scored some effective debating points with the aid of the Cuban and Soviet delegates, who overplayed their hand with the usual crude invective, and he could always point to the obvious aggressions of the Communists. He remained vulnerable because he neglected the reproaches of President Bosch and ducked the basic issue, the charge that we had taken unilateral action in defiance of the U.N. Charter. Other nations, including Latin-American ones, could raise eyebrows at his round declaration of the Kennedy doctrine: "The American nations will not permit the establishment of another Communist government in the Western Hemisphere." Although he might have felt vindicated by the eventual outcome, the democratic election held after his death, he was plainly not happy about this whole affair, nor proud of his part in it. It was one of the actions for which he was harshly criticized by liberal intellectuals.

Another was much more important—his defense of American policy in Vietnam. Here it must first be said that President Johnson inherited this policy from Kennedy, who in building up our military mission had not come under heavy fire. In his own first State of the Union message, in 1964, he barely mentioned Vietnam; at this time Stevenson was troubled because the President was giving little time or thought to foreign affairs. Two years later Johnson was obsessed with Vietnam, which he placed at "the center of our concerns." In the interim he had reversed his policy too. Like Kennedy, he at first insisted that it was not up to us to win the war: "The contest in which South Vietnam is now engaged is first and foremost a contest to be won by the Government and the people of that country for themselves." Then he began sending in American troops, escalating the war, finally bombing North Vietnam. His excuse was that the war was going so badly that more American aid was needed if there was

[8] Martin has since published a book on the Dominican crisis, *Overtaken by Events,* in which he defends the American action.

to be any hope of negotiation; escalation was defended as the quickest way of shortening the war. His dilemma remained that the war continued to go badly. Thereupon he went so much further, eventually sending in several hundred thousand troops, that this may truly be called "Johnson's war."

Unlike President Truman in Korea, who was attacked by the same type of Republicans now supporting the war in Vietnam, Johnson did not ask either Congress or the United Nations for formal approval of full-scale war; he was content with a blank check he had got from Congress authorizing him "to take all necessary measures to repel any armed attack against the forces of the United States and to prevent further aggression." Nor was he candid with the public. As one of his old associates told Philip Geyelin, "You have to ignore the President's own account of why he does things, or even what he has done." Johnson had some excuse in that he was unclear himself just what our objectives were, or how much effort they would require, but in any case he neglected to keep the people fully informed about the operations under way; the military build-up went on amid rumors that would be confirmed after the event. Robert McNamara, who had continued making a poor record as a prophet, now came back from Vietnam predicting that our boys would be home in another year. No doubt he believed what he said, trusting what the generals told him, but thereby he only proved that the judgment of the military cannot be trusted.

The generals had yet to learn the elementary lesson that guerrilla wars cannot be "won" in the ways to which they are accustomed, least of all when the war lacks popular support. The Air Force had not learned either that bombing a poor agricultural country with negligible industry could have nothing like the effects of its vaunted fire raids on Japan; its generals had apparently forgotten that a thorough bombing of North Korea had not prevented the Chinese from coming in and routing MacArthur. In accepting their advice, Johnson showed that he had not learned the painful lesson Kennedy had from the Bay of Pigs. The declared objectives in bombing North Vietnam were to prevent the infiltration of its troops and to induce it to negotiate; soon it became apparent that the policy was having the very opposite effect, stiffening the resistance of North Vietnam while the military themselves complained that still more of its troops were coming in; but then all that the generals could think of was to drop still more bombs.

Stevenson was again unhappy over the war. He was deeply worried by the policy of escalation, knowing the pressures the President was always under to carry it further, even to an all-out war that might bring in China. He suspected what Kenneth Galbraith would say, that "the phrase 'calculated risk' is a military euphemism for total ignorance as to the outcome of a particular action." In any case we were endangering our improved relations with the Soviet, forcing it to join China in condemning our aggression on a Communist country. In defending the war Stevenson could not rejoice in the company he was in, for most of the hawks were not liberals, champions of democracy, or supporters of the cause of the Great Society; he might have guessed that this cause would be among the casualties of the war. Meanwhile Johnson was ignoring the United Nations, where Stevenson was kept aware that world opinion was against us. Only a few client countries openly supported our war, some allies like Britain played along out of loyalty but were obviously unhappy about it, and most countries were explicitly opposed to it. (No European government could survive if it entered the war on our side.) Stevenson must have suffered too from the knowledge that many South Vietnamese peasants were among the victims of our bombs and napalm. But apparently he was most shaken by an affair that did not come to light until after his death—the failure of U Thant's efforts to arrange the negotiations he always preferred to military action.

In the fall of 1964 the Secretary General of the U.N. quietly explored the possibilities of private talks between Washington and Hanoi, to be kept strictly confidential, and got word of Hanoi's consent to his proposal. Stevenson passed on this news to Washington, but for some months got no answer. On his own he then asked U Thant to look into the possibility of a specific meeting place, and shortly informed Washington that Burma had agreed to be the host. Finally, six months after U Thant started his efforts, Washington gave its answer—No. The excuse given was that the South Vietnamese government would surely get wind of the secret meeting and be demoralized. (Readers might try to guess which of the series of unstable governments was in power at that time.) According to Mario Rossi of the *Christian Science Monitor,* Stevenson stated in a private interview his belief that President Johnson had been kept in the dark during the whole affair; though it is difficult to understand why he himself did not inform the President. At any rate, Johnson would tell the American people that "candor" compelled him to inform them that Hanoi had rejected all proposals for negotiation.

Even so Stevenson once more defended the basic policy. "How can I honorably and decently leave this United Nations job?" he asked Eric Sevareid a day or so before he died; but it was not merely a sense of duty that kept him on. He could see no alternative to our continuing to fight once the President had at last indicated willingness to hold negotiations, and Hanoi and Peking flatly rejected any negotiations except on the impossible condition that all American troops be pulled out first. We could not simply leave South Vietnam at the mercy of the Communists, whose brutalities liberal intellectuals seemed to overlook. Stevenson could at least take comfort in the knowledge that the President was keeping the war limited, refusing to let the Air Force bomb Hanoi, and showing more desire for peace by compromise, the only feasible terms. I assume he respected the judgment of our envoy, General Maxwell Taylor, a civilized general whom he had met and admired in Korea on his first world tour. But his chief reason for defending our policy remained his conviction of the need of containing Communist aggression. In a letter written shortly before his death, released some months later by his son Adlai, he answered the writers who in urging him to resign had declared: "By remaining in your post—without speaking truth to power—you have diminished yourself and all men everywhere." Stevenson wrote that whatever criticism might be made over the detail and emphasis of American policy, "its purpose and direction are sound":

I do not think the idea of Chinese expansion is so fanciful that the effort to check it is irrational. And if one argues that it should not be checked, I believe you set us off on the old, old route whereby expansive powers push at more and more doors, believing they will open until, at the ultimate door, resistance is unavoidable and major war breaks out. . . .

I do not believe the opposite policy of retreat in Asia or anywhere else would make any contribution whatsoever to the ideal that violence shall not be the formal arbitrator in world affairs. It is my conviction that American policy is groping its way toward this difficult but essential ideal, and this is the reason both for my support for the policy and for my continuance in a position which gives me some hope of assisting its advance in that direction.

Had Stevenson lived, I assume that he almost surely would have approved the growing demand—at home, abroad, and in the United Nations—that we stop the futile bombing of North Vietnam as the first step toward possible negotiations. As surely he would have felt some dismay over the President's announcements that the United States was committed to imposing peace in Asia and raising the standard of living on that continent—the kind of grandiose commitment, beyond our power, that he had long warned against. I doubt that he would have rejoiced in the Manila conference flamboyantly staged by the President, which impressed only the few governments supporting the war in Vietnam, left even the American people cold. He might well have reconsidered the terrific costs of the war apart from the slaughter at the cost of more than $300,000 a head—the sacrifice of welfare programs at home, of a decent respect for the opinions of mankind, of the improving relations with the Soviet Union. He might have questioned even the "dominoes" theory, with its implication that Southeast Asia is vital to our security—not merely our pride. And so on, through all the reasons for doubting on both realistic and idealistic grounds the necessity of so mighty a military effort to "liberate" an unhappy people, at such expense of their own lives and land, and at such increasing risk of a world war.

Certainly Stevenson would have had more reasons to feel unhappy, such as the President's hard treatment of his good friend Senator Fulbright, his scorn of critics as "nervous Nellies," his continued lack of candor, and his ever plainer inability to inspire the American people or give them moral leadership. Stevenson's associates in his last year disagree about whether or not he was nearing the point of resigning as Ambassador. Some point out that for years he had talked of resigning, and that it was only a matter of mood, with some desire to be reassured; others believe that this time he really meant it. As one who from the outset deplored Johnson's escalation of the war, I cannot feel certain whether Stevenson would have done more good by resigning in protest or by staying on and exerting his influence to moderate policy. But I do feel certain of his basic integrity, or his resolve to do good. It was precisely this, to repeat, that made him suffer. As he wrote in concluding his unmailed letter to his critics, it is always possible for honest men to differ, and he did not impugn the good faith of those who disagreed with him. "I would only ask them, in the name of the courtesies and decencies of a free society, that they should equally refrain from impugning mine."

At the same time, Stevenson was by no means simply a martyr in his last year, forever brooding. In talking of resigning he sometimes gave the conventional reasons, a chance to get some rest and do some reflecting and reading; but as he added to Lillian Ross, "I've been so involved with affairs of my own generation I'd feel a little bereft if I were *not* involved. It's tempting sometimes to dream about a tranquil old age, but I think I'd be a little restive." On his last birthday, an annual ritual that he had celebrated with two dozen old friends ever since he was Governor, he laughed and cried, and poured out his mixed feelings:

> I feel there's so much to do, so much to make up, and I do believe that nothing succeeds like excess. My dearest friends, forgive me my excesses, and I'll forgive you your successes. Give me the benefit of your candor and your criticism, but please keep your doubts to yourself, because I have enough of those of my own.

It would have been pleasant to have had from him a book of memoirs, recollected in tranquillity: it might have been a very rich book. I find it pleasanter to think that to the end Stevenson was unbereft, excessively active, knowing the satisfactions as well as the frustrations of his calling as Ambassador to the United Nations—a title that befitted him more clearly than "President" might have done.

So he was still busy at his calling in his last hours on earth. At an international conference in Geneva he gave a speech in which he made his often quoted observation that we could never again be a squabbling band of nations before the awful majesty of outer space. In London a few days afterward he conferred with Prime Minister Wilson, in an interview on BBC he did his reasonable best to explain and defend American foreign policy, and in a following interview with British newsmen he admitted that America could make mistakes, but repeated his defense of its basic policy. Two days later, July 14, 1965, he collapsed in the street when walking with Marietta Tree, a close associate at the United Nations. She knelt down to breathe into his lips, but his heart had at last stopped. "He died as he would have wished," Carl McGowan concluded a eulogy in the funeral service held in the National Cathedral at Washington, "engaged in his country's business, and mankind's."

12

Stevenson and the Tradition

"Cherish therefore," Jefferson wrote, "the spirit of our
people, and keep alive their attention. Do not be too severe
upon their errors, but reclaim them by enlightening them."

So Jefferson today would be plunged into a battle that
was familiar to him, even though the terrain is different.
The challenge of free men to stay free in a swiftly changing world would absorb all his energies.

—*Adlai Stevenson* at Charlottesville, 1960

Upon the shock of Adlai Stevenson's sudden death in London, genuine
emotion often evoked an eloquence much like his own in the flood of
tributes to him. Many were tributes to the gracious, completely
civilized person I have tried to present in these pages; many to a great
American who, as President Johnson said, "believed in us, perhaps
more than we deserved," and so made us believe in ourselves more
than we had; many to the world statesman dedicated to the cause of
peace and good will on earth, who was admired as much abroad as at
home. "We are a vast company, we friends of Stevenson," Carl
McGowan began his eulogy in the National Cathedral. He sounded
the common grief, for "no one of us is too old to cry." He sounded
the faith in humanity that Stevenson himself so often had, saying that
the echoes of his voice were likely to be heard for a long time: "For it
is the essence of faith to believe that the world in its advancing age
will set no less store than we have upon reason, upon intelligence,
upon gaiety, upon charity and compassion and grace. . . ." And the
many articles and books that began appearing about him, and all he

had meant to us, made it seem more likely that he would be long remembered. On his birthday in 1966 he was remembered piously by a commercial establishment, which published an advertisement in memory of "the gentlest hero of the twentieth century."

Already, however, one may begin to wonder about his fame. In the course of this study I have heard so many expressions of admiration and affection for Stevenson, from people in all walks of life, that I have felt like a member of a "vast company"; but these people were mostly approaching middle or old age. My impression is that at the time of his death he no longer inspired the younger generation as he had in 1952. He is likely to seem old-fashioned to the young people who have been stirring up excitement on the campuses and in literary circles. Among intellectuals his reputation was certainly clouded toward the end of his life. As I write, we are all distracted by all that has happened in the short time since he died, such as the intensified war in Vietnam and the fiercer revolt of the Negroes at home— matters on which his admirers may not look to him for inspiration. And there remain all the reasons for suspecting that he believed in us more than we deserved. "We must wonder," wrote Walter Lippmann, "whether we have buried with Adlai Stevenson some element of the promise of American life." He was admired and loved, Lippmann went on, because "only America could have produced him," and because he represented "the kind of American that Americans themselves, and the great mass of mankind, would like to think that Americans are." The question is: Is this country really "devoted to the American idea he embodied"?

It is an open question, once more. Among other things it involves such incalculables as the extent of his influence, how deep and lasting this was. But if his memory remains green, it will surely be as a symbol of the idealism of America, the still living promise of its life. Meanwhile his importance in his own day—what matters to us— derived from his unswerving loyalty to the democratic tradition come down from Jefferson, Lincoln, and Woodrow Wilson, and his constant effort to adapt this tradition, in the spirit of Jefferson, to the needs of a revolutionary age.

Now, as he knew, there are of course many Americas. Today we have always to begin with the America mirrored in its ubiquitous advertising. "Aesthetes and apologists," declaimed a vice-president of Benton & Bowles, "can rail at its vulgarity, its brashness, its aggressiveness, its insistence, its lack of cultural values, its crass commercialism, its loudness and its single-mindedness—but let them rail"; for these are the qualities "that have built the nation," and "they are qualities of vitality." Others might describe this very practical, businesslike, shrewd America as incurably shortsighted, very slow to learn that the smart trick may pay only for the short run, and that enlightened self-interest calls for more respect for high principle, even some risk of "visionary" idealism. Another America is decent, friendly, well-meaning, in a way humble, yet uncritical, self-satisfied, overfond of platitude and easy uplift, resentful when told its good intentions are not enough, hence always liable to self-righteousness. And so on, to the perennial hope expressed by Barbara Ward in a tribute to Stevenson: the hope of a new kind of man, first symbolized by Benjamin Franklin, who would be an ideal blend of the culture and civility of the old world with the spontaneity, energy, vitality, and good will of the unspoiled new world; and withal a plain man of the people, humble and compassionate, as Abraham Lincoln was.

Stevenson was no such plain man. Like Thomas Jefferson an aristocrat by temperament, he lacked the common touch, and in public life had a harder time because he so often had to deal with crowds; he never learned to feel at home in crowds as did Franklin Roosevelt and Kennedy, other aristocrats. Yet on the whole Stevenson most fully embodied the old hope of a "new man." He paid the crowds a tribute by persisting in being himself and not talking down to them. He was always a democrat at heart, in both feeling and intellectual conviction. While worrying over the shortcomings of the American people more than any other national leader, he retained a warmer faith in them.

All along I have kept suggesting that Stevenson remained prone to a somewhat idealized conception of the American past, and to a possibly excessive faith in the American people. Surely he will not be remembered for any notable contributions to the philosophy of democracy. He never took the time to attempt a political treatise, any more than Jefferson did, and the great deal he had to say about the basic principles of democracy was all familiar, notable only for his style. In his last years he was still committing himself to characteristically simple statements. Addressing the Center for the Study of Democratic Institutions on "The Essence of Democracy: Its Prospects Around the World," he reduced a rambling argument to this credo: "The essence of democracy is the dignity of man. We shall create a free world order on no other basis." A sophisticate might comment that he told an audience of intellectuals what schoolboys may listen to on their graduation ceremonies.

Then one may repeat that great statesmen do not have to be great thinkers, and rarely are. One may consider what Stevenson told a commencement gathering in his last years: "There is something more difficult—something more essential—than comprehending the great complexities. And that is comprehending the great simplicities." One still has a choice in simplicities, including the assumption that power is all that matters, trusting to ideals will never do. My own preference remains Stevenson's belief in the absolute need of idealism to realize the simplicities he proceeded to insist on, that people always come first, the world must be made safe for people, fit for people. At any rate, the case for democracy finally rests on quite simple ideas about what is good for people, and what people are good for. To my mind, no American statesman in our day kept a firmer grasp on these simplicities—and this both because and in spite of Stevenson's awareness of the great complexities.

To begin with, since America was the first great nation to establish direct popular government, with universal suffrage, it *had* to develop a faith in the sufficient good will and good sense of the common people. This faith, historically a very novel one, was proclaimed by Thomas Jefferson. As inherited by Stevenson it may still seem too simple. Some would say that, like Jefferson, Emerson, Whitman, and other typical Americans, he had too little "Vision of Evil," or sense of Original Sin. More would emphasize the woeful deficiencies of voters because of the complexity and gravity of the issues now confronting them. But all are therefore likely to forget another simplicity: that this faith in the people remains absolutely essential for believers in democracy. If it is mistaken, democracy is bound to fail.

Stevenson's faith was at least sober, more so than that of most of the typical Americans. It was backed by the historic achievement of America, most impressive in this century, enabling him to argue that we were defending no mere theory but "a great body of *experience*." It had had to survive, as he said, "some rather disillusioning experiences" in his own career, which sharpened and deepened his criticism of America, and his awareness of the necessity of constant self-criticism. In "The Essence of Democracy" he repeated an elementary historical observation that has been obscured in America by the "self-evident" truths about the natural rights of man, created free and equal: "There is precious little dignity or equality in our natural state." These ideals are not an inalienable birthright but a precarious, hard-won achievement. For nearly three thousand years now Western man has been struggling "to create a social order in which weak, fallible, obstinate, silly, magnificent man can maintain his dignity and exercise his free and responsible choice." As for the evil in man, he cited Reinhold Niebuhr, who has had plenty to say about Original Sin: "Man's capacity for justice makes democracy possible; but man's inclination to injustice makes democracy necessary." And Stevenson never forgot one requisite of faith in the people that Jefferson stressed: they had to be educated. No political leader of his day worked so tirelessly to educate them.

He worked much harder, indeed, than Abraham Lincoln. Since Stevenson idealized the Lincoln-Douglas debates, one may wonder whether he pondered enough some distinctively American features of the political career of his idol. Before the Civil War an ambitious, not too scrupulous politician of Whiggish origins, quite undistinguished except as an orator, Lincoln preached a simple egalitarianism, often in terms of the popular national legend of the success story, that slurred over the harsh realities of American life, and that he was not consistently loyal to. Although he denounced slavery, he was still morally insensitive on the treatment of Negroes, opposing the idea of granting them social and political equality, or in Illinois of granting them citizenship. He won the nomination for the Presidency as a common political type, a safe second-rater, with the help of some unsavory bargains by his managers. As the fatal war approached, he played it safe by remaining silent, making no speeches during the Presidential campaign while his party played him up as a Man of the People, inventing the legend of the Rail-Splitter to go with the log cabin; only Stephen Douglas had the courage to deal honestly with the major issue, the threat of secession. Once the war was on he issued the Emancipation Proclamation as a "military necessity." The least inspiring of the celebrated national documents, this freed only slaves in Confederate territory, specifically excluding those in loyal slave states and Southern territory occupied by Union troops. (As a British newspaper commented, it declared that one could not own a human being unless he was loyal to the United States.) Otherwise no reformer, the Great Emancipator hoped only to restore the Union.

Yet the Abraham Lincoln revered by Stevenson was no less real and remarkable. He was not only the author of the Gettysburg Address but the President sobered by the fulfillment of his ambitions, the great power he now wielded. A man really of the people and for the people, he acquired in the White House more tragic sense of life than any other great leader in history, and with it more humility, charity, and magnanimity. Stevenson knew that Lincoln too had struck his contemporaries as indecisive because of the gravity of the choices he had to make. "Have a heart," he jotted in the margin of a book questioning Lincoln's delay in issuing the Proclamation; "he was only trying to figure out the best way of holding the nation together." Stevenson had a deep sense of both the simplicities and the complexities because he always had a heart. By the same token he had much the same tragic sense as Lincoln, a quality especially rare in American leaders. In particular he was acutely sensitive to the awful responsibilities of great power, and to its inescapable costs, that by decisions made in any grave matters—even when made in a spirit of malice toward none and charity for all—many good people were bound to be hurt. Lincoln was the more somber figure because of the painful decisions he had to make in power, but Stevenson had enough responsibility as a national leader to give him an aura of sadness in spite of his geniality and humor. His humor itself, so often wry, ironic, and self-deprecatory, reflected the kind of comic view of life that with emotion may become a tragic view.

What made him seem like a utopian was his kinship with another President in our quite different century, Woodrow Wilson. Toward the end of his life Stevenson remarked that while he was saturated with Lincoln from infancy, Wilson had become very important to him, for having extended Lincoln's message to the world scene. Again and again he dwelt on the simple truth that "all mankind" is now no abstraction but a political fact, the whole world is a community, there is "no outside," there is in truth but "one world," visible to astronauts. He summarized the message of the beloved Pope John: "The human race is a family, men are brothers, all wars are civil wars, and all killing is fratricidal." The United Nations—or better, he suggested, the *"uniting* nations"—was the indispensable means to a world society under law, and law backed by justice and popular consent, not force alone. In democratic terms, the dignity of every human being on earth had to be recognized. At Notre Dame, which in 1963 had given him its annual Patriotism Award, he concluded his speech of acceptance on the highest note he sounded in this period:

> I can wish no more for your profound patriotism as Americans than that you will add to it a new dedication to the world-wide brotherhood of which you are a part and that, together with your love of America, there will grow a wider love which seeks to transform our earthly city, with all its races and peoples, all its creeds and aspirations, into Saint Augustine's "Heavenly city where truth reigns, love is the law, and whose extent is eternity."

Here indeed a "visionary" was speaking, and a man perhaps more deeply spiritual than Wilson, or any President of our century. Needless to add, this Heavenly city will never be realized on earth; though even so it could be argued that what the youth in affluent America need most is a utopian dream of the future. In any case Stevenson came back to earth when he returned to duty at the United Nations. He was fully aware of the appalling difficulties of building a "free world society," realizing a principle of equality among nations as among citizens, or first of all providing the poor peoples of the world—billions of them—with the social and economic opportunity needed to realize their dignity. His vision was more complex than Wilson's if only because he had lived through a much greater upheaval and was constantly faced with much more appalling dangers. For him it was a "valid question" whether the audacious experiment of democracy could survive this upheaval, during which it has been under mounting attack by totalitarian forms of government. He quickly answered that he had "no doubt" it would prevail, for "it is the most popular form of government yet devised," and in Jefferson's words "the only form of government which is not eternally at open or secret war with the rights of the people." If this "no doubt" came too quickly, Stevenson at once added an emphatic proviso: democracy will prevail only if "we who are its custodians continually re-examine and adapt its principles to the changing needs of our changing times." Again the immense power of America was no answer. As he told the Harvard Alumni Association a month before he died, power had enabled us to form the Western alliance and contain communism, but now it only deepened the uncertainties:

> What power have we to coerce our friends in Europe? What assurance have we that direct action against either Communist giant will not unleash the nuclear war from which we would suffer as much as they? How can we be sure that unlimited support of any authoritarian anti-Communist government may not merely hasten the day when the citizens become Communists as the only means to change? If total isolationism is no answer, total interventionism is no answer either. In fact, the clear, quick, definable, measurable answers are all ruled out. In this new twilight of power there is no quick path to a convenient light switch.

Like Wilson, Stevenson could still sound too optimistic. In viewing the prospects of establishing a free world community under law, he remarked cheerfully that the Founding Fathers must have been as daunted by the task they faced; whereas actually their task was far simpler. But at least no statesman worked harder to keep alive the possibility of such a world community. If his popularity as Ambassador at home owed chiefly to his defense of the "national interest," his following included millions who shared something of his ideal conception of this interest. His popularity abroad was due much more plainly to this conception; to the rest of the world he symbolized the conscience of America. He gave vast numbers of people reassurance, Barbara Ward wrote, that the greatest nation on earth, with an overwhelming, irresistible power, would use this power reasonably, humanely, generously.

Not actually reassurance, I should say—only hope. The rest of the world was too often dismayed by how the United States used its power. There remain the good reasons why so many admirers of Stevenson too were dismayed by his support of President Johnson's policy in Vietnam—the reasons for his own doubts and anxieties. Nevertheless he may still appear to advantage in the company of his critics, in particular the community of intellectuals who at first idolized him and in supporting him acquired more of his own feeling of commitment to America.

Although most sound as if they have retained this commitment, some seem to have reverted to the traditional belief that intellectuals have no real place in the American scheme. More are prone to ambiguous attitudes: resentful because their kind are not in power, yet suspicious of those who are in public life, as if they are sure to be corrupted by it. Such attitudes intensified the criticism of Stevenson for not resigning from his post at the U.N. Thus Irving Howe, who excluded him from the true liberal tradition, implied that this tradition is pretty feeble. The best excuse he could find for Stevenson's staying on in his job was that he had nowhere to turn, "no arena of liberal criticism in which he could speak," since our political life does not provide such support; he was doomed to failure because he "tried to act by civilized standards within the present society." Murray Kempton, who years before had praised him for holding up a light above "this dreary land," similarly saw in the "degradation" of his last years a "summation of the liberals' history"; Stevenson did the dirty work for Kennedy and Johnson because for years the President had been the only hope of his kind of liberal.

In answering his critics, Stevenson might have noted some inconsistency in their devotion to the cause of humanity that he was supposedly betraying. While condemning him to futility or worse, they could seem more futile because their devotion was backed by little apparent faith in the common people of our "dreary land," or any other land. From their accounts of America one might wonder why it was worth saving. Similarly with the literary world. Toward the end Stevenson seems to have been patronized as an antique type, not really sophisticated, and by most of the younger writers he was no more idolized than were his friends Archibald MacLeish and John Steinbeck. A particular reason, I assume, was their favorite theme of alienation, inasmuch as he was never alienated by America or the "wasteland" of modern civilization in general. Others might complain that he did not suffer enough from *Angst*.

Immediately they recall Stevenson's limitations as a thinker. While sensitive to the obvious moral, spiritual shortcomings of America, he was not an acute analyst of them, or of the reasons for the common feelings of alienation. He perhaps did not ponder deeply enough the basic problems of a mass society, ever more highly organized and mechanized. Devoted to the cause of mankind, he perhaps did not brood enough either over the ultimate questions whence man came and whither he was bound, on our little spaceship. As one who often feels troubled but has not had the high experience of *Angst,* I may be too disposed to pass over lightly Stevenson's limitations and to forgive him his possibly too high hopes of man, his basic optimism as a good American and Unitarian. Yet all this is to repeat that he was never a pure intellectual but a statesman, most at home in public life. He saw quite clearly the main reasons for anxiety that should concern a statesman. If he did not worry enough over the plight of lonely intellectuals and artists in our mass society, it could be said that writers have generally compensated by ample self-pity, but in any case he worried more than most of them over the life-and-death issues of international affairs. At the same time he continued to work in the spirit of Eleanor Roosevelt, at whose funeral service he said that she would rather light a candle than curse the darkness. He was saner than most of his critics.

The best in Stevenson likewise shone through his familiar generalizations about the most fundamental challenge of our time, behind the conflict of democracy and communism—the terrific power of modern technology. In his campaign of 1956 Stevenson had risen to its challenge to democracy by his call for a "New America," and for more economic aid to the technologically backward peoples of the world. In his last years he dwelt on the basic implications of the technological revolution: "For the first time in human history, man, Western man, has the power to build society according to his dreams, not his narrow, primeval necessities." Science has given him the power to bring about "a new birth of freedom." Only these unprecedented means force the obvious but neglected question: Freedom *for* what? To what end? "The trumpet still gives an uncertain sound," Stevenson had to reply. "And we still give an uncertain response."

As a statesman he was always most concerned with the plainest danger, the terrible destructive power science had given man. The end might be the literal end of civilization, or of man himself. But as always he was much concerned too with the response of America on the domestic front. Looking back to ancient Greece, he wrote in a popular article: "The great social purposes of a community—its security, the quality of its life and education, the beauty of its public monuments, its images of greatness, its communion with past and future—all these must be expressed in the political dialogue." They led him to consider "the three great distempers of the public mind—reaction, complacency and mediocrity." Reaction, which would presently nominate Barry Goldwater for President, seemed to Stevenson less dangerous than complacency, because of which public opinion might not react at all to the many crises of our time—crises, like the ruin of the American city, that mostly had nothing directly to do with communism. Complacency was breeding mediocrity of vision and aim, as in the popular refrain, "You never had it so good." It was fortifying the conservatism that made the Communists appear to be the bold adventurers and innovators today. At the end Stevenson could say only that he "hoped" a slumbering free society would become "ready again for great purposes and great tasks."

At that critics might again say that he failed to come to grips with the basic economic, social, and political problems of what is now called "postindustrial society" or "technocracy." There was in fact plenty of deliberate innovation in America, since change was being made by the government more directly and consciously than ever before, immediately through the billions it was spending on "research and development." Stevenson did not press the critical questions, about who directed the technology that has given man such immense power over not only nature but human beings, and about what voice the public had—or could have—in decisions about the uses of this power. On problems he did take up he usually remained vague about practical means to their solution. But again this is to say that Stevenson was not an economist, sociologist, or political scientist but a busy statesman, most concerned about foreign affairs. In these affairs he did speak clearly about necessary means. For the rest he was at least sensitive to the changes going on, quick to absorb new ideas about them, such as Galbraith's about the affluent society. And if vague about means, he kept his eye on a more fundamental matter, commonly slighted by the technocrats: the human ends of our extraordinary technological progress.

Among the anomalies of this progress is a sophisticated version of the shallow popular idea that it is an end in itself. For the first time in history it has freed man from a necessary preoccupation with economic needs; yet even serious thinkers make steady economic growth the primary national goal. For Stevenson the end was strictly human values—the good life. He complained that men who talked about putting first things first usually meant more weapons and more consumer goods. He put first such things as "education for excellence, beautiful cities, an open-air world and a society without injustice." An old hand at bodying out the American Dream, he liked "to dream of music and theater in every city, of great festivals of the arts springing up in more and more regions and, above all, of citizens themselves learning to use a growing leisure in making their own art." Since we could as certainly afford to rebuild Harlem as to put a man on the moon, he concluded: "I pray that the imagination we unlock for defense and arms and outer space may yet be unlocked as well for grace and beauty in our daily lives. As an economy, we need it. As a society, we shall perish without it."

Ultimately the human values that most concerned Stevenson were still moral values. The dignity of man that to him was the essence of democracy is a moral principle. Democracy was superior to communism as a form of government not because it is more efficient but because it is based on this moral principle. "Our modern technology of abundance gives us the freedom to act," Stevenson repeated, "—if we so decide"; and the decisions he urged were "moral decisions," among them the obligation to aid the poor peoples of the world. In these terms he restated his faith: "I profoundly believe that at bottom there is here in America a good and generous and moral people."

Stevenson's version of the American Dream may only strengthen doubts about his influence, for by these standards he looks most ineffectual. He stressed the moral decisions we must make in a talk praising the feats of the astronauts, without mentioning that these national heroes had banded together in a profit-making outfit to cash in on their fame. Most Americans take for granted the commercialism that runs through the national life, accentuating the moral slackness and obtuseness, but they seem little concerned about "grace and beauty" in their daily lives, at least if it costs public money; they also accept as natural and normal all the tawdriness, garishness, and ugliness in both cities and countryside, the transformation of America into "God's own junkyard." The "Great Society" fared poorly in the elections of 1966. "For an entire generation of Americans," Lyndon Johnson said in his formal tribute to Stevenson, "he imparted a nobility to public life and a grandeur to American purpose which has already reshaped the life of the nation and which will endure for many generations"; but "nobility" and "grandeur" are not the words for either the President's foreign policy or his conception of politics.[1] They are no more the words for the ruling purposes in Congress, which is bent on reducing foreign aid to a still smaller fraction of one percent of the national income. As for the good life, the House Appropriations Committee typically slashed in half the tiny sum of $14 million that the President requested for the new foundation to support the humanities and fine arts. A Republican leader who wanted to cut out even the $7 million protested, "We got along pretty well in this country for a century or so without spending money for culture and the humanities."

We can never know how much difference Stevenson made in the nation's life. Social and political scientists cannot answer such questions by their quantitative methods. No one, I suppose, would maintain that he permanently elevated the moral and intellectual tone of American politics. I also suppose that no one who studies the political record since 1952 will deny that he had some positive influence, which to me was all to the good. Even so I finally would not make much of it in arguing his claims to greatness. In these terms it would be difficult to demonstrate the greatness of Abraham Lincoln himself. There was precious little of Lincoln's humility and charity in the leaders of the aftermath of the Civil War; the country plunged into the scandalous corruption of the Grant administration; his Republican Party turned its back on the liberal humanitarian in him who had put the man before the dollar, to the end of the century ruling the country in the interests of business; the Gilded Age, in which corruption in both business and politics became routine, had no tragic sense whatever, nor humility either; and the emancipated

[1] Admirers of Stevenson must wonder, incidentally, about the fate of his "buddy" Hubert Humphrey. In a moving telecast after his death, in which Humphrey joined Willard Wirtz, Archibald MacLeish, Eric Sevareid, and Prime Minister Wilson in a commemorative discussion, he was most attractive in the heartfelt simplicity with which he expressed his love of Stevenson. After saying how much Adlai had done to elevate politics, he added, "I always felt that I ought to do a little better because I was his friend." Now as Vice-President, obliged to support the policies of the President, he has made many of his admirers unhappy by doing so with his usual exuberance. But he has also given indications of being somewhat unhappy himself in this role.

Negro was condemned to a century of subjection, intensified by uglier prejudice. The spirit of Adlai Stevenson may no more dominate American life in the years to come. At the end I would maintain only that it was a great spirit.

Still, I believe the nation's rulers must have something of it if America—and civilization—are to survive. In view of the terrific power at man's disposal, let us return to the simplicities—the elementary need of wisdom. Wisdom is not really a simple theme, of course, nor can we ever hope to agree on its dictates in any given problem. But we might agree on its main requirements for statesmen at a time of world crisis. It obviously calls for some understanding of this world, both the dangers and the opportunities confronting us; some breadth and openness of mind, coupled with flexibility and resourcefulness; a measure of simple humanity, a respect for human dignity tempered by an awareness of human frailty and fallibility; a measure of humility or philosophical humor, to guard against self-righteousness; and a measure of skepticism, possibly even of "indecisiveness," at least in preference to absolute confidence in one's judgment. Granted that such qualities are most uncommon in men who seek power, or relish the exercise of it, once in power they are not necessarily corrupted by it but may become humbler and wiser, as President Kennedy did. At any rate, this is the critical question to ask of our leaders in Washington. It is another open question, or so we must hope; but I think most Americans, and more people in the rest of the world, would feel safer were Stevenson making foreign policy. To my mind our best hope lies in his kind of wisdom: a clear intelligence, informed by a sufficient awareness of complexity and difficulty, sobered by a tragic sense, but sweetened by a spirit of faith, hope, and charity.

Or since he was disposed to deprecate such tributes, turn them off with a wry joke, I am content to give the last word to his humor. There is relatively little humor in the published speeches of his last years. The United Nations seldom gave occasion for it, and in other public addresses it often seems a little tired or forced, with some dependence on old jokes. It recalls that he was a harried man, getting along in years, tired, often unhappy. Yet the tone of his speeches was typically still genial, suggesting the good humor he kept to the end. He was never hurt too much to laugh. It may be that he will be remembered most fondly as a civilized man who brought humor into American political life, a rare combination of gaiety, wit, and grace. Both philosophical and earthy, his humor made it possible for him to be as earnest as he pleased without being pompous, as high-minded without being self-righteous. Adlai Stevenson might have welcomed a simple epitaph: He was never a solemn ass.

INDEX

Abel, Elie, 288
Abt, John, 41
Acheson, Dean, 7, 15–16, 94, 107, 111,
    132–133, 207, 289, 292, 299
Adams, Sherman, 139, 206, 208
Addison, Joseph, quoted, 1
Adoula, Premier, 279–280
Advertising, 147–148
Africa, 151, 206, 209, 278–282
Agar, Herbert, 95
Agnosticism, 263 n.
Agricultural Adjustment Administration
    (AAA), 38–41
Air bases, 211, 216
Alliance for Progress, 297
Alsop, Stewart, 291
America First Committee, 44–45
American Farm Bureau, 100
American history, 115–116
American Medical Association, 185
Anti-Americanism, 211, 216, 236, 300
Apartheid, 281
Appeasement, 207, 210, 246
Arabs, 194–195
Arkansas, 182
Armed forces, 191–192
    (*See also* U.S. Army)
Arms Control and Disarmament Agency,
    295
Arvey, Colonel Jacob, 57, 60–61
Ashmore, Harry, 175, 272
    quoted, 176
Asia, 104–105, 110, 151–153, 157–158,
    162, 191, 206, 298, 309
    (*See also* names of countries, as
    China)
Atlantic Charter, 47–48
Atom bomb, 53, 91–92, 94, 293 n.
Attwood, William, 151–152 n., 154,
    251

Bacon, Francis, quoted, 23–24
Baghdad Pact, 133
Ball, George, 50, 81, 113, 164, 264
Bartlett, Charles, 291
Batista, Fulgencio, 136, 207
Bay of Pigs, 259, 282–284, 290, 298,
    306
Belgium, 278–279
Bell, David, 95, 264
Benton, William, 234–235
Berlin, 284, 298, 301
Bill of Rights, 76
Bingham, Barry, 151
Birth control, 263
Blair, William McCormick, Jr., 70, 95,
    151, 264
Bloomington, Illinois, 18, 20–22, 25–26,
    29, 187
Bloomington *Pantagraph,* 26, 29, 32, 34,
    52
Blum, León, 90
Bohlen, Charles, 56
Borden, Ellen (*see* Stevenson, Mrs.
    Adlai Ewing II)
Bosch, Juan, 304–305
Bosses, 88, 245
Bowles, Chester, 292
Bradley, General Omar, 92
Bricker Amendment, 138
Brogan, Denis, quoted, 134
Brooks, Wayland (Curly), 56–58
Brotherhood of man, 228–229
Brown, Edmund G., 9 n.
Brown, Stuart Gerry, 112
Brownell, Herbert, 142
Broyles Bill, 73–75
Bryan, William Jennings, 11, 29, 43
Buddhists, 301
Budget, the, 139–140, 145, 205–206,
    209, 267